*Unknown America*

*Photographs by Gary Settle*

 *Quadrangle / The New York Times Book Co.*

# UNKNOWN AMERICA

## Andrew H. Malcolm

*Additional photographs were provided by*

The Associated Press, p. 37
Ricardo Ferro/NYT, pp. 41, 62
D. Gorton/NYT, p. 179
Gary Guisinger/NYT, pp. 134, 135
Boyd B. Hogen/NYT, p. 248
Ron Kuner/NYT, pp. 28, 29
June Malcolm, p. 11
Ken Murray/NYT, p. 25
Robert Nunley, p. 143

Book design: Alfred Manso

LIBRARY OF CONGRESS CATALOGING IN PUBLICATION DATA

Malcolm, Andrew H.      1943–
   Unknown America.
   1. United States—Social life and customs—1971–
I. Title.
E169.02.M336   1974      917.3'03'924      74–77946
ISBN 0–8129–0485–0

*To June (like the month)*

# CONTENTS

## F A L L

# W  I  N  T  E  R

# ACKNOWLEDGMENTS

I owe many thanks to many people for their aid, both directly and indirectly relating to this book. Without them all this would not have been. I am deeply indebted to my parents, Ralph and Beatrice Malcolm, for their support, especially during early uncertain times; to Arthur Hughes for his excitement for words; to Abe Rosenthal for the assignment; to Seymour Topping for his confidence; to Henry Lieberman for many lessons; to Gene Roberts for the chance; to Dave Jones for his longstanding support and understanding of an idea and an approach; to other national desk editors, including Bob Semple, Irv Horowitz, and Tom Wark, for their suggestions and aid; to Jerry King for his guidance; to Gary Settle for his keen eye and companionship; to my family—and especially little Spencer—for their patience; to *The Times*'s researchers for their backup; and to everyone else who helped—and understood.

# INTRODUCTION

"Well, if you're from *The New York Times,*" they inevitably say, "why are you way out here?"

The answer is simple: to see what life is like wherever I happen to be.

As a national correspondent for *The New York Times,* it is my job to roam the country to report and write on those little-known facets of life in the heartland that will help millions of *Times* readers better understand their own country—an immense country, as the saying goes, separated by a common language.

It is a varied nation with enough cultures, subcultures, and sub-subcultures to populate a half dozen nations. These cultures, these nuances, make up the fabric of life in the United States today. Some are changing. And that is news. Some are not changing. And that is news. Some are happy. That is news. Some are sad. And that too is news. But together they are the seeds for hundreds of stories that, it is hoped, shed some new insight on a little-known America.

In New York City, for instance, a violent August thunderstorm might postpone a picnic or bicycle ride in Central Park. In Good Thunder, Minnesota, on the other hand, it means money in the pocket, a timely irrigation of crops that produce a good harvest to help pay for the new tractor. In Chicago the ring of a telephone means simply that someone is calling. In Squaw Gap, North Dakota, where telephones arrived not so long ago, a telephone was something you saw on television or traveled 65 miles to use.

To some people, a buzzard is a filthy scavenger that lives off carrion. To thousands of humans who flock to Hinckley, Ohio, one March Sunday each year, the buzzards are simply nature's garbage-men and, more importantly that day, a sure sign of spring. A 500-pound bomb is something airplanes drop to kill people; to some people, however, a lethal bomb is something you make at work after bundling a toddler off to nursery school. Superman may be a lifeless comic-book character, but he is also the potential economic savior of residents in Metropolis, Illinois.

To some people, a turkey is something to eat; in Daviess County,

Indiana, a turkey is something to grow and race. Beer cans and postmarks are considered disposable items by many; to some, they are things to treasure. A town whistle can be a bothersome noise-maker that disturbs sleep, but in Canton, Illinois, it is an important and reassuring community bond that marks the beginning, middle, and end of each working day.

To some people, a roadhouse is a place to buy gasoline—sometimes—and grab a hamburger on the way to somewhere else. In Datil, New Mexico, the roadhouse is the heart of the community, albeit a community that covers hundreds of square miles and parts of two states.

And so it goes from Beallsville, Ohio, and Pumpkin Center, Indiana, to Smoot, Wyoming, and Pumpville, Texas, from Thief River Falls, Minnesota, and Evening Shade, Arkansas, to Millstone Hollow, Kentucky, and West Frostproof, Florida. Most of these places I found fascinating. Others, of course, are great places to live in, I am sure, but you wouldn't necessarily want to visit them. Each, however, highlights another little-known—and to me, exciting—aspect of a well-known nation. A discovery for some, a rediscovery for others.

You will discover these people and towns and cities and crossroads and fields just as I did on my journeys. From the timelessness of a windmill to the timelessness of a desert mountain, you will take a voyage of your own here through a year in the life of a special nation peopled by special people. It is a year that begins, quite naturally (in the most literal sense), with spring. For that is the time that nature, unknowledgeable about man's printed color calendars, starts her own year, her own annual rhythm of life. Moving slowly but inexorably over the land, the seasons form a backdrop for the doings—and undoings—of humans.

The ideas for these stories came from a myriad of sources—from friends and family, from intriguing road signs and curious mentions in other publications, from overheard conversations and fellow correspondents, from editors and readers, and often from simply perusing a road atlas and wondering just what could possibly be in a place called Santa Claus, Indiana. (The answer, surprisingly, was Santa Claus.)

My method, if that's the word for the approach, follows a general pattern. First, AT&T stockholders will happily note, come a series of fairly lengthy telephone conversations, a set of pre-interviews with residents, experts, officials, or nobodies who know the town, area, or subject to be explored. I try with every story to shed as much as possible of the outsider's prejudices and preferences, the blinders that could keep me from seeing a way of life as those who live it see it. More than any one thing I have tried not to apply my standards—or lack of same—to their lives and work. After all, what I personally think about buzzards or getting up at 4:45 A.M. or hanging around an ice-cream stand all evening sipping Cokes and swatting mosquitoes is absolutely irrelevant.

After the phone calls comes perhaps my favorite part—the actual travel—more than 200,000 miles of it in more than two years by car, train, commercial jet, pickup truck, snowmobile, and even a sturdy (thank goodness) old monoplane with Joe McPhillips, the trusty pilot who saved me a seat next to the rest of his cargo for Beaver Island: 21 cases of beer strapped securely in the other seats like the precious packages they were.

My stays in these communities lasted anywhere from a few hours in Mentone, Texas, to several days on Beaver Island when no planes could land in the fog. That was the place with so much snow that I had to sit on the roof of the snowbound phone booth to talk with my editors in New York. Regardless of the length of the stay, however, I try to immerse myself totally in the scene, the lives, the homes, the hopes, the despairs, the economy, the health, and the people of the locality. No detail can be too small to jot down in my spiral notebook, my own weathered security blanket to which I confide all names, numbers, thoughts, addresses, snide remarks, reminders, and impressions. Thus, for instance, a note on the size of the Sacred Heart phone book seemed meaningless at the time but ended up in the story as an offbeat way of perhaps providing some perspective on life for distant city folk with five volumes of phone books.

Once past the initial hurdle ("Well, if you're from *The New York Times* . . .") my stays have quickly—and fortunately—become not official visits by some ambassador of a faraway national newspaper, but more like stopovers by a new friend. Universally, the people—if still somewhat curious—are flattered by an outsider's interest. At times this has led to interviews of me, the interviewer, on local radio stations or page-one stories in local newspapers about my story for another newspaper.

I've often found potential news sources in bigger cities to be initially suspicious of a reporter. In the smaller communities I've visited on assignment from *The Times*'s Chicago and San Francisco Bureaus, I have found that people suspect the best until proven wrong—from the waitress in Coon Rapids who sat down at our table to chat a while to Betty Strommer in Sacred Heart, who had me stay in her home and then forwarded my forgotten shirt (freshly laundered and ironed).

Even public figures, accustomed to the blinding, depersonalizing glare of television cameras before thousands of forums, somehow seem to change when they're "down home." "Hubert didn't tell me you were coming," said Muriel Humphrey at their rural Waverly, Minnesota, home. Suddenly, a swimsuit-clad senator, then a Presidential candidate taking a weekend off, hopped from the bedroom. "You're not going to wear that old beige swimsuit today?" chided Mrs. Humphrey.

"Why not?" said her husband, who then turned to me: "Let me show you around." And we walked along the lakeshore and into the woods, where Secret Servicemen in Brooks Brothers suits stepped from bushes and talked into their two-way radio rings, giving superiors progress reports on their assignment's whereabouts. "You know," nonchalantly remarked the man who had been in public life longer than many can remember, "at night you can walk anywhere around here and no one is going to shoot you."

In fact, if there's any problem covering the lives of America's heartland, it is probably getting some people to stop talking about their town or work or hobby or the weather or the livestock or the mountains or their crops or their vacation or whatever. After all, I normally get only 1100 words, or 1.5 newspaper columns, for each story. As I keep telling my editors, that ain't much space to describe a way of life.

Sometimes, however, especially late at night in a quiet motel room, 1100 words can seem like an awful lot to write. Our office secretary, Sabina Torgersen, knows my traveling requirements by heart now—a desk, a phone, a nearby pop machine, and a bed, in that order of importance. There, once I have exhausted all possible procrastinations, I take red pen in hand and decipher my notes, underlining important facts or impressions, circling the more important things, scribbling stars by the very important things, and underlining, circling, and starring things of cosmic importance. By some notations, I cleverly write "Qte" to keep me from forgetting some unforgettable quote.

Then with pipe in mouth, a Pepsi at hand, and typewriter at my fingertips, I start to write. Some stories, like the tale of Wyoming's Betty Evenson, come fast, as though I'm transcribing them for someone else. Others don't. And the poor people in the next motel room get impatient with my typing and knock on the wall. Generally, however, I find that writing isn't any worse than major surgery, and after four hours, two soft drinks, one pipeful of tobacco, and six sheets of paper, it's done. Often, so am I. And I ask myself that familiar question: "Well, if I'm from *The New York Times*, what am I doing way out here?"

By morning, however, the written story has fermented for several hours and seems to have improved by itself. Whenever possible, I like to try out at least parts of them on my wife, June, a journalism-school graduate whose opinions I find invaluable, if often humbling.

Then, I telephone a special number in New York City. It's a tape recorder, and I dictate the entire story into it, complete with all punctuation marks, capital letters, and unusual spellings (to, two, too, and Thieu can all sound alike). It is a somewhat bizarre experience, talking to a machine for a half hour. It's an experience that has drawn some strange stares from those waiting to use the phone. And it once prompted my older son Christopher to greet me by saying, "Hello comma caps Daddy period paragraph How are you tonight question mark close quote."

With the story safely "filed" to New York, I feel great. For when you get right down to it, I love to write. Or, rather, I love having written. To think that I've lived an experience and by my selection and arrangement of words, phrases, sentences, and paragraphs perhaps have communicated a feeling, an explanation, or a better understanding to someone holding the newspaper hundreds of miles away, well, to me that is just about the most exciting thing that could happen. Of course, that feeling is before I read, reread, and re-reread the story in print and realize all the other far better ways I could have put things.

For reasons of space and the pressures of other news some of my stories appear in the paper somewhat shorter than my original golden prose. Like most other reporters, when I see those in print, my reaction usually registers somewhere around 5.3 on the Richter scale. And for that reason, it is with great satisfaction and pleasure that I have restored these cuts in the versions that appear here, many of which are expanded and include details I had no room for in the original story as published by *The New York Times* and distributed by The Times News Service.

But whatever minor frustrations there are, I have discovered 10 times as many satisfactions. Like the opportunity to work with real professionals on the national news desk in NewYork. And the opportunity to visit unusual places like Tuweep, Arizona. And the opportunity to do exciting things like steer a giant ore boat or climb up a windmill or drive a tractor or hunt rattlesnakes or retrace John Dillinger's last footsteps or go fur trapping or "streaking" or go to a sub-zero, midwinter weiner roast on a snowmobile or fly over the Grand Canyon with a man who has a 57-mile driveway. (And for this they pay me?)

But best of all really is the opportunity, exhausting and demanding though it is, to make new friends by the score. To use my press card as a ticket to talk with—and be talked at by—hundreds of people like Tom Wagner, Guy Skiles, Betty Evenson, Pearl Hutchinson, Mabel Kiser, Roswell Garst, Ed Remmick, Shirley Hoag Eden, Jimmie Kunkel, and the other fascinating Americans who took some time to spend with me.

In fact, one of my most rewarding moments was when I happened to revisit the FitzSimmons farm, the subject of one story included here, several weeks after the original piece appeared in *The Times*. I rang the doorbell. The screen door opened. And Bonnie FitzSimmons called back to the rest of the family: "Hey, everybody, Andy's back."

And she didn't even ask me why.

A.H.M.

Spring, 1974

# S P R I N G

*What was I doing in the middle of winter
in the middle of Lake Michigan in the
middle of an Irish colony in the middle of
its Saint Patrick's Day celebrations?*

# BEAVER ISLAND, MICHIGAN

When Walter and Vera Wojan marked their 25th wedding anniversary here the other day, virtually the entire island turned out at the Shamrock Bar to help celebrate. The next night everybody celebrated the birthday of Phil Gregg, Lloyd McDonough, and Rosie Connaghan. And the next night they had another party to finish off the food from the first two parties. Wednesday they had a party when the mail plane could not land in the fog. Yesterday they would have had another if it had landed. And today? Well, today was very special. It was Saint Patrick's Day, the biggest event of the year here where 170 people, mostly Connaghans, McDonoughs, and LaFrenieres (their mother was a Boyle), pass their friendly lives in joyful isolation 32 miles out in Lake Michigan.

Almost everyone on Beaver Island claims Irish blood to some degree, and many are related to the hearty Irish fishermen who settled on it 116 years ago. Like many Irishmen they favor a good time, most notably in the long winter when there's little else to do. It is not that Beaver Islanders are especially wild. It's just that they live on Beaver Island, a forested dot twice the size of Manhattan, with 1/9000th its population, 300 miles northeast of Chicago—an island where extraordinary things are a regular part of life.

It was once the royal capital of King James Strang, who was probably the only king crowned in the United States, probably the only king elected to the Michigan House, and, it would seem safe to say, the only king–state legislator to be assassinated. A Mormon who had split with Brigham Young, he arrived on the island in 1846 and, until his assassination, ruled over his 2600 followers as king of their Promised Land.

Then there's Beaver Island's public school (it closed early for today's festivities) where all four teachers are Roman Catholic nuns and the 63 pupils generally score in the top 2 percent of Michigan's students. And here, the island's Catholic priest and Protestant minister take each other's congregations at vacation time.

Somehow this all seems normal on Beaver Island. For the hectic urban existence that consumes the lives of the majority of Americans is a long way off. In fact, it is a hair-raising 15-minute flight away over shifting ice floes. "We don't want to set her down there," commented Joe McPhillips as he pointed to the huge melting ice chunks and slate-gray waters whizzing by just 400 feet below. Joe (everybody goes by his first name out here) has flown mail, supplies, and people to Beaver Island for 27 years, and his little red airplane has yet to let him down, so to speak.

That's good because at this time of year he is the sole transportation for the island (the ferry does not start until April 17). Which means two recent passengers shared their seats with 21 cases of beer ("They're stocking up for Saint Pat's"). Everyone in the tiny town of Saint James was busy when Joe landed at the deserted airport, so they sent the 67-year-old doctor, Joe Christie ("I also pull teeth"), for the beer.

The bar is presided over by Archie LaFreniere, Vernon and Pat's brother. Together they dominate the "L" listings in Beaver Island's three-page phone book. Although there are 117 listings in all, it seems everyone is related somehow. "You see," explained Archie Minor, an ore-boat sailor awaiting spring, "Pat LaFreniere is my father-in-law. Archie is my wife's uncle. Jerry LaFreniere is my wife's cousin. Carol is Jerry's wife. And Buddy McDonough is a cousin."

Vernon LaFreniere runs the general store ("If We Don't Have It, You Don't Need It"). He was born here in 1914 and quickly learned one of the island's cardinal rules: stock up for winter. So before the boat stopped December 27 he laid in, among other things, 800 rolls of toilet paper, a ton of sugar, and 5 coffins. Islanders cannot get appliances or furniture until the spring boat. And if, as sometimes happens, an islander dies on the mainland, the body must be shipped back sitting in one of Joe McPhillips's plane seats right next to the beer and passengers.

Archie LaFreniere prepared for the long winter, too. He stocked about 16,800 cans of beer. Others store gas for the island's 65 snowmobiles that take "snow safaris" on these dying winter Wednesday and Sunday afternoons. Back in the woods, the riders cook steaks, roast marshmallows, pop popcorn, and, of course, swallow a drink or two. Or they eat a different course at different homes, moving from house to house in long lines of snarling snowmobiles. "We just have the greatest time," said Betty Anderson. "We have so darn many parties here," said Doc Christie, "that we've refined partying to an art."

Today's festivities included a wienie roast, foot and snowmobile races, and a dinner with everyone bringing a different dish. In the evening (and into the morning) they bent the old elbow a bit at the Shamrock, where you ring the big bell if you're buying a round. Actually, today's party began last Saturday in Chicago, where about 300 ex-islanders gather annually at Saint Kevin's for a Saint Patrick's dinner dance. Recent proceeds helped finance the convent for the island's public-school teachers. The Dominican nuns wear religious garb, teach four grades in a classroom, and confine religious instructions to Tuesday evenings (when 55 of the 63 students attend).

"I don't know how we do it," said the principal, Sister Rita Wenzlick, referring to her students' high state test scores. Neither does the United States Senate, which sent a staff member to investigate last fall. Perhaps it's the steady drill on fundamentals, individual instruction (largest class: 9) or the teachers' experience (average: 15 years). It's certainly not the salaries (about $8,000), which teachers elsewhere stress so much.

The nuns were invited to the public school in the 1930s when the island's commercial fishing industry began to die and many residents left the island. Many still do leave, initially for college, then for a career. "There's really not much opportunity for any advancement," noted Mr. LaFreniere (Vernon). "But I love it here. There's hustle and bustle. No crime. Where could a criminal go? It's just a good life."

Added Archie Minor: "I always say any town with more than one street is too big. And we've got just one street."

*My mother used them. My mother's
mother used them. And my mother's
mother's mother used them. But your
daughter won't.*

# MONTICELLO, IOWA

A little piece of the past died here the other day. And when it passed on, quietly and with no fanfare, there was just one person left to cry. "I ran the company the last few years," said Mrs. Shirley Hoag Eden, "and, you see, well, I guess maybe I didn't do a very good job. Or something happened." And she stared at the floor.

Mrs. Eden is the friendly 54-year-old great-granddaughter of William Hoag, a Chicagoan trapped here by blizzards in 1872. To while away the winter, the wily Mr. Hoag thought up a utensil that would ease the lives of millions and support four generations of Hoags. He invented the feather duster. The turkey feather duster to be exact. And over these 102 years Mr. Hoag, Gertrude Pickett, Harv Harford, Pearl Claus, Edna Doyle, Anna Seehusen, Ellsie Kilias, and hundreds of other residents of this northeast Iowa community turned out millions of feather dusters—in some years half the world's production—for the globe's housewives, janitors, maids, librarians, and, in the early days of the automobile, their meticulous white-coated drivers.

It may be difficult for a non-Hoag to understand an emotional attachment to a bunch of once-worn turkey feathers, even the dark-bronze, striped ones so highly prized in eras gone by. But steam cleaning these feathers and sorting them by length and dyeing them bright colors and tumble drying them and splitting them and bundling them together on homemade handles of wood, all this was once a way of life for the Hoags and many of Monticello's 3669 residents. "It's about all I know really," said Mrs. Hoag.

There are hundreds of old, once-rural Midwestern communities like Monticello, which was founded in 1836, that have gone through similar traumas. Slowly, one small step at a time, change

7

creeps into these elm-shaded towns. The Ma and Pa grocery store is bought out by the A&P. Phyllis's Feminine Fashions goes out of business, an economic sacrifice to the department store in the sprawling shopping center by the growing city that was once a two-day ride away. Now it is just 30 power-steered minutes down a paved highway. One day the town realizes that it has been years since anyone parked a tractor on Main Street and that most of its men and women are earning a living in a factory in some metal prefab building near the old depot, which is now a boutique.

The old family farmers and the craftsmen of buggy whips and the town blacksmith were yesterday's casualties. Now in Monticello the bell has tolled for the fabricators of feather dusters. And in some brutally efficient way it is perhaps fitting that the Hoag turkey feather-duster factory at 410 North Maple will soon be turning out computer circuit boards. "We estimate that within three weeks we'll have a whole new industry under way here," said Duaine Bollwitt. He is the building's new owner and head of Electropath Inc. "We've already laid new floors for our machines and we'll soon be turning boards out right and left."

He spoke as a utility crew knocked its way through walls of handmade bricks to rig high-voltage lines for the electric heaters that will replace the old Hoag steam boiler. Earlier this winter that elderly boiler, the heart of the three-story plant's heating, feather-cleaning, feather-splitting, and feather-dyeing systems, had failed.

Mrs. Eden was prepared to pay the $10,000 repair bill. But one night she got to thinking. Specialized vacuum-cleaner attachments and metal cans of aerosol furniture polish had cut deeply into feather-duster sales to homemakers over the years, even though turkey feathers are natural magnets for dust. Mrs. Eden's costs had mounted steadily, too. Labor once cost 10 cents an hour for men and 7.5 cents for women; now the minimum is $1.60. And the dusters sold for around 69 cents. Turkey feathers, which once went for 15 cents a pound, now cost $3 a pound, a substantial increase if you're buying 150,000 pounds of feathers a year.

At one time the dark-brown feathers were plucked by hand from turkeys naturally bred in open, outdoor ranges. Now, however, more turkeys are raised on special chemical foods in crowded, climate-controlled buildings. Special machines rip the feathers from the slain birds as they move along the automatic disassembly line that entombs them in plastic bags. Moreover, market analysts decided that white-feathered birds were more attractive to con-sumers. So the computers crossbred generations of turkeys until, now, natural-colored feathers are mostly gone.

Then, too, Mrs. Eden's partner and brother, Stuart, recently died. And Louis, the other brother who helped, developed serious eye and asthma troubles. Mrs. Eden's oldest son, Ronald, had left Monticello to run a bowling alley and race midget cars in Craw-fordsville, Indiana. So the business burden became too much for one woman.

And a few weeks ago Mrs. Eden gave up. One month later the 12-page *Monticello Express* gave the closing seven short paragraphs on page 11. After all, the Hoag Duster Co. employed only 12 persons at the end, far fewer than the Cuckler Steel Span Co., the Energy Farm Implement Co., the Georgia-Pacific carton plant, or the 23 other industries in Monticello, which was dubbed "The Pittsburgh of the Prairies" by someone who obviously had never seen the Pittsburgh of the Alleghenies.

A few firms line the town's old brick streets, named Cedar, Elm, and Oak. Most, however, are out in the new industrial park, where one new street is named Plastic Lane. Up on Paradise Hill, the best sled run in Jones County, the old wooden toboggans have been replaced by plastic roll-up sleds. And down at the foot of the hill, Mrs. Eden walks around the old factory.

"We used to jump out of the lofts there," she said, "and land on burlap bags full of feathers over there. When I was six, Maude Arduser let me hand out the pay envelopes right here." Some of the factory's floors are still littered with soft little feathers. The file drawers are lined with 1922 newspapers. The worn, wooden work chairs still stand by the feather-splitting machines where the workers left them. And the wall calendar hasn't been changed in months.

"When we closed," said Mrs. Eden, "I went home and had two bourbons and cried for hours. I felt like I was letting the family down after generations." Then she handed a visitor a yellowed newspaper clipping from 1951. It was from *The Cedar Rapids Gazette*, and it pictured a healthy Louis Hoag smiling and making a turkey feather duster. "As long as there is dust," Mr. Hoag was quoted as saying, "there will be a demand for feather dusters. And as long as there is a Hoag and a turkey with feathers, the Hoag Duster Company will continue to do business."

*Hell hath no fury like a small town*
*pushed around. The residents of Canton*
*were anxious to tell me why.*


# CANTON, ILLINOIS

The town whistle blew here today. And that simple, steamy blast brought smiles to the faces of Lee Allaman and Orlene Johnson and Edward Lewis and Florence Thixton and Ray Walter and even old Al Sheets. It was further proof—if any was needed—that the end had come for The Great Whistle War, a sudden skirmish that taught the state government, a giant corporation, and much of a cheering Middle West just how strong an aroused community can be when its institutions appear threatened.

It all began on December 7, a day that will live in infamy here. On that date, just three days before Canton's 148th birthday, an antinoise-pollution squad from the Illinois Environmental Protection Agency infiltrated this town to measure the decibel count of the giant deep-throated steam whistle on top of the International Harvester plant. Later EPA officials said some disgruntled but unidentified residents had invited the agency in—a claim that everyone here knows is historically a favorite ploy of aggressors.

Soon after the test, the factory was told officially that its whistle, which blows seven times each weekday and can be heard clear over in Lewistown, might violate new noise-pollution codes taking effect next August. Not wishing to alienate neighbors, and since computers, time clocks, and union washup regulations had long since eliminated any corporate need for the 61-year-old whistle, Robert Nelson, the plant manager, shut the whistle down.

His decision came 45 minutes after *The Canton Daily Ledger's* deadline. But for news that big, the presses were held. And like Minutemen summoned in the night, Canton's residents answered the call of the silenced whistle.

Led by Lee Allaman, 7000 persons—one-half the town's population—signed petitions within 48 hours. They wrote state representatives. They called state senators.

"The government," said Edward Lewis, "is into too many little aspects of life—airplane passenger searches, gas and speed limits, and now the whistle. Next, it'll be the churches."

*The Daily Ledger* called for open defiance of the state government, saying the ruling was "a silly bureaucratic abuse of power." And Mary Mickalonis wrote a poem:

Give us our whistle, it's been part of our town
For three score and one never letting us down.
They will hear us exclaim every day, every night,
The IH whistle is OUR special right.

Actually, in the Middle West town whistles or civic sirens are common. They sit perched on top of tall poles in thousands of towns and cities, waiting to blast a call to work, the noon signal, or the evening curfew for teen-agers.

Over the years the whistle and its regular signals become more than a mere mechanical message. Subtly, almost unconsciously, it becomes a part of the fabric of life, like getting up in the morning. Because everyone hears the signal simultaneously, it becomes a kind of community bond, a common denominator for thousands of daily routines and a reassuring sign that life is progressing on schedule.

Watches are set by the whistle. Husbands go to work by it. Children, even those in the most secret of secret clubhouses, are to be home by it. Wives start dinner by it. And here, it is said, Mrs. Clarence Hossler's deaf milkman could hear the whistle when it was about to rain and warned her not to hang out her wash.

If a town's whistle or siren blows at any unusual time, that can only mean trouble—a house or grass fire or, still worse, a tornado. Even more alarming, however, is when a town's whistle does not blow at all.

Canton, which is 200 miles southwest of Chicago, is a three-square-mile settlement named for Canton, China, which settlers believed is directly under here. This Canton, once a stop on the Funk and Walker stage line, is a friendly kind of town where the employees of the movie's popcorn stand think to put up a hand-lettered sign: "Caution—Salt Pours Fast."

Old but well-kept homes line the snowy sidewalks. These days, biting blizzards may still burst across the surrounding prairies and strip mines. But soon the summer humidity will hang heavily over the cornfields like a wet towel in a sauna bath.

Change comes so slowly to communities like Canton that when it finally eases in, change doesn't seem like change at all. It seems, well, normal.

Back in 1910, for example, reformers agitated for the removal of the horse-hitching posts in the square. Village merchants, who liked the free horse parking by their front doors, branded the agitators as "newcomers," that is, people who had lived here less than 15 or 20 years. Then one night the street lights mysteriously failed, and in the morning the posts were gone. Someone put them back, though. And only over the years did the hitching posts give way to today's penny parking meters.

So it was not surprising that the sudden silencing of Canton's whistle caused the biggest stir here since that April day in 1855 when 200 women hid axes under their shawls and marched downtown to destroy the Sebastopol Tavern.

When the whistle, said to be just like the *Lusitania*'s, failed to blow at 6 A.M., Janet Starcevich overslept. Lee Allaman's regular predawn cup of coffee tasted funny. John Beale's watch was behind all day. Ray Walker wasn't sure exactly when to wake his sleeping son. The coffee-break regulars at Edward Lewis's soda fountain straggled in separately. One man stood up at a church service and urged the congregation to tar and feather the still unknown whistle opponents. And Mrs. Thixton, who was Mr. Allaman's first-grade teacher a half century ago, didn't start her day as usual—remembering her deceased father who had worked right under the whistle for decades.

"In our community," said Mr. Allaman, a 57-year-old township road supervisor, "you're born to that whistle, and you die to that whistle. Buildings may come and go, and that's progress. But we wanted our whistle to blow."

As a result of the furor, which included some loud words along the bar at Matt Sepich's tavern, Jim Reid, an EPA official who grew up to the sound of the whistle in Oconomowoc, Wisconsin, denied that he had ordered the whistle silenced. The factory turned the whistle back on. *The Daily Ledger* toned down its call to arms. There was talk of a legal variance for Canton's whistle. And everyone got back on schedule.

But just in case the message didn't seep down to those government fellows in Springfield, nearby East Peoria's city council passed a resolution vowing total solidarity with Canton. "We have two steam whistles ourselves," said East Peoria's Mayor James Spinder, "and I'd just like to see the state try to stop them."

*In my childhood in Cleveland a sure sign a new year had begun was the sudden disappearance of those giant iron-ore boats from their winter moorings in the Cuyahoga River. But I never knew where they went until I boarded the Cason J. Callaway.*

# ABOARD THE S.S. CALLAWAY

Archie Minor passed within six miles of his wife, Mary, and their home on Beaver Island early this morning. But he didn't see them. The same thing will happen tomorrow and about twice a week now. But chances are he won't see either one until some time next year, probably the first week of February. For Archie Minor is a Great Lakes ore-boat sailor, one of about 7200 on the five big lakes and 1500 in U.S. Steel Corporation's giant fleet.

As wheelman on this lumbering 647-foot ore carrier, Mr. Minor and 35 others are about to complete their first trip of the season, a sometimes harrowing 812-mile journey through 15-foot ice, rain, snow, sleet, clogged locks, and fog. They are more than a day late, and they carry a few wounds from a crushing battle with the elements. But they accomplished their mission. They brought 17,248 tons of iron-ore pellets from the stark mineral ranges of northern Minnesota to the blazing furnaces of U.S. Steel's South Chicago works. There they will unload and head back north to continue the lonely, lucrative life that draws them voluntarily from families and homes to ride an itinerant floating steel box on these treacherous waters.

"You have to be a little crazy in this job," said the *Callaway*'s master, Captain Guido Gulder, who at 64 has sailed these lakes since 1927 and has now begun his last season.

Although it seemed to be a mild winter, it is a late spring with the worst ice in decades riding the northern waters in giant, shifting chunks. As a consequence, many of the Great Lakes's 206 ore vessels have yet to leave winter berth. But U.S. Steel in recent years has extended its ore-shipping season. So last week 5 of the 42 vessels it will sail this year, including the 20-year-old *Cason J. Callaway*, left Milwaukee for the grubby loading docks of Two Harbors, Minnesota.

It was not an easy passage upbound, though the empty craft could ride up on the ice and break it. One vessel, the *Arthur M. Anderson*, straggled into Duluth for engine repairs after stranding herself on the ice for several hours. But within 12 hours of the arrival of the other four boats, 960 railroad cars had dumped into the yawning cargo holds some 67,000 tons of ore—enough to make 29,094 automobiles.

Then on a sunny Sunday afternoon, the more powerful *Callaway*, an eighth of a mile long, led the way from the harbor for the *Philip R. Clarke*, the *Leon Fraser*, and the *Enders M. Voorhees*. If anyone in the convoy got stuck, the theory was, those behind could help.

"It's kind of nice to get away from civilization again," said Captain Gulder as we headed out into Lake Superior.

The four sailed along the lake's north shore where strong winds had blown the ice south. In the darkness millions of small pieces of ice clinked together in the slight swell. Occasionally a large piece, blown down from Thunder Bay, thudded against the hull, but mostly it was quiet, very quiet. Crewmen quickly picked up the old routine of sleeping, eating the plentiful good food, writing letters, watching a fading television signal, then standing their four-hour watch on the bridge, in the engine room, or on maintenance crews.

"It's a real good life for a young single man" said the 48-year-old Mr. Minor, "but it gets harder to come back each year." He earns $3.53 an hour, has 16 hours of overtime each weekend, and gets free room and board. A captain earns about $3,000 per working month. Claude Vest, the second mate, earns about $400 a week. "I don't have a college education," Mr. Vest said, "so where else could I earn that kind of money?" Each winter he spends his vacation in Mexico.

But money isn't the only attraction. "I love sailing for the challenges," said John Vondran, the first mate. "We run our own little city here, and when we're out in the lakes, you lose track of the days and nothing else matters but the boat. No commuting.

No clock-punching. I can't quit. And anyway, when I'm home, I'm home more than other fathers."

But home was a long way away at 2:30 P.M. Monday as an upbound Canadian boat reported very heavy ice in Whitefish Bay. At dinner the captain takes a rare dessert. "It's going to be a long night," he says. It went this way:

6:31 P.M.—The four vessels close up and decrease speed. Radar shows ice ahead.

6:50 P.M.—Change course, seeking "the track," the path broken through the ice field by previous upbound ships.

7:00 P.M.—Ice flecks in the water.

7:05 P.M.—The first ice cakes slam into the bow. The captain is encouraged; the ice seems soft.

7:21 P.M.—We hit the "big ice." The cakes, some of them hundreds of feet long, are jammed almost solid in the narrowing bay. Even at only six knots an hour the ship shudders. Inside, the thunder is constant and deafening as the fragments bump and grind along the hull while others surge out and slip on edge before smacking down in a freezing spray.

The bow slices into the ice, sending cracks shooting off in all directions. "As long as it cracks and moves, we're okay," the captain says.

9:00 P.M.—Fewer cracks. Engines at full speed. The *Callaway* slows.

9:20 P.M.—The ship is stuck. The captain radios the *Clarke*, which veers off to port and stops. The *Callaway* reverses, leaving her rivet imprints in a V-shaped wall of ice, then charges in again. Progress. "What's this all doing to my paint job?" mutters John Stanbrook, a deckhand.

11:00 P.M.—The "track" closes in on the *Fraser* and *Voorhees*, pinching them to a halt.

11:20 P.M.—We pass three upbound Canadian ore vessels. They, too, will soon be stuck solidly for the night.

12:08 A.M. (Tuesday)—The *Callaway* and the *Clarke* heave to until dawn.

5:20 A.M.—In the frigid early morning darkness both the *Clarke* and the *Callaway* head for the Sault Sainte Marie locks and the 22-foot drop to Lake Huron.

An icebreaker has freed the *Fraser* and the *Voorhees*, but there are many more hours of ice ahead down the Saint Marys River. And fog. Thick and soupy, it envelopes the ships as they ease into the Straits of Mackinac. The men on the bridge turn from the windows to the radar screen, its green sweeping light adding an eerie touch to their serious faces. On the radio, ships exchange tips on ice conditions ahead. The foghorn blasts every few minutes, its ponderous tones quickly absorbed by the gray fog.

Then, suddenly, an answering horn dead ahead. "That's the Mackinac Bridge," says Mr. Vondran. And minutes later part of one steel span creeps from the fog. Mysteriously, it hangs in the air, stretching from one thick cloud to another with no visible means of support. A truck emerges from one cloud and hums across the gratings until it disappears on the other side. Slowly, the bridge falls astern and is swallowed in Lake Michigan's mist.

Twenty hours out of South Chicago a flock of northbound robins, apparently befuddled by fog, lands on the southbound boat and begins hopping about the steel hatch covers, listening for worms.

Mr. Minor, at the helm, glances at the radar screen. "That blip there is home," he says.

Below decks Mr. Vondran has discovered some dents and a six-inch gash in the hull's half-inch-thick steel plate. "It's not dangerous," he says, "but you can't play with ice."

*Spring means different things to different people. In Florida I found bugs and college students, not necessarily in that order.*

# WEST FROSTPROOF, FLORIDA

It may not have been official until 1:13 P.M. yesterday afternoon, but spring came to this central Florida crossroads several days ago.

"I knew it was here again," said Mike Hatchett at the Route 27 Truck Stop, "as soon as I seen Hubert's truck pull in with those damn lovebugs all over the front."

Mr. Hatchett, who pumps 10,000 gallons of fuel a day in this tiny community where trucks outnumber people, was not referring to any psychedelic decorations on Hubert Gunter's giant diesel rig. He was talking about the lovebug, a cousin of the fly that for no evident reason has multiplied in recent years into stupendous numbers across the northern half of Florida—where the heavily sweet scent of spring orange blossoms now hangs in the air.

For reasons a team of entomologists has yet to determine, the lovebug is attracted to highways. Winged blizzards of them smash into motor vehicles, suddenly fogging windshields, fouling radiators, and, at times, closing roads.

Although the lovebug is not loved here, he is—like the first robin, forsythia bud, or cricket chirp up North—seized upon by many humans as a sure sign that once again spring is moving slowly over this land, each day pushing winter's cold curtain a few more miles north.

In about six weeks' time, spring will ease its way north past Atlanta, the Appalachians, the great cities, and the Great Plains, and on into Canada. Farmers will take to the fields, city folk to the streets, and millions of life-styles will change until in six months the sun passes back over the equator and winter's pall again begins to cover the land.

It seemed in recent weeks that spring had come early to much of

the land after an unusually mild winter. The weather was sunny
and warm. Frozen soil thawed. Tulips broke through. And as far
north as southern Indiana the grasses began to green. But there
were foreboding signs elsewhere. Last week many weather-wise
migrating birds, returning north like rich folk to their summer
homes, went into a holding pattern over Tennessee and Kentucky.
And then three nights ago the false spring ended with snow
flurries, freezing rains, and powerful winds paralyzing parts of states
from Illinois east to northern New York, burying the tulips and
grasses, and befuddling thousands of robins, who vainly sought
worms in snowdrifts. It was conclusive proof that the sun will not
be hurried in its journey north.

The sun may not be hurried, but in the springtime Florida's
natural phenomenon certainly are. Not only are the lovebugs a
memory one day and a swarming nuisance the next, but Shirley
Scott's azaleas bud one day and blossom the next. Moreover, in the
spring Florida's unnatural phenomena also become hurriedly apparent. While the robins, whippoorwills, phoebes, and wood ducks
instinctively leave for the North, Homo sapiens moves south, as if
by instinct.

This month more than 2 million will visit Florida, part of the
27 million who throng here annually, 78 percent of them in their
own cars. In the next three weeks more than 600,000 college
students will migrate to the beckoning beaches, jamming the
highways from New York, Pennsylvania, Ohio, Michigan, Indiana,
Wisconsin, and Illinois. The youths descend like locusts, devouring
all the hot dogs, hamburgers, french fries, and beer in their path
and shedding their winter coats and sweaters as they go. A half
million of the youths will head for Daytona Beach alone (population 46,000), where the police, local bars, and 425 motels are
braced. "Here they come!" exclaimed one resident.

"If these are college students," one policeman noted, "then it
must be spring." Police Chief Robert Palmer long ago wrote to
every college campus east of the Mississippi River outlining city
regulations. Municipal trucks loaded with musicians will cruise
Atlantic Avenue and the 23-mile-long beach in the current 72-
degree temperature, keeping the youths busy as each spends an
estimated $16 a day.

"We want to keep them happy," said a chamber of commerce

officer. "Some day they'll come back with their families when they're really making money."

Mixed in with the hordes of sweatshirt-clad youths, who already choke roadside rest areas and Interstate interchanges as far north as Atlanta, are a few families on the road to Disney World. Their sedate station wagons and campers seemingly drift among thousands of battered Volkswagens, shiny sports cars, and modified hearses. It is all that a motel manager could dream of. As one reservations clerk put it early this morning as he scanned his computer printout of available rooms, "I'm sorry, sir, but Florida is filled for the night."

Tourists are not the only ones on the move here, however. Hoboes and migrant workers are heading north again. More planes and rental cars are moving south. The jet set's yachts are starting north. And the *Pleica nearctica* are moving in all directions. They are the lovebugs, the little understood, but aptly named insects that spend most of their four-day life-span fornicating in flight. Unfortunately for the insect and for drivers, lovebugs become so involved with one another that they are apparently unaware of where they are going.

"When you're doing 60 miles an hour with a 40,000-pound load of car batteries," says Mr. Gunter, the truck driver, "it's really something to hit a cloud of them damn lovebugs. You can't see a thing even with the washers on all the time."

Roadside rest areas install special hoses for motorists to wash their windows and stained clothing. Drivers smear the front of their vehicles with baby oil or Vaseline to facilitate removal of the lovebugs, while others rig special nets in front of radiators and truck refrigeration units. Even so, the bug corpses had best be removed promptly. For if they are not, the concentrated protein that once was a lovebug will eat away car paint, a fact that car-wash firms advertise blatantly along with their prices—seasonally adjusted upward.

"We really don't know much about these little fellows," admitted Dr. Louis Kuitert, a University of Florida entomologist who is trying to spawn a lovebug abatement program. "Somehow, though, man has altered the environment in the last five or six years and they've grown out of control."

"It's another one of the joys of spring," added Mr. Hatchett.

*Meanwhile, up in North Dakota . . .*

# BISMARCK, NORTH DAKOTA

The North Dakota National Guard has been told by officials in Washington that it must recruit 20 blacks this year to balance its membership racially. There is just one small problem. According to a population study by the Guard here, there are only 20 eligible blacks in the entire state.

The incident grew from the National Guard's 18-month-old effort to increase its black membership nationally. But for many persons in these Midwest regions, the North Dakota situation was further proof that Washington bureaucrats, 1535 miles southeast, know little if anything about life beyond the Potomac.

"My first reaction," said General LeClair Melhouse, the state's National Guard commander, "was 'Where are the blacks?'" According to the latest census statistics, this rural state along the Canadian border has 2496 Negro residents.

General Melhouse provided the following breakdown:

• Of the 2496 blacks in North Dakota, 2346 (including dependents) are members of the Air Force at bomber bases at Minot and Grand Forks and at radar sites scattered throughout the state. "Active military personnel would seem to be unlikely prospects for an enlistment in the National Guard," one official here noted. That leaves 150.

• Of the 150, more than 60 are women. That leaves 90.

• Of the 90, about 40 are either under age 18 or over age 45. That leaves 50.

• Of the 50, more than 30 are college students, many from out of state on athletic scholarships and presumably with little interest in remaining in North Dakota for a six-year National Guard enlistment.

• That leaves about 20 eligible blacks, some of whom may be physically unfit.

"The way I figure," General Melhouse said, "if you don't have the man, well, then you can't very well recruit him, can you?"

A year and a half ago the National Guard's new chief, General Francis S. Greenlief, ordered the number of blacks in the Guard (then 5893) to be doubled within the year through special recruitment efforts. Since then, each state unit has had to report its minority enlistments monthly. And General Greenlief has appointed a special adviser for minority affairs. By the end of January this year the Air and Army National Guards had 11,965 Negroes, or 4.7 percent of the 480,108 members. But there were none in the North Dakota unit. "We do have one mulatto," one official proudly noted.

So in Washington, National Guard officials studied the latest state census figures for black populations to determine what proportion each state Guard unit should have. "Somehow they came up with 20 for us," General Melhouse said, "although according to our calculations, proportionately we need a little bit less than one entire black."

North Dakota's main minority is Indians, who make up 14,369, or about 2 percent, of the state's 617,761 residents. There are now 13 Indians among the state Guard's 3500 members. That is less than 1 percent. When the letter came out from Washington a few weeks ago, however, there was no mention of Indians, just blacks.

"Actually," General Melhouse said, "we had a black guardsman once. He was a transfer student from New Jersey on a basketball scholarship out here. But he's been gone a couple years now." So the general wrote back to Washington, "If we can find a black, we'll attempt to recruit him."

The general dispatched the state Guard's full-time recruiter, Major Nelson Stave, and his personnel officer, Colonel Edgar Johnson, to speak at college campuses, Indian reservations, and schools to increase minority enlistments. "We've had no particular luck yet," Colonel Johnson said. In fact, not one new black has enlisted.

In recent days in recognition of the difficulties of recruiting 20 young blacks in a farming state where blacks total four thousandths of 1 percent of the population, Washington officials have revised the quota for the North Dakota National Guard.

Now, General Melhouse is to recruit just 10 blacks.

*A couple of weeks later Mabel Kiser*
*discovered spring in her kitchen.*
*We talked about it.*

# MILLSTONE, KENTUCKY

Mabel Kiser was cooking breakfast in her modest little home down the hollow here the other morning when she realized something special was happening. Warm sunshine was streaming in that little window over the kitchen sink and shining on the side of the icebox. The sun hadn't done that since last fall, when it forsook these mountains for the winter.

"Each year when I see that happen," the 60-year-old Mrs. Kiser said, "well, then I know spring is here."

It is a happy annual event for Mrs. Kiser, who, like millions of other Americans, suddenly realizes one day that another year has gone and that once again spring is easing slowly and quietly over the land, each day moving a few more miles north. It takes about six weeks for the green of spring to inch north from Florida's orange groves to North Dakota's wheat fields.

Already car washes in central Florida, 800 miles south of here, are "seasonally adjusting" their prices for the long lines of drivers eager to wash from the car bodies some of the area's mushrooming colonies of lovebugs. In Atlanta, about half the leaves are out now, although they just had snow in Macon. Near Chatsworth, a few farmers have broken ground for the first time this year and LuLu's fireworks stand is sprucing for summer holiday sales. Around Knoxville, motel owners are cleaning and painting the swimming pools while some schoolboys have already tried out their fishing poles.

Here in the Cumberland Mountains of Appalachia in eastern Kentucky, where the smell of coal-burning furnaces hangs in the air, the leaf buds have just started to emerge, giving the apple trees and beeches and maples and oaks that familiar soft green misty look. Purple phlox line the roadside. The craggy rock faces of the mountains are shiny wet from the unusually heavy rains that have pushed many rivers to flood stage. Joe Gose can pump gas now without a coat on, and little Timmy McCray has already gone barefoot once, down to the creek to watch the waterbugs skitter across the warming stream.

"I tell you we're happy to see spring come," said Blaine Kiser, a retired coal miner who is Mabel's husband. "Winter is no fun here. It's raining. People aren't out much. But in the spring the sun gets to coming out and people just feel good again."

One of 14 children of a coal miner, Mr. Kiser, who is now in his 63rd spring, never had much time to notice things like the seasons. He finished the fifth grade, then entered the mines down the road where he swung a pick in shafts often only three feet high. He visited Cincinnati once but spent most of his life right here near Millstone (population: 576) just two hills away, as distance is measured in these parts, from his birthplace. Here he entered the mines; bought his own land; met his wife-to-be; helped build his own house with timber from a relative's land; dug his own well, which he uses to this day; and raised his son and daughter, who, like most local young people, have gone to northern cities for work.

The Kisers' home is a single-story, six-room wood structure with a tin roof where each room's lights are carefully extinguished as people move to other rooms. It is situated on a two-and-a-half-mile rutted, pitted clay road that local residents maintain is still passable. The single-lane road, originally a mule path, has one tire track two feet higher than the other. It is given to sudden dips, steep slippery hills, and floods. The water from spring rains rushes along it from Claude and Jake Bentley's home down past the Kisers' to Widow Cook's place and then Buster Bentley's house. "The road isn't too bad," Mrs. Kiser said. "The water has gone down some."

Mr. Kiser tends his garden down by the old outhouse, which the family used until the mid-1950s. Under the watchful supervision of Cain and Brownie, the dogs, he has just planted his potatoes, onions, and cabbage, and, now that the sun is shining on the kitchen icebox, he figures he'll get his green beans planted in about two weeks.

Soon Mrs. Kiser, who studied alone to earn her high-school diploma at the age of 51, will be out in the garden, too. "I'm just a country child," she said. "I love to watch living things." And there are many more living things here in the spring. She will plant a lot

of flowers—for their own beauty to be sure, but more because they attract butterflies. "Have you ever watched a butterfly for a while?" she asked. "They are so carefree." Or she will listen to the peewee birds, so-called for their song. They returned last week. Or she will watch by the old log barn where two colonies of black ants are perpetually at war, grappling, biting, and pushing their opponents off the logs in their annual spring offensives. "But my greatest spring pleasure," she said, "is to stand under the big old apple tree when its blossoms are full-blown and listen to the bees. My, but they sing pretty."

In recent years Mrs. Kiser has also spent much time in an abandoned mobile schoolhouse as director of the Millstone Sewing Center, a federally funded project that gives local women intermittent employment repairing old donated clothes and preparing new outfits for Letcher County's needy families. However, the dismantling of the Office of Economic Opportunity by the Nixon Administration seems to place the popular center's future in jeopardy. To her dismay, then, Mrs. Kiser may soon have more time for those "thinking walks" she used to take with Old Beck, the mule.

"In the winter when it snows," she said with much enthusiasm, "it seems like the whole earth must be covered by silence. And in the fall—oh, every season is my favorite—in the fall everything is going to sleep for a while. When I was young, you know, sometimes I'd chase a falling leaf and try and kiss it in the air. Some days that was the most important thing in the world to me."

But now it is spring again and Mrs. Kiser is as excited as ever. "Every spring," she said, "I thank the Lord because I am old now and each year is one more that I might not have again." Mrs. Kiser paused. "Oh," she said, "April, April, linger longer."

*Everyone's heard of the swallows of*
*Capistrano. But they'd be just*
*appetizers for Hinckley's birds.*

# HINCKLEY, OHIO

The buzzards returned to Hinckley today, pursued by 25,000 curious sightseers eager, for some reason, to glimpse the bald-headed birds that live off rotting flesh. Capistrano, California, whose swallows also returned today, may have a prettier name, a famous song, and a more attractive bird. But Hinckley, a crossroads community 23 miles south of Cleveland, still has its 75 beloved buzzards. And annually, in what the local newspaper calls "the social event of the year," Hinckley along with much of northern Ohio celebrates the return to the roost of their area's buzzards, who have spent the winter in Florida.

Mysteriously, the birds always seem to return on the Sunday that local citizens hold their lucrative annual Pancake Breakfast. One year there were 70,000 people here for pancakes and buzzards— about 17 times the entire town's population. Today's crowd included Mrs. Lola Jane Forsythe, who predicted the time the first buzzard would be sighted, and thus won a three-day trip to, of course, Buzzards Bay, Massachusetts. (Some said second prize was six days in Buzzards Bay.)

The buzzards were not exactly swarming over Hinckley, but the park rangers said at least seven had arrived. Other people swore they had seen more of the ugly birds, nature's own special janitors, soaring in the sunny sky. Still others were skeptical. But that really didn't matter. Everybody celebrated the coming of spring anyway with buzzard pins, buzzard sweatshirts, buzzard medallions, buzzard hats, buzzard paperweights, and buzzard bumper stickers. They came from California, Washington, New York, and Ohio on bicycles, motorcycles, helicopters, and foot and in cars, some marked "Hinckley or Bust." They walked in the woods, necked in the cars, and slipped in the mud puddles. And traffic backed up over three miles, bumper sticker to bumper sticker.

"I really don't know why I'm here," said Ed Driscoll, who returned early from vacation to see the buzzards. "It's just something to do outdoors on a nice day after staying indoors all winter." "I suppose it's sad we don't have anything better to do," said Rich Basch, who along with a friend has driven over 200 miles round-trip from Toledo for the last three years. He has yet to see a buzzard. "So what," he said. "Everybody here is happy."

There are about 40 buzzard roosts in Ohio and others in the East and South. And there are numerous theories as to why some buzzards have chosen to homestead in Hinckley. One is that the soaring birds were curious to see the thousands of humans who come here every spring to stand in the park's mud and peer into the sky for no apparent reason. Another dates from 1818 when Medina County farmers decided there were too many animals here. So they slaughtered more than 300 deer, 21 bears, 17 wolves, and other game in one afternoon. Presumably tales of that feast have been winged down from buzzard generation to generation. Probably the best theory is that the local ledges provide ideal up- and down drafts for the five-pound buzzards (technically turkey vultures) to glide on.

With a five-foot wingspread, a hooked beak, and a guttural hiss, the buzzards seem menacing. They are, however, very shy of

humans. Their eyesight, though, is about eight times sharper than man's, enabling them to see swarming flies on a dead animal from several hundred feet up. Sharp-eyed or not, the nation's buzzard population has dwindled somewhat as farmers no longer dump dead animals in their fields—and as frustrated hunters illegally pick off buzzards for target practice.

*Spring in the city is a subtle thing.*

## CHICAGO, ILLINOIS

Spring came to Ron Ohlsen the other day as he crept along this city's Edens Expressway in a warm afternoon's traffic jam. Suddenly, he realized he could hear a radio in the next car because, for the first time since last fall, his own car window was rolled down. Spring seems to come more subtly to millions of Americans in northern cities than it does to the more sparsely populated countryside.

Down in Florida it is hard to miss the frolicking college students. In Georgia it is hard to miss the azaleas. In the Cumberland Mountains of eastern Kentucky the leaves are out fully now, and in Millstone the other day Mabel Kiser heard a bee. In southern Indiana the farmers are breaking up the soil that will soon receive millions of corn seeds. And in Gary the reddish steel-mill smog stands out starkly against a blue sky instead of blending with winter's sodden clouds.

To Mr. Ohlsen, a Dictaphone salesman, spring's arrival here means he can open his car window without getting a face full of slush from another lane. Now it is daylight when he starts home from work. Now he can hang his suit coat on a hanger in the back seat. And soon the traffic jams are caused by cars overheating instead of cars skidding.

Elsewhere in this metropolitan area of more than 7 million people, spring arrived in myriad ways. Drive-in restaurants reopened. Sidewalk cafes primped. Commuter shuttle boats returned to the Chicago River. Fishermen, young and old, again lined the city's breathtaking waterfront as one by one the pleasure craft, from the smallest sailboat to giant yachts, tied up at harbor floats. Apartment dwellers in the lakefront high-rises dusted off their binoculars for another season of scrutinizing scantily clad sunbathers on the beaches below—where five-year-old Malcolm Morison has already scampered in the warming sand.

In Arlington Heights, "For Sale" signs blossomed overnight on front lawns as businessmen prepared for the annual rash of corporate transfers. Dozens of commuters also began again to ride their bicycles to the train station. In the more rural northwestern suburbs, where mailboxes are still anchored in old milk cans, squads of belching construction trucks wallowed across mushrooming garden-apartment projects in mud-filled fields that last fall yielded their last corn harvest. In the exclusive suburb of Kenilworth, uniformed maids left their coats behind as they walked the dogs, and grounds keepers on the lakefront estates hosed down their owners' white stone birdbaths.

Downtown, Marvin Harris, a 35-year-old Good Humor man, was back cruising on Rush Street. He "just happened" by the Ogden Elementary School at its 3 P.M. dismissal and was engulfed by welcoming youngsters clutching sticky dimes. Down the street, Farrell Potman, a neon-sign cleaner, was on the job. "Now the work begins," he said. On the South Side, around the University of Chicago, the tall bare trees were starting to bud. Nearby, coatless gaggles of youngsters ran up and down giant mounds of debris from deteriorating buildings.

But spring can be a fickle season here, too. As one store clerk put it, "I thought we had spring last Monday." Last week there were several warm days and then a blizzard buried some suburbs with drifting snow, closing roads and offices. Downtown there was a cold, driving rain. Historically, this week is one of the year's most dangerous—the peak time for tornadoes. Civil Defense sirens blew warnings in numerous communities, but there have been no reports of damage so far. The city's 6000 miles of local streets and alleys, however, have suffered much damage, not from tornadoes but from what weather experts classify as this winter's 43 storms. All week long, James J. McDonough, commissioner of streets and sanitation, had 45 crews out filling potholes.

Mr. McDonough has a foolproof system for detecting the arrival of spring in Chicago. On one day every year, the trash his men collect jumps abruptly from about 4000 tons a day to 5500 tons as city residents begin spring housecleaning, gardening, and mowing their lawns. This year that day was Monday. City crews then began removing snowplows and salt spreaders from 600 trucks. "As far as my department is concerned," the commissioner said, "winter is officially over and spring is here."

*There's a new rite of spring, and it's
as old as the Garden of Eden.*

# MEMPHIS, TENNESSEE

"It just felt so good!" she said. And she bounced up and down and waved her arms all over and then got dressed. The crowd cheered lustily. And Janet's "streak" was over. It was but one of thousands of streaks run on and off the nation's college campuses in recent days as the country's latest fad—running nude through public places—streaked north with the warm rays of spring. Streaking, a pastime first popularized by Adam and Eve and later politicized by Lady Godiva, is being fueled by a certain annual spring silliness and a perennial news media eagerness thirsty for refreshing stories.

The precise social significance of streaking is as yet unclear. But some academics, none of them known streakers, say the fad is an innocent asexual flaunting of social values, an updated version of wearing long hair, or a nonviolent way of demonstrating the generation gap. There may be, however, a simpler explanation: it's fun.

Although the novelty of nudity will surely fade in many places soon, the current epidemic of epidermis has already developed its own etiquette, national ratings, fashions, and, of course, ardent opponents, many of them anonymous. Streaking has also led to numerous humorous incidents, a few police confrontations, and generally favorable comparisons with some more violent campus antics in the 1960s.

Here in Memphis, a bustling mid-South river city not noted for its wild exuberance, streaking has prompted an awakening of school spirit at Memphis State University. A 62-year-old conservative institution, Memphis State has 20,000 students. However, 18,000 of them live off campus, which makes for little communal spirit.

It was something of a surprise, therefore, when David Fowler, MSU's quarterback, and Tony Marchetti, an offensive guard, appeared out of uniform near a girl's dorm. Some police in uniform caught the pair, but streaking had struck. And for nights afterward dozens of streakers dashed across campus, drawing guffaws, applause, and cheers.

Four nights later, more than 4000 persons—oldsters in wheelchairs, young marrieds with infants, and college students themselves—gathered in 75-degree spring weather to have a good time. They did. At 8:24 the night's first two streakers streaked, the start of the school's bid to be ranked No. 1 nationally in streaking. For the next four hours more than 200 nude men and women dashed about from one side of the mall to the other, over bushes, through crowds, up on rooftops, and out on limbs. The delighted mob of spectators washed back and forth across the field seeking streakers, reserving their loudest cheers for streaking coeds.

Few streakers came to streak, however. For a true streak is a spontaneous act among strangers or a dare between friends like Rocky Janda and Dwight Lee. Modestly stripping in the men's room of the sociology building, the pair burst out the door and up the ramp toward the throng. They had good streaking form. They were appropriately undressed, wearing only tennis shoes and socks. Like good streakers, they waved their arms in the air and shouted. In one motion, the crowd's heads swung to the action and a cheer erupted.

Like other participants, they discovered the heady exhilaration that accompanies streaking: first, the sense of daring, then the nervous anticipation as you undress, the last fleeting moment of fear before you start, the wet grass underfoot, the pounding heart during the dash, the smiles of spectators flashing by, the wind brushing against your cheeks, and the warm sense of accomplishment as you dress—uncaptured—at your goal.

"Wasn't that great?" Mr. Janda asked a fellow streaker. "It really felt super, like for once in my life here I accomplished something. And it didn't hurt anybody."

There are those who disagree. "The entire thing is asinine and silly," said William C. Tatum, the dean of students, who was home sick in bed. Others, also absent, are offended by such public pubic displays. Some phoned threats to school officials. Others wrote newspapers: "If young people are taught they are animals long enough through the theory of evolution," reasoned Mrs.

Helen T. Puckett, "they'll soon begin to act like them." But President Billy Mack Jones left most crowd control in the hands of student leaders like Rick Carter, a 24-year-old pig-tailed ex-Marine who is student-body president. He kept the crowd—and therefore the streakers—on campus.

There was a band playing "Moonlight Becomes You." Some students dedicated streaks to gaggles of giggling girls who pretended to cover their eyes when, moments later, the boys galloped by. And as some sort of indicator of progress, there was even an integrated streak. There were also a few arrests for indecent exposure, some fines, and one student was seized for urinating in public. However, Memphis students explained with an understanding nod that he was from Vanderbilt.

"There's nothing sensuous or freaky about streaking," said Betsy Garrett. And anyway there is little time for leering. Streakers favor darkness and, by definition, they streak by. Suddenly a naked body is flying at you and just as suddenly it is gone. As one coed put it, "You don't have time to look at the face, too."

"Streaking is a deliberate effort to flout an older society's different view of nudity," said Delton Pickering, the Methodist chaplain here. And the more brazen the streak the better. Thus, when 450 students in a psychology class here discussed streaking, it was inevitable that a pair of streakers, a man and a woman holding hands, would dash across the auditorium stage. And as Memphis Police Director Jay Hubbard urged a student throng not to streak, three naked students felt compelled to streak by behind him.

In Northfield, Minnesota, Laura Barton, a Carleton College coed, streaked across a stage during a curtain call for Shakespeare's *Measure for Measure*. "I was the first girl to streak at Carleton," said Miss Barton, "and I was the first to streak a play." In Columbia, Missouri, more than 600 streakers claimed a new world's record at the University of Missouri. And one engineering student was booked on a new charge: indecent exposure with intent to streak.

There were reports of reverse streaks—persons getting dressed and racing through nudist colonies. And streaking even hit high schools. "It's better than sitting around the Dairy Queen," said one teen-ager. At Memphis's Bartlett High one youth successfully streaked the cafeteria, wearing only shoes, sunglasses, and a ski mask. A female onlooker, however, made a positive identification, police said, and a young man was later arrested.

With the end of streaking not in sight, so to speak, perhaps Gene Pace, a 24-year-old Memphis State senior, had the best explanation of the fad. "Maybe," he said intently, "maybe you don't need a reason to streak. I mean what kind of reason is there to play basketball or anything else?"

*I'd seen about 30 springs come and go. But*
*that was less than half the number*
*Roswell Garst had known.*

# COON RAPIDS, IOWA

Thin trails of soft dust rise slowly into the warming air here these days behind the red and green and tan tractors that grind their way across the rolling miles of open earth, delicately dropping one corn seed every eight inches. Just as they have done every year at this time for decades. The red-winged blackbirds are back, too, like always, sunning themselves on the quiet roadways. In town, business has fallen off again, as it usually does in May when everyone but the shopkeepers is out in the fields.

And another spring has come to Coon Rapids, a backwater farming town where almost nothing changes but the seasons. With its quiet Main Street, dotted with dirty pickup trucks, Coon Rapids is like thousands of Middle Western American towns on the brink of another humid summer.

Once, just once, it was plucked from obscurity—when Nikita Sergeivich Khrushchev drove the 69 miles from Des Moines to visit the sprawling farm of Roswell Garst, Coon Rapids's most prominent businessman, farmer, banker, storekeeper, landowner, and promoter. That was during the Soviet Premier's 12-day visit to the United States. It was a historic visit not reciprocated by an American President until today. But Mr. Khrushchev's visit was 12 summers, 13 falls, 13 winters, and 13 springs ago. And since then, at least on the surface, not much has changed in Coon Rapids, where rabbits still bound across the few residential streets.

It is a town of 1381 souls who live in small, white-shingled houses along clean, shaded avenues called First, Second, and Third. It is a friendly town where a waitress sits down with patrons to take their orders, where strangers are greeted with a "Howdy," and where, unlike the big cities, people suspect the best of others, until proven wrong. It is a town where you park in the middle of the street, where few people think to lock their cars, and where talk

centers seriously on the weather, which is always the first, not the last, item on local radio newscasts. It is a town of no stoplights, no jail, and no movie.

"People don't get excited around here," said Gwen Sorensen. "It's not their nature. And there's not much to get excited about." Not since Sept. 23, 1959, when 500 people vainly lined Main Street to see Mr. Khrushchev; Adlai E. Stevenson, Jr., one of his escorts; and other dignitaries who never got downtown but left after visiting the Garst spread a half-mile away.

There is, however, plenty of work, thanks in large part to Mr. Garst who owns or manages 3000 cattle and 4500 acres of land and is involved in some way with the seed company, the dry-goods store, the feed company, the insurance agency, the bank, and the grain elevator. "You take Garst out of Coon Rapids," said one resident, "and this place would dry up like a cotton ball." It's been like that since the beginning, way back in 1869 when the town was founded on a sleepy bend of the Raccoon River and Edward Garst opened the general store. About the only time, Mr. Garst lost out was when he wanted to name the town Coon Riffle.

His son, Roswell, carried on the energetic family tradition, becoming not only a successful hybrid-corn farmer and business-man but a zealous, self-appointed agricultural missionary to the Soviet Union and Eastern Europe, where he spurred many farming reforms and invited the Soviet Premier to visit his home. "I told Khrushchev we two farmers could solve the world's problems a lot better than any diplomats," Mr. Garst said the other day.

A lot of water has flowed over the Coon Rapids since that visit. Mr. Khrushchev and Mr. Stevenson are both dead, and Mr. Garst has survived a bout with throat cancer. Although he lost his larynx, Mr. Garst, who is 74 years old, still can talk nonstop with the aid of a battery-powered vibrator held against his throat. But because he must breathe through a hole in his chest, he cannot swim. So the Garsts' swimming pool, where everyone gathered for a picnic that warm September day in 1959, has been filled in for a vegetable garden for Mrs. Garst. Her husband, whose early pioneering work and successes in hybrid-corn farming attracted the Russians' atten-tion, still maintains a lively interest in world affairs.

There are some other changes, too. The years have seen the town's population decline a bit; there are fewer small farms here-abouts, and Mr. Garst's two sons and a nephew now run the ever-prosperous businesses. In 1959 the grocery store sold five pounds of sugar for 38 cents and eight 12-ounce cans of corn for $1; today sugar costs 71 cents and the corn is five for $1. And the wages Mr. Garst pays his workers have increased—though not enough, accord-ing to many.

The weekly newspaper, *The Enterprise*, still doesn't publish news of local traffic violations, though, or much about crime, which strikes infrequently. "We had two break-ins the last two nights,"

said Gerald Tribble, who is half the police force, "so someone else must have gotten on to drugs." Like the chief, William Augustus, Mr. Tribble takes a rather relaxed, friendly attitude toward law enforcement. "Hey, Terry," he called to a passing driver, "your taillights are out. Better get them fixed."

He spoke as he sat the other evening in the police car in its regular parking spot at Fifth and Main, where almost everybody passes by. As usual, it was an uneventful night. The most serious call involved a teen-age couple picking tulips from the waterworks garden. Mr. Tribble gave them a stern warning. "Kids are always kids," he said as he cruised the darkened streets where you could almost feel the town going to sleep.

The City of Los Angeles, the passenger train, doesn't roar through town every night any more. But the 11:48 freight is always right on time and rumbles off to the East, leaving a string of red track signals in its wake. Then, as usual, by midnight the silence here is stunning.

The people are asleep. The blackbirds are asleep. Even the cornfields, soon to be green again, are asleep. And out on the edge of town, right where Mr. Khrushchev drove past, the only sound is the soft creaking of the 12-foot revolving corncob that still says, "Welcome to Coon Rapids."

*Something strange was afoot—a*
*barefoot—at this gas station.*

# ORLANDO, FLORIDA

The driver pulled into the gas station here on Orange Blossom Trail near the Florida Turnpike.

"Fill 'er up, sir?" asked an attractive young woman, who was obviously a male attendant's visiting girlfriend.

"Check the oil for you?" asked another woman, who simply couldn't work here.

"That'll be $4.85," said a third female, who obviously could not hold a traditionally male job like gas-station attendant.

But all three women do.

They are the only employees of the Turnpike Texaco Gas Station, where even two German shepherd guard dogs are female. And each day the women prove to several dozen startled—and sometimes chauvinist—motorists that females can pump 1000 gallons of gasoline, change oil, and check tire pressures as well (or as poorly, depending on your opinion of auto mechanics) as any male grease monkey.

So what if occasionally they don't know where to pour oil or how to open a hood. Some travelers, usually males, are so surprised—and charmed—by the feminine gasoline attendants that they even leave tips.

"These girls sure do help business," said James Simpson, the 52-year-old owner who does the station's heavy mechanical labor. "They like this kind of work and the customers like them liking their work. I think, too, the girls know how to get along with people better than men."

It was also a pragmatic step to begin hiring only women last fall. Qualified laborers are difficult to find locally, where many residents are retired and not looking for work. And other laborers can easily find more lucrative construction jobs in this fast-growing region near Disney World. "The girls are more reliable and conscientious than men. I couldn't be happier. In fact, I'm looking for a couple

40

more girls," said Mr. Simpson, who plans to order hot-pants uniforms for them soon. The women—Sue Ailes, Kathy Kidwell, and Vicky DeMore—now wander about barefoot in any informal apparel that suits them, from slacks to cut-off jeans and halter tops.

The three were drawn from their homes by Florida's sunshine. Once here, they needed some income. They get $100 for a 53-hour week, plus 10 percent commissions on their sales of oil, food, fruits, toys, pony rides, and even horses, which are for sale at the station.

It wasn't entirely the money that prompted Miss Kidwell, who is 21 years old, to apply for the job. "It sounded kind of different," she said. "I vowed I wouldn't go back to Ohio without a suntan, so I wanted to work outside. Work doesn't seem like work outdoors." She quit college after two years and first got work here as a maid. That lasted one day. Then there was a short stint in an orange-juicing factory where she monitored the flow of open, but full, cans of orange juice. Once she turned her head away for a few moments and when she looked back, there were 50 cans of orange juice all over the floor. That job lasted three days.

There is less pressure at the gas station, but there are problems. "I didn't know where the oil thingy [sic] was at first," Miss Kidwell said, "and sometimes I still have a hard time opening the trunk, I mean the hood, to check the engine."

Many dumfounded motorists won't even let the women check under the hood, apparently unable to believe they are capable of such simple chores. Some double-check each measurement. Others refuse to believe the girls are employees. One woman driver refused to let the 20-year-old Miss DeMore add a quart of oil until Mr. Simpson reaffirmed the need.

"A lot of people won't accept what a girl says until a man agrees," complained Miss DeMore, who comes from Augusta, Georgia, and is thinking in terms of eventually becoming a bartender or a barber for men. "It's very annoying," she added. "I never thought much about this women's lib stuff until now."

There are other problems. The long hours preclude much social life. There is an occasional fresh traveling salesman. Every night at home there are long scrubbing sessions with mechanics' soap to remove oil from fingernails, long hair, and bare feet. And then there are what Miss Kidwell calls the "yechy awful bugs" splattered on windshields.

But that doesn't bother the 19-year-old Miss Ailes, who comes from Morristown, Indiana. "Even with all that dirt and grime," she said, "I always feel like a female, especially when I'm reaching way across those wide windshields and I look down and see a whole carload of guys leaning forward to watch."

*I never understood why cowboy hats*
*came in all those strange shapes. I still*
*don't, but it was fun trying.*


Virtue may flourish in an old cravat,
But man and nature scorn the shocking hat.

—Oliver Wendell Holmes


# DEL RIO, TEXAS

"Down in this here country," drawled John Stockton, "you'd just as soon do without boots as not wear a hat. Why, a hat is a bare necessity." He is, of course, right. Down in this here country, a Western hat—better known in the East perhaps as a cowboy hat—sits perched up on just about every head big enough to wear one. And a few that aren't.

For much of Western history, the cowboy hat has been an all-purpose tool. Its wide brim made just about the only shade to be found in these magnificently barren parts. A sturdy, dependable hat was, in effect, a portable tree that protected the cowhand's neck and head from the rain, the sleet, and the sun that almost daily bakes much of the Southwest and, in the summer, the plains to the north. At times the Western hat made a good bucket, an uncommon wallet, or an out-of-the-way place to stash an extra pistol. Tipped over the eyes, it created a tiny pocket of darkness for a midday snooze and kept bugs off the face. Or, waved vigorously in the air, it could startle ponderous cattle herds into a long drive to the railhead.

Over the years, in fact, the cowboy hat has become as much a part of the Western tradition as the horse. Even today an experienced eye, squinting out from under a wide brim, can tell much about a person—man or woman—by the Western hat on his head—its style, color, crease, angle, degree of dirtiness, and how it

**43**

is doffed. In recent years, however, the traditional Western hat has also taken on some aspects of fashion, its height, crease, and width changing with the seasons like lapels.

And now at this time of annual Western hat model changeovers, there are growing signs, too, that the cowboy hat once worn by no self-respecting city dude past the age of nine, is becoming increasingly popular among adults throughout the country and overseas. "There's no doubt about it," said one smiling Texas hat manufacturer, "the East is going Western."

Some say the new national popularity of Western hats—as well as Western-style boots, pants, shirts, and jackets—is caused by a changing American life-style with greater amounts of leisure time. Western attire is, to be sure, casual and quite comfortable, especially for popular outdoor activities such as horseback riding and camping. Others trace the popularity, at least in part, to a certain romantic image of strength and self-reliance created by such advertisements as the Marlboro man, whose rugged face, shaded by a Western hat, looks out from billboards and the back covers of millions of magazines.

Whatever the reasons, Manhattan stores, among others, report growing sales of Western hats. Harvey Kane, owner and president of Worth and Worth, said he sells more Western hats on Madison Avenue than many stores in the West. "Western wear is popular," he said, "because of today's casual living and dress. And people are wearing Western hats more because they add class to their image. The other day here I had customers from Germany, Denmark, and the United Nations, and one Japanese man bought eight Western hats." In Garland, Texas, home of Resistol Hats, Inc., Corlyss Rider said a large number of orders now come from Germany. "Apparently it's a real fad there," she said. "We get letters saying, 'Send me a cowboy hat like James Stewart wore in such and such a movie.' And that 'Bonanza' TV show sells a lot of hats, too."

A Western hat costs anywhere from $4 to more than $125. True cowhands, however, rarely wear an expensive hat to work, for horses' hooves can just as easily crush a $100 Stetson as a $4 straw job. The cost of the hat depends on the brand and amount of beaver fur, felt, or starched straw involved. There are hundreds of styles with each manufacturer dubbing each design according to his own whim. They include cattleman, little dogie, Fort Worth, cascade, high chaparral, deputy, sundowner, ridgetop, trail boss,

ranchman, open road, bull rider, rodeo pro, Winchester, ace of spades, hoss, pony express, timberline, and Marlboro country. There is an equal variety of crown heights, brim widths, and creases to fit a man's or woman's face and figure. Generally, a tall man equals a short hat. Recently brim widths widened right along with lapels, and crowns have risen. Gary Rosenthal, president of Stetson Hat Company in Saint Joseph, Missouri, says young people are buying up his firm's new seven-inch-crown Tom Mix hats. With the trend to fashion wear, Western hats are also being made in colors other than the traditional gray, brown, and black. Resistol, for one, now sells cowboy hats in lemon, red, skylark blue, lavender, and watermelon pink, shades that must make deceased gunfighters writhe in their sandy graves.

Western hats now are big business. Hat companies compete to have winning rodeo riders, the Western hat-fashion setters, wear their hats. Teen-agers in this Mexican border town wander through Western hat departments after school like their city counterparts browse through record or tape stores.

Expensive hats are often bought in lots and given as business gifts, in lieu of liquor. For such men as cattle and horse traders, their hat is a most important wardrobe accessory, given the impact of first impressions. "If you walk into a trading session with a hat that makes you look like some kind of fool," said Mr. Stockton, who helps run a Western-wear store here, "well, you're just going to get taken, that's all."

Hat-shopping is also an important, drawn-out ritual, requiring much thought. Mike Wallen walked into Prosper-Martin's, Mr. Stockton's store, the other day looking for a new dress hat. He was wearing a dirtied mass of black felt that had obviously been stomped on by half the cattle in West Texas. Mr. Wallen had sprayed the hat countless times with starch and sugar water so it would keep the proper form. But he had carefully preserved much dirt and accumulated fingerprints on a certain spot on the front of the brim. To the knowing, this marked him as a true cowhand. For he always took his hat off with the same fingers in the same place. Dudes don't.

Old-time cowhands generally favor the narrower, lower Western hats that were popular in their youth. The younger Westerners here go for the taller, wider hat styles that have been working their way across this vast state in the last three years. Bankers and merchants, of course, still favor the "LBJ hat," the conservative gray hat that President Johnson often wore.

Dudes, sometimes called Drugstore Cowboys or Rexall Rangers, often wear their nice, clean hats at an extreme jaunty angle, sideways, forward or backward. True horseback riders, however, know that such angles invite a stiff prairie wind to whip the headgear into the next county. Nonetheless, some angles are permitted. In bars, for instance, the greater the tilt the less the sobriety.

Mr. Wallen tried on several hats, discussed the crown heights and brim widths with Mr. Stockton, then left the store to savor his decision like the veteran Western hat buyer he is. "He'll be back," said Mr. Stockton, "he'll be back."

*If you have to go to North Dakota, they say, don't go in winter. So I waited until spring. And then I met Ed Remmick.*

# GACKLE, NORTH DAKOTA

Ed Remmick owned 217 cattle last night. This morning he owned 220. "All winter long," he said, "you just wait and wait and wait and wait, not doing much of anything. But then those calves start a-coming and you get real busy and, well, you just know it's spring again."

Spring, an exciting time of new life on the farm, has finally reached this little central North Dakota community. About six weeks ago it began its annual trek north, easing its greening way over the land. It was then that college students, one-half million strong, migrated south to Florida's beaches. Here in the north, officials of the Shawnee National Forest have recently closed the main road for 60 days to give wildlife a chance to migrate safely to their summer homes. And the geese have flown over Wisconsin heading north.

In North Dakota the arrival of spring is not celebrated so much as is the departure of winter, that time of year when ice-cream cones freeze harder outdoors than they do in the refrigerator. If you don't like the weather, the saying here goes, then wait six months. So the 47-year-old Mr. Remmick, his wife, LuAnna, and their children, Michael, 17, and Mona, 13, waited through the long, cold winter. Then one day the mallard ducks were back on the pond. The laundry didn't freeze solid on the clothesline. The forecast of snow was wrong. And if these plains had trees, they would have been budding. Then, of course, the calves started to arrive—a crucial time of the year in this rural state where livestock outnumber humans five to one.

Mr. Remmick, clad in a plaid lumberjack shirt, denims, and baseball cap, walked out to the pasture one morning at 6 and there he found a calf, less than two hours old, barely standing on shaky legs. It took one step and collapsed in an 85-pound, brown-and-white heap. The sight of the calf wasn't exactly a surprise to Mr. Remmick. He has a little black book with formulas telling him when to turn the heifers loose with the bull to produce calves on what date. A June 10 mingling, for instance, means calves on or about March 26. Mr. Remmick tries to time the calves' arrival for after the last snow, but as early in good weather as possible to enable maximum summer growth. Sometimes he is wrong, and the wide-eyed, wet calf must be taken from the cold outdoors to the dry, warm basement, much to the consternation of its mother. More often, Mr. Remmick's calculations are just right. "This is the best year I can remember," he said.

In addition to the calves, Mr. Remmick has 100 Hereford cows or heifers, ranging in age from one to eight years; 7 bulls; and 100 Holstein milk cows, which he bought last fall speculating that they would increase in price by this spring. They did and will be sold soon. Together, the herd is worth about $100,000 at today's prices. But as Mr. Remmick noted, "There's no guarantee about farming. We could have a drought or epidemic and they could all be worth $40,000. It's a gamble."

A large number of the cows have had their spring calves. One was stillborn, but another heifer had twins. Each night Mr. Remmick visits the pasture every two hours, checking the one-year-old heifers. Often they need help with their first calf or both will die. As soon as a calf is born, its mother licks it vigorously all over. This gets the calf's circulation going well and puts the mother's scent on the animal. In a crowd of dozens of calves, all seemingly exact duplicates, the mothers invariably find their own.

After 10 days or so the mother and calf are turned from the corral into a pasture with other mothers and calves. There the mothers munch grass or hay while their calves romp and tumble with one another across the hillside, exploring every new flower, butterfly, and bee. Sometimes they all snooze in the warming spring sun, sprawled over the grass like so many sunbathers. But let a storm or human or dog approach the herd and the mothers are instantly awake, searching for their offspring by sniff and bellow. Cautiously, and with many glances over the shoulder, the mothers guide the curious young ones to the other side of the hill. In six weeks, the valuable calves will be vaccinated, branded, dehorned, castrated, and dusted with a powder to keep flies away.

When the grasses turn browner in the fall, which in these parts starts promptly on Labor Day, Mr. Remmick begins his early-morning trips to the pasture with fresh hay. The cattle quickly become accustomed to this tasty ritual and, in fact, gather by the gate to watch for him shortly after dawn. As he leaves the back door, he is greeted by a chorus of welcoming bellows. By then all Mr. Remmick's crops are harvested. Having started 20 years ago with 320 acres, he now farms cattle, wheat, flax, and alfalfa on 2500 acres, an area three times the size of New York's Central Park. From his house, his land stretches as far as the eye can see.

By late fall Mr. Remmick will have chosen two dozen female calves or heifers to replace his aging cows. He is expanding his herd by 10 percent because the price per pound is good these days and because Michael starts college in the fall and the Remmicks need extra income.

In about six months, this spring's calves will be weaned and separated from their mothers for the first time. It is a traumatic event for the calves, their mothers, and the Remmicks. The calves are put in another corral near the house where they are fed oats to fatten them for the slaughterhouse the following spring. The mothers gather on the other side of the fence. And for three solid days both sides bellow at each other day and night. "They really go at it," says Mr. Remmick, "and we don't get much sleep. But after three days the cattle get hoarse and quit."

Ninety days later the calves, by then weighing 550 pounds, are sold to a feedlot for final fattening. By that time, of course, the ducks are gone for the winter, the cows are pregnant again, and the bulls are in a separate pasture resting.

Despite the income the cattle sale brings, auction day is not necessarily the happiest of the year. "It's easy to get attached to an animal," says Mr. Remmick. "You help it get born into this world, care for it when it's sick, and see it grow up. By sale day it's become a part of the family. But if you're not careful, you could get emotional about something around here every day of the year.

"So to me," he adds, "I just try and keep that cow in my mind as Number 78. That's all."

*For me a ghost town is irresistible.
Especially one with a shiny modern
tourist center.*

# LANGTRY, TEXAS

The judge gazed at the man's body laid out in the sunlight for an official inquest. There was a fresh bullet hole in the middle of the man's forehead. "This hombre," the judge ruled, "met his death by being shot by a person unknown who was a damn good shot."

The murder victim has remained anonymous. But the magistrate, who died in 1904, was Judge Roy Bean, the fabled "Law West of the Pecos," the smelly saloonkeeper, sheep rancher, and part-time judge. His questionable legal decisions and nefarious ways earned him—and this former frontier town—a fame that prompted a television series and lately a movie starring Paul Newman, *The Life and Times of Judge Roy Bean.*

The judge "might have been a murderer, a robber, and a thief," recalled Beulah Burdwell, a longtime resident here, "but he was good at heart."

He was also good for business. In fact, Judge Bean is about the only reason that Langtry, an almost imperceptible ghost town in the isolated sandy wastes of West Texas, is still on any map. And there is a stagecoachful of stories about him, as many as half of which may be true.

It was Judge Bean, the unscrupulous old four-flusher, who discovered a corpse wearing a revolver one day. He confiscated the gun and fined the body $40—the exact contents of the deceased's pockets—for carrying a concealed weapon.

It was Judge Bean, the amateur legal expert, who freed a cowboy accused of murder because the judge could find no law that specifically prohibited killing a Chinese.

And it was Judge Bean, with more brass than a bedstead, who outraged an Easterner in his saloon one day. The young man had ordered a beer and put a $20 gold piece on the counter. Judge Bean promptly deposited it in his cashbox. When the stranger protested,

Saloonkeeper Bean replied, "I'm telling you that any galoot from New York with no more sense than to pay for a 35-cent beer with a $20 gold piece ain't got any change coming." When the young man's protests grew louder, Judge Bean fined him $19.65 for disturbing the peace.

In those days, when Langtry was known as one of the wickedest cities in the West, thousands peopled all four of her dusty streets, lined with stores, bars, and homes. But now a strong chilling wind blows in off the range, gushing through the broken windows of Jesus Torres's old saloon, and W. H. Dodd's old home before flapping a piece of metal roofing on what once was Jimmy Merritt's general store. Many of the houses are gone. Others are steadily decaying. And the population continues to age and decline. Four years ago it was 120. Last summer it was 55. Yesterday it was 40.

Just about everybody left in Langtry has something to do with the memory of Judge Bean. "The railroad built this town," said Jack Skiles, long a resident here, "but it's the late Roy Bean who's keeping it alive." Judge Bean keeps Mr. Skiles's family, for instance, because Mr. Skiles is the supervisor of the state's modern air-conditioned Judge Roy Bean Visitors Center. It lured 84,000 tourists off the main highway this year to see the judge's restored saloon and to buy ice cream, potato chips, cowboy hats, and gasoline. In return, in the tradition of Judge Bean's victims, the strangers leave a few dollars behind.

Most of the railroad workers left Langtry along with the steam engine. But it wasn't always so for the little town on the 300-foot cliff over the Rio Grande. Word that the Southern Pacific Railroad was stitching the Southwest together and would meet the Gulf, Harrisburg, and San Antonio near what is now Langtry prompted a boom here that saw 5000 pickpockets, railroad workers, gunfighters, gamblers, and game girls pour into the newborn sultry sin center on the Mexican border. The railroad came for the soft spring water to quench its thirsty steam engines. The others came for harder stuff. And they had a fair choice. In the 1880s there were 23 saloons in Langtry.

Sometimes as many as three men died violently in a single week—about one-half as many murders as New York City now has on an average day. To clean up the mess, the Texas Rangers had the wily Roy Bean commissioned as a judge. Between drinks and

semi-annual baths, he held court in his bar, the Jersey Lily. Its sign read: "Judge Roy Bean Notary Public Justice of the Peace Law West of the Pecos Ice Beer." Mr. Bean was no hanging judge. Instead, on paydays he favored heavy fines, which he kept, or expulsion from town with no money, horse, or weapons—a formidable punishment in those days when civilization was 100 rugged miles away.

The judge had one soft spot—Lily Langtry, the beautiful English actress known as the Jersey Lily whose pictures he had seen in a magazine once. He said she was "as purty as a red heffer in a flower bed." He wrote her often and told everyone he had named the town for her (though nonromantics said it was for George Langtry, a railroad engineer). He was always inviting Miss Langtry to Langtry, where he said he had built a little opera house for her to perform in. Finally, on a United States tour she did come, but the judge had died just a few months earlier.

A few people here can remember those days when drunks were chained to the hanging tree until sober and when civic dances went on all night. The trains stopped wherever passengers waved them down in the countryside. It was a frontier town into the 1930s, when residents still carried six-shooters. But soon there was not much to dance about. Mechanization reduced the railroad crews. Modern medicine reduced the need for cowboys to ride the range daily in search of sick sheep or cattle. And the changing economics of agriculture dictated bigger ranches and fewer ranchers.

The attractions of city life, including full-time employment, grew too strong for many. Although electricity came in 1950, the telephone did not arrive until 1967. As for television, any resident who wants to see astronauts on the moon still must drive more than 60 miles to Del Rio and rent a motel room. It's 217 miles to the dentist and 240 miles to some high-school basketball games. In the summer the temperature can get up to 113 degrees in the shade, if any shade can be found.

"It's a rather harsh place to live," said Mrs. Wilmuth Skiles, who teaches at the area's school, 30 miles away. "We miss some cultural things, music and art," she added. "The children should be around people of different types more. And we get too set in our ways."

But there are some compensations. Every family, for instance, is self-sufficient. Most build and wire their own homes. Once a month they all gather at the old school for a movie. There are baseball games out at Pump Canyon, goat fries by the river, hunting, fishing, caves and relic-strewn old railroad camps to be explored, and boats to float down the Rio Grande.

"Out in these parts," said Mr. Skiles, "we enjoy nature. We're pretty much on our own. We don't have to depend on anybody else for anything. We've got a lot of freedom. And you can go anywhere you want whenever you want." Then he turned his pickup truck off the dirt path and made his own road home through the sage.

*On the other hand, Schaumburg is no*
*ghost town. It's . . . It's . . .*
*Well, it's something else.*

# SCHAUMBURG, ILLINOIS

"I SAID," he said, "WE USED TO KEEP THE BEES OVER THERE."

Like just about everyone in this northwest Chicago suburb, Ellsworth Meineke, the former farmer, was shouting. It is the only way to be heard outdoors here, for everywhere one turns a giant earth-mover belching black smoke is growling its way through a field, its metal mouth swallowing cubic yard after cubic yard of fertile farmland. Cornfields are becoming apartment developments; country lanes are turning into two-way, four-lane thoroughfares with radar-enforced speed limits; and bean fields are becoming backyards. Acre by acre, once-sleepy little Schaumburg is being molded into the ultimate American suburb—a 23-square-mile Tomorrowland whose residents even now regard downtown Chicago as a place to drive through once a year to see the Christmas lights.

It is a transformation occurring to varying degrees these days around the fringes of many decaying American cities. And it is a transformation that creates an entirely new city with its own symbols, sights, and sounds. Such a suburb is an "outer city" where people say things like "That lake was a cornfield 18 months ago" or "I see Dave got the windows in" or "The new police station will go over by that silo." The present, it seems, exists only as another construction phase.

In Schaumburg, Chicago's fastest-growing suburb, the municipal motto should be "Semper Muddy." Streets are littered with dirt clods tossed from the giant rubber treads of earth-movers, dump trucks, and diesels hauling flatbeds full of new sewer pipes. Recently Schaumburg reported 18 cement mixers worked 20 straight hours hauling enough gray goo to form the Midwest's largest single cement slab. (It *was* a cornfield; it *will be* the new Motorola headquarters.)

It is a city where sidewalks end in weeds, where "Choice Land For Sale" signs seem to outnumber people, where few trees measure over two inches in diameter, and where more houses were built last year than in all of Chicago.

"In short," said Mayor Robert O. Atcher, "this is a fairytale town." The mayor is a balding, 59-year-old former songwriter ("I Want to Be Wanted"), country singer, and radio broadcaster who grew up in Kentucky's Hardin County like another of Illinois's adopted sons, Abe Lincoln. Mr. Atcher spoke in his office, the converted chauffeur's quarters over the garage of the old Jennings farm, where the walls are lined, not with prominent people's pictures, but with bronzed shovels from countless groundbreaking ceremonies. ("You can't miss the City Hall," his secretary had said. "It's the white house across the parking lot from the big barn.")

Next month, however, Schaumburg officials will move into a new city hall. "THIS WILL BE MY OFFICE," shouted Mayor Atcher as he stepped over some spilled nails.

He was shouting because a cement truck was dumping a load nearby and Mike Koldos, a carpenter who lives in Chicago and works in the suburbs, was banging a plank in place. "ACCORD-ING TO PLAN, THE WALLS SHOULD GO UP NEXT WEEK," the mayor said.

And therein lies a special difference between Schaumburg and other exploding suburbs. For Schaumburg did not just happen. It was planned—by Schaumburgians.

It all began in the early 1950s when a few affluent Chicagoans fled the city for the quiet of western Cook County. They settled in Schaumburg, for 100 years a crossroads community where local German farmers retired to live on a road called Easy Street. Before long, however, the newcomers detected developers sniffing around. They were worried. "It was clear that suburbia was coming," said Mayor Atcher, "and our goal was to control the hodgepodge mess of developments."

So in 1956 the village was incorporated. Population: 130. The new town fathers promptly slapped a five-year moratorium on all development, pending completion of scores of extensive studies on soil, water, land use, financing, zoning, sewage, traffic, and other concerns foreign to farmers. "Schaumburg was never planned as a normal suburban community," said Mr. Atcher. "We saw what they had become." The new town devised a long list of rules. Developers had to build and maintain their own streets. They had to install 54-inch sewers, twice as big as necessary for the developments planned, but just right for the developments that officials knew from their studies would follow. Schaumburg has no downtown. It is being built from the outside (cheapest land) inward. Zoning regulations encourage 10 moderate-size shopping centers, sensibly spaced so all residents can walk to shop.

The water study showed Schaumburg atop a massive aquifer with supplies for generations. Just to make sure, though, the city is building 100 surface lakes on gravel beds to resupply the underground lake. Officials even foresaw energy shortages. Half the 16 water pumps are electric and half gasoline-powered. And in case there's ever a long drought, two new deep wells are going down. One, of course, is gas; the other is electric. An esthetics committee is designing legislation to remove ugly, tall commercial signs. And Mr. Meineke heads a group to open a 200-acre virgin prairie park.

Perhaps most impressive is Schaumburg's financial foresight. Its $7-million income now comes from building permits, and the town's share of state gasoline and sales taxes, much of the latter from 3 big furniture stores, 13 automobile dealers, and Woodfield Mall, the world's largest enclosed shopping center. There is no city property tax. To assure its independence, Schaumburg, which is on two major expressways near O'Hare International Airport, zoned its northeast corner for office buildings, covering just 20 percent of the town. Yet in 15 or 20 years, when the building boom is over and the income from construction permits drops, this business sector is expected to pay two-thirds of any city property tax.

From 130 residents in 1956, Schaumburg grew to 1000 in 1960, 18,830 in 1970, and 33,000 today. By 1990, the plans say, it will have its maximum desirable 230,000. Each day 11 new residents move in. The average income is $15,000 a year. And, significantly, only 4 percent of the population works in downtown Chicago, the city 32 miles away that spawned this suburb.

All of which is not to say that Schaumburg's life is trouble-free. Road construction is behind schedule. The mosquitoes have been bad. There is no post office. And more people mean more crime.

Ten years ago a runaway cow was a serious incident. Now there's shoplifting and robbery, and the other day Schaumburg almost had its first murder case. Fortunately, however, the body was dumped 14 feet inside Hoffman Estates, the next suburb north.

Land values have skyrocketed, too. In the mid-1800s Mr. Meineke's land went for $1.25 an acre. Twenty years ago, it cost $250. Today it is more than 100 times as much. Which is why the 74-year-old Mr. Mieneke sold off his 8 million bees and 38 acres of clover for an apartment development next to his old gazebo. "I hate to see this country change," he said.

"So do I," said Mayor Atcher, as he looked over a vast development where tractors skim off valuable topsoil before building. The development's name is Walden. "I came out here to escape the city," he continued, "but you can't. You can just try to control it. We have 8000 homes now and 2000 apartments and 22,000 jobs. It's going faster than we thought, but all according to plan."

Then, an air hammer opened up, drowning out the mayor's words. He leaned toward a visitor's ear and shouted. "I SAID," he said, "THIS IS ONLY THE BEGINNING."

*I never knew Wendell Willkie.*
*But I met his son.*

# RUSHVILLE, INDIANA

Just about every road that finds its way into Rush County somehow ends up heading straight through this humid little town of about 7000 people. Historically, that's understandable. Rushville is the county seat, and that means it should be a convenient horseback ride away from the other towns that dot the Hoosier countryside, the backyard of Wendell Lewis Willkie, the unsuccessful Republican candidate for President in 1940. But as this little town celebrates its 150th anniversary—honoring Mr. Willkie, of course, even though he was born a few miles north, up in Elwood—the days of riding a horse to the county seat have become, like Willkie himself, a part of our history.

Change is stalking Rush County and Rushville and Fountaintown and Gwynneville and the other little disc-and-harrow towns and villages brushstroked onto the flat green corn country 40 miles south and east of downtown Indianapolis. These towns, once the vital supply points and social centers for farm families, are being transformed into bedroom communities and bothersome 30-mile-an-hour speed zones for the thousands of workers who still live in the county but earn their living in the city's factories. "Indianapolis is getting closer all the time," said Robert Crawley, editor of *The Rushville Republican*. Rush County, a 260-square-mile area that has supported every Republican Presidential candidate since 1856, seems about to become exurbia.

"Open your eyes to the future," brash, strapping Wendell Willkie told his fellow Americans. "Help us build a New World." Mr. Willkie was married here, owned farmland here, and had his national campaign headquarters here; his son is president of the bank here. On the surface, the New World that Willkie saw seems little different. The roadside litter is not yet beer bottles but empty fertilizer bags.

"But looks are very deceptive here," said Philip Willkie, Wendell's only son. Today there are more swimming pools in the backyards, more vacationers head south for Florida, and the used-car lots are starting to squeeze out the farm-implement dealers. Local officials estimate about 40 percent of the county's 20,000 residents, steady since the Civil War, now work in factories in Indianapolis or budding industrial centers like Shelbyville, Anderson, and Connersville. And land development for industry and housing, a sure sign of approaching suburbia, is nearing Rush County. Land prices, for years about $500 an acre, have risen to $750, on the way to the $1,500 that an acre commands close to the city.

To be sure, agriculture still dominates the county job picture, but it's a kind of agriculture that John Arnold, the first landowner in Rush County, named for Benjamin Rush, a signer of the Declaration of Independence, would hardly recognize. The farms must be bigger now to support a family. A new tractor costs about $12,000, so more farmers are contracting out part of their work to others who already own the necessary machinery. And more and more farmers, some say up to 50 percent, are also holding full-time factory jobs. Like John Ed Harrison.

A tall, blond 27-year-old father of two boys, John Ed Harrison lives eight miles south of here on a 460-acre farm. He rises daily at 6 A.M. for his chores and, these days, plants corn and soybeans. At 4 P.M. he drives a few miles into Milroy, where he works until midnight for Harcourt Outlines, a maker of school supplies. The factory work earns him $8,500 a year while the farm income, which he shares with his widowed mother, brings Mr. Harrison $2,000. "Anyone who wants to farm like I do has to have another job to support himself," said Mr. Harrison, who hopes eventually to acquire enough land to farm full-time.

Like a few hundred other local citizens, Mr. Harrison took a few hours off to join in the week-long sesquicentennial celebrations, which included a "giant parade" that took two hours to pass by, a square dance, antique and dog shows, a local art exhibition, home tours, plus an ice-cream social at the First Presbyterian Church. Many of the local men grew beards for the celebrations, while numerous women wore the bonnets and long, gingham dresses of another era.

There was also "the gigantic historical spectacular 'One World,'" a dramatic presentation of the county's history that included a pig chase; a segment on Poots, the local cow that made the Fox Movietone newsreels in the 1930s because she could pump water; and a tribute to Mr. Willkie, whose book *One World*, a plea for unity among nations, prompted the show's title.

The festivities also prompted hundreds of reminiscences about Willkie, generally among the town's elderly population. "He was a great man," said 69-year-old Louis Simon as he left the shady grave site. "You know I was the ring boy at his wedding. That was a long time ago though. And I reckon things have changed a lot."

On April 10, 1974, Philip H. Willkie died.
He was buried not far from his father.

*I'd just finished reading* Jonathan Livingston Seagull. *And then I met The Breakfast Flock.*

# SAINT PETERSBURG, FLORIDA

The air lanes around Saint Petersburg–Clearwater International Airport are becoming increasingly crowded—with sea gulls. Fresh from a stale snack of garbage at an expanding county dump nearby, thousands of the graceful gray and white birds have at peak times in recent weeks taken to gliding the one mile to the airport to relax and frolic on the warm cement runways provided by Pinellas County taxpayers.

No one is talking of killing the scavengers, not with the continuing popularity of Richard Bach's book *Jonathan Livingston Seagull*. Besides, the birds, who are no doubt members of Jonathan's Breakfast Flock, are a major tourist attraction on nearby gulf beaches, where they mooch picnickers' sandwiches on the fly and daintily take proffered pieces of bread from vacationers' hands.

In fact, the gulls have become so tame that they hardly bother to blink at the creatures in airport uniforms who run out on the runways, waving their arms and shouting at them. They don't even blink at the automatic scarecrow device that periodically fires small, explosive charges to frighten them away. Bobo Hayes, the airport manager, reports that the birds have learned the firing intervals, and just before each explosion all the gulls duck, so to speak. Then continue their fun.

Unfortunately the sea gulls' newfound playground is a potential hazard. In recent weeks at least three aircraft have plowed into bunches of the birds, killing some, denting the airplanes, and ruining two jet engines. The 2000-acre airfield has three major runways, ranging up to 8000 feet, and handles an average of 500 flights a day, according to Mr. Hayes. Much of the traffic is private and corporate jets, chartered tourist flights from Canada, and planes carrying Florida cattle for export. "We haven't had any injuries or serious accidents yet," said Mr. Hayes, "but it is potentially a very serious problem. And we must take immediate steps."

So local officials, including County Administrator Lowell C. Wikoff, are considering a trash compactor to help clean up the gulls' feeding ground. The machine, much like those that crush old autos into tiny metal cubes for recycling, takes an average truckload of 1.5 tons of orange peels, paper, and coffee grounds and turns them into a compact cube of solid trash about 3 feet square. "Any gull would break his beak working on one of those," Mr. Wikoff said.

The moisture squeezed from the trash would be added to the county's sewage. According to Mr. Wikoff, though, the area's treated sewage effluent is being sold to private buyers, such as golf-course operators, eager for nutrient-rich irrigation water in this sandy area. And there are now so many buyers of sewage, Mr. Wikoff said, that soon the county will have a shortage of sewage to sell. The compacted trash cubes would be laid three deep in a landfill project covering 160 acres, which are now mostly marsh but will someday be a public recreation area complete with a golf course, a lake, and a soap-box-derby ramp. In a way, the birds have done their county a favor, helping convince officials to start a solid-waste program years before it had been planned. The compactor would increase the dump's life-span to about 20 years instead of the 5 or 6 years now envisioned.

Apparently, news of the free daily feast has been spreading by word of beak in the gull world and the birds' numbers increase daily. The gulls now arrive for brunch at 10 A.M. sharp, just as the first truckloads arrive with the refuse from 50,000 humans in Clearwater and 280,000 in Saint Petersburg.

"I suppose," said one bulldozer driver, "they think we're spreading this stuff out just for them."

# SUMMER

*People in the public eye, I thought, must
need some time to themselves. Fortunately,
the Humphreys did allow one
visitor one weekend.*

# WAVERLY, MINNESOTA

Ten-year-old Frank Dorsey was strolling the curbless streets of this little town of 600 today, casually chucking copies of a local newspaper onto porches. Eugene Cheveliar, 71, was chopping down the canary grass along his property line and planning some afternoon fishing. Little Steve Demarais was unsuccessfully trying to teach his dog Tippy to sit.

And Hubert H. Humphrey, 61, was taking a dip.

The Presidential candidate was relishing a rare respite from the campaign trail that by nightfall would take him back into the public eye at yet another political meeting in San Antonio, Texas, 1251 miles from here. It was a deliciously private weekend for the Minnesota Democrat, the constant campaigner who has taken his share of political buffetings. It was the first time he had seen his children and grandchildren in more than a month, and the first time he had been home since Christmas. "It's been quite a year," he said.

It was a June weekend and Mr. Humphrey could busy himself with caring for his lawn and trees and cars—routine chores for millions of Americans but a real treat for a harried Presidential candidate. But it was a weekend that didn't really get started until 2 A.M. Saturday when he and his small caravan of Secret Service guards drove 40 miles west from the lights of Minneapolis, around Waverly Lake on County Road 9 to the township road that is paved to a point just beyond the Humphrey driveway.

At his lakefront home—a four-bedroom, paneled ranch house built in the mid-50s—his wife, Muriel, was waiting, somewhat disappointed because the Senator was to have arrived around noon Friday from a speech in Pittsburgh. He had suddenly decided to return to Washington for a news conference, however, and then fly to Oklahoma City, where he told shouting delegates at the state Democratic convention that he favored many changes within the country, "but not just changes for change sake, not visions with no chance of success."

Saturday, Mr. Humphrey slept until 11, when his wife cooked his favorite breakfast—bacon, eggs, orange juice, and toast with honey. "It was the first time I had good food in five months," he said. Then he made a tour of his 22 acres, picking up some litter here or a weed there, pausing now and then to listen to the birds he cannot hear in his Washington apartment. "Whenever I get exhausted and tired," the former Vice President said, "this is the place I always think about. It's so quiet. The air is so clear, the trees so green. At night you can walk anywhere around here and no one is going to shoot you."

Later he tinkered with the three antique cars he loves to tune and drive to shop at Franske's Fairway Supermarket in town. After a swim he prepared for the wiener roast he and Mrs. Humphrey held for a few neighbors.

Sunday, Mr. Humphrey slept almost until noon. "Why is it," he asked a visitor, "breakfast eggs taste so much better in the country?" Afterward, he puttered about the yard, tending the dozens of trees he has planted. Then another swim and a 25-mile drive to his daughter's home at Lake Minnetonka, where four grandchildren had planned a surprise "tea party," a belated celebration of Mr. Humphrey's birthday on May 27. The adults sat in little chairs in the children's playroom and were served Kool-Aid and cupcakes. Then each child did a little tumbling or musical act. A quiet chicken dinner at the home of friends followed.

Monday morning it was not hard to tell the quiet weekend was over. The telephone began ringing at 6 A.M. It was a West Coast political friend who thought it was 8 A.M. here. Mr. Humphrey telephoned a local farmer and bought 10 sheep to help keep his grass down. There were other calls to friends, political allies, and his Washington office, where work progressed on the week's schedule. Tonight Mr. Humphrey is to be in San Antonio at the Texas State Democratic Convention. Tomorrow he flies to Columbia, South Carolina, and then back to Washington for a couple of meetings with aides.

His schedule will continue much like this—meetings in Wash-

ington and around the country with delegates, potential supporters, politicians, and labor leaders—until the 1972 Democratic
National Convention in Miami on July 10. "I think, frankly," he
said, "I have a good fighting chance. There are around 600 delegates yet to be chosen. It's worth the effort. After all, it's not the
same grueling physical and financial pace as the primaries."

Then he made another inspection of the yard and went for a
final dip, in a beige swimsuit that Mrs. Humphrey maintains
should have been thrown out years ago. At poolside they discussed
some household matters like buying a new rug for the guesthouse.
At one point Mrs. Humphrey said the house needed some
painting.

"Already?" the Senator asked.

"I tease him about that," Mrs. Humphrey said to a visitor. "He
thinks I spend too much."

"Muriel is worse than Nixon on deficit spending," Mr. Humphrey said.

Then he dressed, retrieved his glasses from his wife's purse, and
headed for the door.

"Try not to get too tired," she said.

"I think I'll see you Friday night," he said.

*One state away from Waverly, it seemed*
*another politician could have all*
*the peace and quiet he wanted.*

# MITCHELL, SOUTH DAKOTA

The World's Only Corn Palace, a very distinctive four-story Moorish structure covered with corncobs and prairie grasses, is undergoing its annual redecoration these days. The pictures of Mother Goose nursery-rhyme characters, made by nailing 10,129 pounds of colored corncobs to the outside walls of the civic center, are being replaced by pictures on the theme "Relaxation in South Dakota."

The weather has been unusually wet this year. Already, more than 15 inches of rain have fallen, the total average annual rainfall. Back again, too, is the heat that seems to suck the perspiration out.

And of least interest around here, or so it seems anyway, is the fact that George McGovern, the local preacher's son who did so well on the high-school debate team and used to live over on Second Street, has been nominated for President of the United States.

It is true that *The Daily Republic* yesterday gave him a seven-column headline on page one. No one at the paper, which changed its name from "Republican" during the New Deal, can remember the last time that size headline appeared. (And no one could say what Mr. McGovern must do to earn an eight-column headline.) Otherwise, not that many people seemed to care. For Miami Beach and Washington and all those places beyond Sioux Falls are a long way from Mitchell and the quiet lives of its 13,400 residents here in the southeast corner of South Dakota.

"We're just not a noisy bunch," said Mrs. Wilma Flynn, the reference librarian.

"You'd think the town might be a little excited," said Wayne Unzicker, Mitchell's sole foot doctor and a former mayor, "but we're just placid Plains people. It's our nature."

68

Few people in this normally Republican town even read the Senator's book. *War Against Want,* Mr. McGovern's 1965 book with a foreword by President Johnson, has not been out of the library since Sheryl Wilcox checked it out for one day two and a half years ago. Yesterday, however, a sign was erected along Interstate 90 noting that Mitchell is the South Dakota Democrat's hometown. With its empty railroad station, pizza parlor, bars, gas stations, and well-kept houses with screened front porches, Mitchell looks like hundreds of other towns across mid-America.

Mr. McGovern moved here when he was six and left after graduating from and teaching for a spell at Dakota Wesleyan University. He went to Congress to represent a district where corn and extreme temperatures seem to dominate life. On a mild winter's day the thermometer can sometimes get up to 20 below or so. On July and August nights, the temperature has been known to plunge as low as 90. The grasping heat turns metal seatbelt buckles into miniature hot plates that blister careless fingers, and it sets sane citizens to seeking shade. Shade is, in fact, a prized commodity on the prairie where miles of flatness are only occasionally marred by groves of trees. One local campground even advertises, "Swim, Showers, Shade!"

One of the tree clumps is Mitchell, a town founded in the Dakota Territory in 1881 and named for Alexander Mitchell, president of the Chicago, Milwaukee & St. Paul Railway who, it was hoped, would run his tracks through here. He did. The town, with its elm-shaded streets named Duff, Sanborn, and Sixth, is the last settlement of any size for 300 eternal miles going west and the first sign of civilization on the return trip. So, thanks to the interstate, Mitchell gets a steady stream of rumpled tourists seeking water, gas, and air-conditioned motel rooms. Mitchell also has a hog slaughterhouse and a few light industries, but it concentrates on being the retail trade center for about 100,000 persons sprinkled over eastern South Dakota.

Business in the clothing and hardware stores is good now as it usually is when ample rain gives farmers good growths of oats, wheat, grazing grass, and, of course, corn. That crop has provided fodder for many corny jokes. The radio-TV station is KORN. The baseball team is the Cobs. The basketball team is the Kernels.

And then there is the World's Only Corn Palace. It is, to say the

least, a striking structure whose brightly colored minarets, domes, and corncob panels definitely set it apart from the downtown stores and small, white, single-family homes nearby. Built in 1892, it was patterned after a similar venture that failed in Sioux City, Iowa. It looks like just the place for a political rally by William Jennings Bryan, which it once was. Besides being a civic center, it serves as a gymnasium, convention site, and, in the summer, tourist attraction.

Last summer, for some reason, more than 600,000 visitors toured the World's Only Corn Palace, which local people call the Big Birdfeeder because so many squirrels and birds eat the decorations. The Corn Palace's attractions are two hot-dog stands, a display of African animal heads that a local resident bagged in 1965, seats for 3500 people, a few Indian teepees, a picture of the Lennon Sisters, and what is probably the world's largest nonair-conditioned curio shop. Covering an area the size of a large basketball court, the highly profitable shop sells, among other things, Corn Palace dishes, Corn Palace straw hats, Corn Palace sweatshirts, Corn Palace ash trays, Corn Palace spoons, Corn Palace coasters, Corn Palace taffy, Corn Palace salt and pepper shakers, Corn Palace puzzles, Corn Palace toothpick holders, and Corn Palace collapsible plastic cups. The tours are free, but business attracted to the World's Only Corn Palace last year totaled around $300,000.

The last full week in September is Corn Palace Week, when the new structure's corncob decorations are officially unveiled, and the seven blocks of Main Street are blocked off for a carnival. Every night there is big-name entertainment such as Eddie Arnold or Lawrence Welk, the North Dakota musician who played gigs here as a boy. In 1904 the festival had John Philip Sousa who, once he saw Mitchell, refused to let his band off the train until he got his $7,000 fee in cash.

Mitchell also has a new airport runway used by four daily flights that take on about two passengers each. Like countless other rural communities, however, Mitchell has learned that it takes more than a Corn Palace or new runway to keep its energetic young people, the vital fuel for any municipal future. The chamber of commerce is energetically soliciting new firms, but meanwhile the town must count on its offspring returning voluntarily.

One returning offspring is Dr. Unzicker, who enjoys Mitchell's quiet ways.

Dr. Unzicker abandoned an urban practice in Chicago for Mitchell, where he works four days a week, quits each day at 4:30 P.M., and is on the golf course at 4:35. "It's an easy life," he said. "It's an easy life."

*Another political party wanted just peace. But then the children's caucus issued its demands.*

# SAINT LOUIS, MISSOURI

The People's Party, a shifting coalition of radical-left groups around the country, chose Dr. Benjamin Spock, the noted pediatrician and antiwar activist, as its Presidential standard bearer today. One of his first acts as the official candidate was to acknowledge that he had absolutely no chance of winning in November. "But that's not our purpose," said the 69-year-old candidate. "We're out to build a grass-roots movement. Our national campaign is not to see how many votes we can get, but to call attention to our local movements and inspire some to join us there."

As its Vice Presidential candidate the party selected Julius Hobson, a 50-year-old black educator and former member of the board of education in Washington, D.C.

While there was some post-nomination talk of unity, it was clear that the party, formed after the 1968 election, was deeply split over its selection of Dr. Spock. A number of Southern delegates wanted to support Senator George McGovern who, while not ideologically ideal in their view, at least had a chance to become President. The nomination and the wild cheering of the 100 delegates as the television cameras looked on highlighted the closing sessions of the party's four-day convention in the downtown Gateway Hotel.

More than three of those four days were spent in patient political platform debates, building official policy positions to suit the views of member factions. Dr. Spock's platform calls for, among other things, the immediate withdrawal of all American troops abroad, free medical care as a right, closure of all tax loopholes, a guaranteed allowance of $6,500 for a family of four, legalization of both abortion on demand and marijuana, and an end to all discrimination against women and homosexuals.

In its endless debates and procedural wrangles, the People's Party convention seemed much like any other political party. But there were some distinct differences. It was, for one thing, most informal. Dr. Spock was the only participant to wear a necktie. The delegates, many of whom favored long beards and bare feet, were mostly young, very earnest, and dressed in blue jeans. Speeches were impromptu and informal. At one point the acting chairman announced, "All right. All right. All those in favor of Danny's amendment to the agenda say aye." At least one speaker noted that the energetic Dr. Spock played an influential role in the upbringing of the young people who were now nominating him for President.

Then there was the liberation caucus for children, 10 of whom were full delegates. A group of them, aged 6 to 12, called Dr. Spock in yesterday to hear their demands, which included a full-time babysitter to escort them around the city and escape from the "dull, boring adult speeches."

Dr. Spock bought them some comic books instead.

The convention this week was at least the second held here by a People's Party in 76 years. In 1896 the People's Party, popularly known as the Populists, held its national convention here but decided instead to endorse the Democratic Party's nominee, William Jennings Bryan. There was no such endorsement this week.

"We are out to build an independent political movement," said Dr. Spock, who hopes to be on the ballot in about 20 states. "That means we are independent of both political parties. Both of them got us involved in Vietnam. Neither one got us out. Both are beholden to industry, both bore new tax loopholes. So it is inconsistent," he continued in an interview, "to be building an independent radical party and then endorse another party's nominee."

Dr. Spock also emphasized the importance of political involvement at the local level. Then, as the convention ordered, he signed his own resignation as President to take effect if he wins but does not remove all American troops from Indochina within 90 days of his inauguration.

The radicals' convention ended with a dinner dance for all delegates.

*Dr. Mudd's name was, well, mud.*

# CHICAGO, ILLINOIS

"Free Dr. Mudd."

While that political slogan is hardly on the lips of every American, it has lately aroused several thousand citizens who have proudly pasted it on their car bumpers, thereby joining the 107-year-old fight to clear the name of Dr. Samuel A. Mudd, the country doctor sentenced to life imprisonment for setting the broken leg of John Wilkes Booth. Dr. Mudd was the poor man whose travails are said to have prompted the expression, "Your name is mud."

Now, in what supporters say will be the final attempt to clear the Mudd name, Senator Philip A. Hart of Michigan and Dr. Mudd's 71-year-old grandson plan to send a petition to President Nixon on the anniversary of President Lincoln's assassination by Booth. The petition will seek a Presidential declaration that Dr. Mudd was "innocent of any crime in the circumstances surrounding the death of President Lincoln." Senator Hart will also introduce a similar Congressional resolution.

This latest historical footnote to Lincoln's death culminates almost a half century's work for the grandson, Dr. Richard D. Mudd, who is also a country doctor. A spry resident of Saginaw, Michigan, Dr. Mudd has spent thousands of hours and dollars on research, speeches, and writings to expunge the blot on the name of the grandfather he never met. His cause has been supported in numerous resolutions by state medical and historical groups. But his efforts have been stymied where they count—in Washington, D.C. "I suppose I'm crazy," Dr. Mudd said in an interview as he packed for the trip to the nation's capital, "but the whole conscience of America must purge itself of this horrible injustice."

His grandfather's travails began on the night of April 14, 1865, when a disguised Booth and an accomplice rode up to the Mudd house outside Bryantown, Maryland, about 30 miles southeast of Washington. Booth had caught his spurs in the flag bunting while leaping from the Presidential box at Ford's Theater and had

74

broken his leg. Dr. Mudd treated Booth, who left a few hours later, but not before Mrs. Mudd had seen his false beard slip off once. The next day, after the Mudds learned of the assassination, they notified the authorities of the suspicious pair. Five days later Dr. Mudd was arrested as a conspirator.

The doctor was tried and convicted by a military commission, as were seven others. Four were hanged; four went to prison for life. According to Don E. Fehrbacher, a noted Lincoln scholar at Stanford University, "There is a feeling among historians that the evidence against Dr. Mudd would not have been strong enough to convict him at another less emotional time."

Four years later Dr. Mudd was pardoned by President Andrew Johnson after the doctor valiantly tended fellow inmates during a yellow-fever epidemic. But to many of Dr. Mudd's 280-odd living descendants, who include Roger Mudd, the television reporter, a pardon was not an exoneration. Since then, lawsuits have challenged the constitutionality of Dr. Mudd's trial by military authorities when civilian courts were in session. But federal officials, including President Lyndon B. Johnson, apparently have been reluctant to set a precedent that could also exonerate the real conspirators. Despite countless letters and visits by Dr. Richard Mudd, they have not acted.

In the 1930s Hollywood filmed *The Prisoner of Shark Island* with Warner Baxter in a sympathetic portrayal of Dr. Mudd, who died in January, 1883, at age 49. In 1959 Congress approved a memorial to Dr. Mudd at his prison in the Dry Tortugas off Key West, Florida, but the bill made no mention of his guilt or innocence.

Recently, Dr. Richard Mudd, who plays handball four times a week, has made almost 40 appearances a year, appealing for public support for his cause. One visit was to Utica, New York, where civic leaders proclaimed April 19 as "Sam Mudd Day." "I don't think there can be any doubt about my grandfather's innocence," Dr. Mudd maintained. "How could Booth know in advance that he would need a doctor that night? If Granddad was a conspirator, why would Booth, who was quite a good actor, wear a disguise and give a false name? And why would Granddad report it at all? He wouldn't, of course. And I think this is a good time for the President to do a little something for an old country doctor."

In a tribute to Dr. Mudd's dogged, documented pursuit of justice, an aide to Senator Hart said, "This Mudd business has been the subject of numerous hours of legal meetings and talks here and with the White House. Why, our Mudd file is thicker than our ITT file."

*To Charles McLean, I discovered, we*
*drivers are just another blip.*

# CHICAGO, ILLINOIS

"We don't have rush hours any more," said Charles H. McLean, who runs the world's busiest road. "We just have rush periods. And they keep getting longer and longer and longer."

Charles McLean was describing this area's 235 miles of freeways and, specifically, the Kennedy Expressway. But he might have been talking about almost any of the nation's expressways, those fearsome, multilane urban maelstroms that have become as much a part of American city life as the almost continuous traffic jams that clog them. A relatively new institution, as history goes, these costly cement ribbons have in a single generation changed metropolitan living patterns, displaced thousands of residents, employed thousands of others, and killed thousands more. And they are creating a technology that many thought would not arrive until 1984.

Here in Chicago, a city whose economic existence has depended on the business of transportation since stagecoach days, state experts have developed a computerized system of monitoring traffic on the city's seven expressways. Now, a controller can even follow the progress of a funeral procession by scanning a panel of blinking lights. Traffic experts call Chicago's $5-million system "the coming thing." "Illinois has taken the lead," said Constantine Sidamon-Eristoff, New York City's Transportation Administrator, whose men are studying Chicago's system. A similar network has been installed on parts of some expressways in Los Angeles and Houston.

In Chicago, the system consists of electronic sensors buried every half mile in each expressway lane. Twenty times every second a General Electric 4020 computer in Oak Park, a western suburb, queries each sensor. Their reports on traffic flow are translated into green, yellow, or red lights on a map of each expressway in a downtown control room. A green light means traffic is moving 45 to 60 miles an hour, yellow means 30 to 45 miles an hour, and red means heavy congestion, vehicles standing idle, or traffic moving up to 30 miles an hour.

"See that red light in lane 2 near Austin Avenue on the inbound Kennedy?" a controller asked a visitor. "That's Ron Lehner's repair crew filling cracks, and traffic has backed up." The controller, Kenneth Chlebicki (better known as K.C.), punched a button on the panel. It flashed the lights and sounded the horn in Mr. Lehner's parked truck, summoning him to the radio. He confirmed his location. Minutes later the light turned yellow. Traffic was moving again. But the light at Foster Avenue turned red. The crew had moved down the road.

The light by the Roosevelt Road ramp on the Dan Ryan Expressway kept flashing between yellow and red. "A lot of trucks get on there," K.C. said. "They can't accelerate as fast as the cars." Another almost constant yellow light registered by Taylor Road. "Those are cars slowing down to read all the signs there," he added, "as they head into the Spaghetti Bowl." The Bowl describes the myriad ramps that carry some 400,000 vehicles every 24 hours between the Ryan, Kennedy, and Eisenhower expressways.

The sensors also indicate immediately where a stalled vehicle or accident or debris is backing up traffic. Emergency vehicles, standing by at appointed posts, can then be dispatched by radio. Moreover, once a tie-up is detected, the computer adjusts entrance-ramp lights to reduce the flow to the troubled area. In the system's first three years, Mr. McLean said, such controls reduced congestion up to 60 percent and accidents up to 18 percent. The city's expressway fatality rate per 100-million vehicle miles is now 1.4 compared with 2.6 nationally.

But that's not all the sensors have taught controllers. By watching the lights Mr. McLean, who is regional operations engineer for the Illinois Transportation Department, has learned that most Chicago Bear football fans come from the affluent northern and northwestern suburbs. He can tell when spring has arrived. For several days each spring the angle of the setting sun shines in the eyes of homebound motorists at a turn by Nagle Avenue on the Kennedy Expressway. So the drivers slow down, and the red light glows. He can tell that the number of reverse commuters, city residents who work in the suburbs, is growing each month. And it used to be that on Sunday afternoons traffic and the red lights did not build up until early afternoon. Nowadays, however, more city dwellers are leaving for a country drive earlier in the morning. "I guess fewer people are going to church," said Mr. McLean.

In fact, traffic volume grows constantly. "These roads were designed for 1500 vehicles per lane per hour," Mr. McLean said. "Now we're often getting 2000." Each day drivers here log 12 million miles of expressway travel. The Kennedy handles 267,000 vehicles a day. By comparison Los Angeles's Santa Monica Freeway carries 226,000, Detroit's Ford Freeway takes 178,000, and New York City's busiest expressway, the Long Island, handles 159,000. Los Angeles and Houston have installed sensors, too, and, like Chicago, use stoplights at ramp entrances to control vehicle volume near tie-ups. Los Angeles also uses television cameras in helicopters and electric signs with changing messages. Under consideration is the use of heavy-duty helicopters to clear accident scenes quickly.

Mr. Sidamon-Eristoff admits New York City is "way behind" the Chicago traffic-monitoring system.

The city has instead spent its funds on computers (five IBM 1800s supervised by an IBM 360/50) and overhead sensors to control 500 traffic lights on arterial streets like Queens and Northern boulevards, Metropolitan, Jamaica, and Roosevelt avenues. The Illinois system will be used soon, however, on part of the Van Wyck Expressway and in future major reconstructions of New York's freeways where some traffic volume is still counted by a man standing by the road.

Sheer volume is not the only expressway problem in Chicago. There is Lake Michigan, which affects the weather. Some days the sun will shine brightly on one expressway while rain floods another and a blizzard stifles travel on a third. Not too long ago Paul Costanzo, an emergency patrolman, was run down in a snowstorm as he set out flares near an accident, the third such patrolman to die since 1961. Co-workers have left an earlier casualty's demolished truck in their work yard as a monument to their colleagues and the fatal fury of an expressway. Each year almost 50 persons die in 13,500 accidents on Chicago expressways. Studies show the most dangerous time is a rainy Friday night at 7 P.M. on the Dan Ryan.

Another problem is litter. Mr. McLean says it costs the state 63 cents to pick up a discarded beer can. But expressway debris also includes fenders, TV sets, a truckload of steel shavings (which caused 50 flat tires), frozen chickens, and an occasional human body. Then there was the truck that spilled thousands of foldout photos from *Playboy* magazine. That debris, however, was removed by helpful male motorists.

There is also the "gapers block," that peculiar phenomenon that causes curious drivers to slow sharply at the least distraction, from a major accident to a mini-skirted secretary on a bridge overhead. "We've had tie-ups," said Mr. McLean, "as thousands of people watched an old lady pick dandelions on the roadside. One mother stopped her car to recover a daughter's dropped doll. The shock waves of that slowdown worked their way back along the express-way for an hour and a half."

Given such difficulties, why do so many people still prefer to drive to work? "I figure," said Mr. McLean, "that the daily commute in the car is the only solitude a lot of people have left today."

Does Mr. McLean take the expressway to work? "No, sirree," he said, "I don't drive on those things. I'm not crazy."

*Speaking of blips, there's a place in
North Dakota that no one could call from
anywhere. Not until telephones arrived.
I wasn't far behind.*

# SQUAW GAP, NORTH DAKOTA

There's a strange clicking sound in Squaw Gap these days, coming from within the new, pink cement-block building over by the crumbling community hall. Every so often a workman visits the windowless structure, but the clicking continues. And that's just fine with everyone here. For that sound, about the only unnatural one heard for scores of miles in this rugged, rolling corner of North Dakota, symbolizes the end of isolation for the few people of Squaw Gap and the beginning of a new way of life.

It is the sound of an automatic telephone switching center. Six months ago, it brought to 93 families here their first telephone service.

Spread over 1000 square miles of northwest North Dakota, these people lived in the largest inhabited area of the United States without phones. For years they have had electricity, dishwashers, television sets, washing machines, and air-conditioners. But until Dec. 15, 1971, a day etched in local memory on a par with Pearl Harbor, they had no phone service. Then, at 1:30 P.M., Mountain Standard Time, with more than 200 excited people in attendance at the community hall, Squaw Gap—after 23 years of trying—was connected with the rest of the nation.

The telephone has already revolutionized life here, saving countless hours, many dollars, much wasted effort, and probably a few lives. It has made better friends of some and caused friction with others. It has boosted business for many, saved at least one rancher from costly disaster, and probably spurred a couple of teen-age romances. "The phone," said Sharon Whited, "is simply wonderful." All this with no thanks to the Bell System, which, despite dozens of meetings, petitions, and pleas since 1948, maintained that it could not economically serve Squaw Gap's cattle ranchers and wheat farmers.

Squaw Gap, an area and a town named for a now-fallen rock formation resembling a squaw, is indeed isolated. It appears on no road maps. The "town" consists of a T-shaped, dirt-road intersection with eight buildings—four of them outhouses. The town's population on a winter weekday evening is one. On the weekend, it's none, because Mrs. Ethel Franz, the schoolteacher for four students, goes back to Sidney, Montana. Even Sidney is more than 40 dusty miles away across the stark buttes and rolling grassland, where cattle, deer, and antelope graze and the only sound is the swishing of the grasses in the 30-mile-an-hour prairie wind.

It is an area that is 45 times bigger than Manhattan. But it has about 1/26,000 the number of phones. It wasn't long ago that the residents were doubtful about ever getting any. "Here I could watch astronauts go to the moon on color TV," said Ray Macik, "but I couldn't phone my next-door neighbor." Then someone wrote the Reservation Telephone Cooperative, a small, independent system in Parshall, North Dakota. With a hefty loan from the federal government, its officers said they could bury about 200 miles of cable and give everyone a private dial line for a $50 membership fee and $12 a month.

Last September, the digging began, skepticism waned, and excitement rose. One night in early December, Mr. Macik's wife recalled, their newly installed but dormant phone suddenly rang. Instant bedlam engulfed the house—children shouted, parents cheered, dogs barked, papers flew. It was only a workman testing the line, but it signaled progress.

On December 15, Mrs. Franz canceled classes and Squaw Gap staged the biggest do here since 1916, when Buffalo Bill Cody is said to have passed through. The historic first call, to Secretary of Agriculture Earl L. Butz, was disconnected by a Washington secretary. But after that afternoon, life here will never be the same.

When Mr. Macik's order of 100 baby chickens arrived in Sidney, the agent could call him instead of mailing a postcard. That saved several days and probably several chickens. Mrs. Whited can now make advance appointments by phone at her beautician and her children's doctor instead of taking a chance. Vernon Goldsberry's quarter-horse business is up 50 percent now that he can advertise with a phone number. "People don't like to write any more," he said.

Melvin Leland now knows exactly when a truck is due to pick up his cattle so he won't waste time hanging around the house with the animals penned up and losing weight. And his wife, Luella, shares a telephone coffee break twice daily with her sister, Betty Wersland. Mr. Goldsberry's wife talked with her brother in Portland, Oregon, the other day for the first time in 15 years. Mrs. Loretta Tescher's morale had sagged every winter when she was snowbound for days and the mail came once a week or so. "Now it's just wonderful," she said, "I can chat with a neighbor and it lets me put off my housework." More important, it saved her family several thousand dollars. About three months ago, 2 of their 500 cattle died unexpectedly. Although snowed in, the family could telephone the veterinarian with the symptoms. He diagnosed it as a form of food poisoning and saved dozens of other cattle, many of them pregnant, from the same feed.

Around midnight just a couple of weeks ago, lightning cracked into Milton Brunsvold's field. Soon the horizon was lit by the ominous glow that can mean only one thing out here—prairie fire. Within minutes, 100 men, summoned by an impromptu telephone relay, were dashing the flames with wet gunnysacks. The fire burned 160 acres. Four years ago, a similar blaze roared across 3000 acres before couriers in cars could round up enough help. In other times, people perished, unwarned of such fires or of flash floods.

There are, however, some problems with the telephone. Almost every call is long distance, so monthly bills hover around $50. Some children away at college have discovered, to their parents' dismay, the collect phone call. And some farmhands, juiced up after a Friday night at a Sidney bar, still think it is hilarious to telephone their boss at 3 A.M. to discuss the marvels of modern communication.

"Sometimes," said Mr. Macik, "I'd like to know how to turn this fool thing off."

*They use telephones in Chicago's*
*towering Hancock Center, too. But*
*there they telephone earth.*

# CHICAGO, ILLINOIS

Thomas Ramsier awakened in his downtown apartment here yesterday and buzzed Charlie, the doorman downstairs, to find out what the weather was like. It's not that Mr. Ramsier is blind, has an inside apartment, or no windows. It's just that he lives above the weather. For Mr. Ramsier is one of 1700 affluent tenants whose home is the John Hancock Center at 100 stories and 1107 feet, the world's tallest residential office building, a city within itself.

And as often happens on these warm summer mornings, with a cool breeze off Lake Michigan a block away, the towering Hancock Center was enveloped for a time in clouds and fog. Some tenants threw open their curtains to face a solid gray wall. Others felt like they were in an airplane. "You wake up literally on top of the clouds," said Mr. Ramsier, "while back down on earth it's raining."

The mammoth, three-year-old structure cost $95 million and was the largest investment ever made by its owner, the John Hancock Mutual Life Insurance Company. It is the modern way to live over the corner grocery store and the bank—and the hairdresser, and the swimming pool, and the department store, and the airline office, and the 1200-car garage, and the sauna, and the ice-skating rink, and all those restaurants, and 28 floors of offices.

To urban planners, such a "vertical city" represents a ray of hope for rejuvenating downtown areas now virtually abandoned after 5 P.M. Floors 1 through 5 of the Hancock Center are stores and a bank, 6 through 12 are for parking, 13 through 41 are offices, and 42 and 43 store equipment for some of the 50 elevators in the building. On the 44th floor, right where many buildings end, there's the grocery store, pool, "sky lobby," and a restaurant. Floors 45 through 92 are apartments topped with more equipment, restaurants, and television apparatus. Twin 349-foot TV antennas start at the 1107-foot level.

The management calls the building a "megastructure." Actually, it resembles more of a giant glassed-in oil derrick with room each day for 4000 office workers, 1700 residents in 705 apartments, 1000 visitors, and upward of 10,000 other shoppers and pedestrians. Its 46,000 tons of steel form a building, which, if laid on its side, as some critics would like, would be longer than the longest ship ever built, the carrier *Enterprise*. Daily its 1250 miles of wiring carry enough power for a city of 30,000. To Mr. Ramsier, though, it's all just home.

But it's a high home that takes some getting used to, like commuting to work on an elevator, or watching the traffic helicopters hum by under your breakfast-room window, or feeling that famous wind that sways the building 18 inches at the top and knocks people over on the ground.

"Big John," as the local newspapers like to call the building, is the tallest in a whole brigade of luxury high-rise apartments that march north of Chicago's Loop along the scenic lakefront. From its observation platform, tourists who pay $1.25 can see the smog over four states—Illinois, Indiana, Michigan, and Wisconsin. There is also a spectacular view of summer thunderstorms, tornadoes, and, with the binoculars that are standard equipment for most tenants, any careless sunbathers on nearby roofs or the Oak Street Beach to the north.

The residents, who pay up to $850 a month for four bedrooms, seem attracted, however, more by the building's convenience to their work. Ludwig Skog, for instance, takes a 12-minute bus ride home every noon to lunch with his wife, Jane. From their 46th floor apartment, they can watch their son, an ironworker, putting up a new apartment building across the street.

Mrs. Louis Agatstein, a widow, wanted to be near the downtown cultural activities she attends frequently. "Being fogged in is not the most pleasant experience I've ever had," she said in her 49th floor apartment, "but the view is incomparable. Even my bathroom has one of the most beautiful views in the world."

Mrs. Martha Needham, whose 91st floor apartment lets her live higher than almost anyone else in the world, probably has the easiest commutation—88 floors straight down to her office in Bonwit Teller's. Every morning she watches the sun come up over Michigan, then joins her two teen-age children in the breakfast nook, where they wave to the passing helicopter pilots. Then she crowds on a local elevator, where the businessmen all read newspapers just as they would on the subway. At floor 44, everyone changes to the express. At street level, they brace themselves before bursting out onto East Delaware, where, if they are lucky, the formidable gusts of wind that whirl in off the lake and barrel down the building's sides will have subsided slightly.

The wind was quite a problem during the building's construction. Once, it carried two 55-gallon drums off into the neighborhood, and it frequently lifted tools from worker's hands or pockets. Nearby doormen took to wearing hard hats. Even indoors the wind rushing ahead of the high-speed elevators has destroyed many a hairdo.

Most tenants seem to like living there, but they have some complaints. One thought there should be a tennis court somewhere. Walking a dog is a major expedition, another said, while barefoot children and bicycles on the elevator bother others. Many also feel the tenants are less than friendly and have yet to meet the people living on the other side of the wall. For a while each night some residents of the lower apartments had the beam of the 2-billion-candlepower beacon of the Playboy Building racing through their living rooms every minute or so. But now a shield blocks that off. Everyone could also do without the long lost friends who drop in to see the tourist sites. Even the delivery boys ask to look out the window.

"It really is beautiful," said Mrs. Ruth Wyatt. "Sometimes you can just see the tops of the high rises sticking out of the clouds like candles on white frosting." Yet she still needs to get away sometimes. "It's all so artificial," she said. "You can't open a window, only a slot. Everything is done by pushbutton. After a bit, you feel like you're living in a space station or a filing cabinet with a view. And you just have to get on the ground for a while."

Even on the ground, though, there are some problems. For every so often, the sky is a beautiful, cloudless blue—except for a soft, white ring of moisture that fondly encircles Big John. Residents dread those days, for they inevitably mean someone in the neighborhood will pull an alarm and dozens of firemen will race through the structure seeking the phantom flames.

Despite Big John's drawbacks, Mr. Ramsier, who, like many tenants, didn't bother to hang any drapes ("Who could look in?"), plans to stay in his 57th floor apartment. "Living in the Hancock Center," he said, "establishes you right away as prestigious. This is real living."

*Trivia Quiz:*
*Q: What was the last movie*
*John Dillinger saw?*
A: Manhattan Melodrama.
*Q: Where was it playing?*
A: *At Chicago's Biograph Theater.*
*Q: What's it like there today?*

# CHICAGO, ILLINOIS

He came out of the Biograph Theater at 10:45 P.M., wearing a white silk shirt, gray flannel trousers, white shoes, and a girl on each arm. He lit a cigarette, his last, as they moved to the left down Lincoln Avenue.

A man stepped from behind a post.

"Hello, John," he whispered.

The man in the white shirt whirled.

He reached into his pocket.

Guns blasted.

He crumpled in a dirty alley.

And John Dillinger died.

The flamboyant killer, called Public Enemy No. 1, the arch-criminal of the century, had paid, as the press noted in banner headlines 38 years ago this evening, his debt to society.

He died as the result of a tip to federal agents by a mysterious woman in red who told them Dillinger was seeking relief from Chicago's 101-degree temperature in the "Iced Fresh Air" of the movie house at 2433 Lincoln, on the North Side, about two miles north of the Loop. On the Biograph's screen he had seen *Manhattan Melodrama*, starring Clark Gable as an outlaw who went to the electric chair.

Tonight the same projector in the same theater showed *The Grissom Gang* and *True Gang Murders* ("See the real killers slain in an orgy of gang warfare"). Even the same air-conditioning unit provided the Biograph's iced fresh air.

Like many urban neighborhood theaters today, however, it is not the same business. William Durante, who bought the Biograph in 1968 and hands out black business cards recalling Dillinger's death, says he is losing up to $1,800 a month on the theater, which has specialized in recent years in classic old films like *Wings* and *Public Enemy*. "The neighborhood theater is dead, just like Dillinger," Mr. Durante said as he stood by the miniature Dillinger museum in his theater lobby. "Why should people walk city streets at night when they can drive to a suburban movie without fear or watch TV free at home?"

He has maintained a homey atmosphere in the 990-seat Biograph, where old easy chairs line the lobby and penny candy is still for sale. But Mr. Durante is lucky if 100 people buy his $1.25 tickets each night. "I'd like to stay open to show today's generation what life and movies were like decades ago," says Mr. Durante, who runs eight other movies, "but in another year I'll have to make a hard decision. If this pattern continues, I just don't know. You're in business to make a living, right?"

So, too, was John Herbert Dillinger, in his fashion.

In just one year Dillinger, Baby Face Nelson, and the rest of the gang had excited, aroused, and appalled a nation with their daring bank robberies, gunfights, and jailbreaks. Dillinger, the Hoosier farm boy in the bulletproof vest, shot his way out of numerous police traps, robbed countless banks, escaped from jail using a hand-carved wood pistol blackened with shoe polish, and was responsible for at least 20 deaths, including that of an East Chicago policeman cut in half by machine-gun fire.

"Johnny was not near as bad as he was painted," his father, John Dillinger, Sr., once said.

On that hot and humid night of July 22, 1934, the robber-killer-jail escaper went to the movies with his girl friend, Polly Hamilton, and her friend, Anna Sage, who wore a red dress. Perhaps it was the $25,000 reward on John Dillinger's head—or her pending deportation to Romania—that prompted Anna Sage, a former brothel keeper, to tip off Melvin H. Purvis, chief of the Department of Justice's local Dillinger detail. It was planned that Miss Sage would wear a red dress for recognition at the theater.

Dillinger entered the Biograph at 8:40 P.M. and, despite some excellent plastic surgery, was recognized by the agents outside. He sat in the middle seat of the 12th row, near the exit. The 16 agents outside were so nervous that the Biograph's cashier became suspicious and called the local police. Mr. Purvis frantically shooed them away.

Then Dillinger emerged. As the trio began walking, Miss Sage dropped back. Mr. Purvis, who was standing in a nearby doorway, lit a cigar. That was the signal. The agent stepped out. The shooting started. Mortally wounded with four bullets, Dillinger staggered to the alley and fell forward.

The shooting drew hundreds. They dipped handkerchiefs, newspapers, and skirt hems in his blood for souvenirs.

Dillinger was taken to Alexian Brothers Hospital, which refused to accept him as a patient because he was dead. So, carefully guarded, the corpse lay on the grass outside until a deputy coroner ordered it to the morgue, where there was a near riot as the curious clamored to see the body. Though he had applied acid to burn off his fingerprints, Dillinger was identified at the morgue by officials, many of whom posed for pictures like hunters beside some slain big game.

His death drew a three-column, front-page headline in *The New York Times* and banners in journals around the world. In Mooresville, Indiana, his father, a farmer, collapsed on hearing the news. A few days later, he went on a personal appearance tour.

On July 11, 1974, Mr. Durante closed the Biograph's doors for the last time. The final film was titled "Sleeper."

*"I live in Metropolis," he said, "and we've adopted Superman and, well, he's just changing everybody's life down here." Yea, sure thing, I said. But I went anyway. Great Caesar's Ghost!*

# METROPOLIS, ILLINOIS

The glove plant here closed. Other firms laid off workers. Young people left town. Construction dropped. Retail sales declined. Metropolis seemed doomed!

This was a job for . . .

Look! Up on the water tower! It's a bird! It's a plane! It's Superman!

Yes, it's Superman, the fictional comic-book creation who, disguised as Clark Kent, mild-mannered reporter for *The Daily Planet*, came to earth with powers and abilities far beyond those of mortal men.

Now the Man of Steel has been summoned to rescue this economically faltering community, which has officially adopted Superman as a hometown hero and prime tourist attraction.

Already his image—on local signs, T-shirts, the budding Superman Museum, and on national television—has begun to change life in Metropolis, a city of 6900 that late last year seemed to have more than its share of municipal woes. Coincidentally, Metropolis, as anyone who was young once knows, is also the name of the fictional city in which Superman overcomes what seem to be more than any one place's share of strange monsters and other problems. So why not, reasoned the real Metropolis's fathers, capitalize on the town's name and give out a Superman of Metropolis Award for civic contributions. It would create goodwill and perhaps put the nation's only real Metropolis on the map. That's all, just a little paper award.

But Metropolis did not count on the imagination of Clark Kent's colleagues in the media. In January, when a wire-service reporter heard of the award, he sensed a good feature article. His

eager questioning produced an offbeat, bright story for hundreds of newspaper editors in the January doldrums. It also triggered an article by a competing wire service, which triggered a batch of radio interviews, which triggered some magazine pieces and a network-television news report, which triggered thousands of letters, which triggered the biggest boom that this sleepy little Ohio River town has ever known.

Already, tourists flock here daily to buy Superman souvenirs and see the beginnings of the Amazing World of Superman Museum, which includes Clark Kent's phone booth and the original Superman suit worn in the TV series by George Reeves. But more importantly, the fictional character has, through his strange powers, radically changed the lives of Metropolis's citizens. Some still seem stunned.

Encouraged by a new superoptimism, residents and merchants are painting and fixing up. There are plans for a 1000-acre, $50-million Superman Land here with a 200-foot-tall statue of the Man of Might. (Cars will drive between The Hero's legs.) More new housing is going up. Industries are making serious inquiries for plant sites. Next year there may even be a postage stamp on Superman's 35th birthday. And the local newspaper, *The Metropolis News*, has, of course, changed its name to *The Planet*. "Before

Superman came," said editor Sam Smith, "Metropolis was a dying town. Now almost overnight there's a spark, a contagious enthusiasm, and a boom like I've never seen in all my years."

On the surface, Metropolis's tourist attractions seem somewhat less than compelling. The town is reputedly the site of the world's longest single-span railroad bridge. It is the burial site of Robert Stroud, the Birdman of Alcatraz. It was the hometown of Marvin Steele, the American paratrooper snared on a church steeple during the Allies' 1944 landing in Normandy. And it is the site of the newly renovated Fort Massac, named because settlers in the 1800s balked at staying in an encampment called Fort Massacre. It is safe today, though. On front lawns children's toys remain overnight, unattended and umolested. The shady streets, some of them curbless, are lined with unlocked cars. But the streets are busier now, thanks to Superman.

His latest saga began with the arrival in Metropolis of a strange visitor from another state. When Bob Westerfield, an energetic former halfback with the Cleveland Browns and the Green Bay Packers, moved here from Kentucky, he was shocked to see no sign of the Action Ace. So, last winter, at Mr. Westerfield's suggestion, the chamber of commerce approved the Superman Award. Sam Smith notified a reporter for United Press International, who called Mr. Westerfield, who recounted the following conversations:

Are you going to do anything besides have the award? the reporter asked in a typical follow-up question.

What do you mean? responded Mr. Westerfield.

Well, said the reporter, are you going to put a big picture of Superman up on the water tower?

Hey, that's a great idea, said Mr. Westerfield.

So when The Associated Press called, Mr. Westerfield announced that a big picture of Superman would soon go up on the water tower.

Anything else? the AP reporter asked. Like, oh, a sign at the city limits?

Hey, I like that, said Mr. Westerfield.

Then, with those stories in hand, it was the turn of CBS News.

When are you going to do something we can film? a producer asked.

Well, said Mr. Westerfield, thinking very quickly, the city is officially adopting Superman on Friday.

We'll be there, said the producer.

And they were—along with a half-dozen TV camera crews, 4 magazine reporters, 25 newspapermen, and around 4000 spectators, some of them sitting in trees, all of them excited by the outside attention. They gathered in the drizzle at Fourth and Metropolis, where Carmine Infantino, head of National Periodical Publications, which owns Superman, was to introduce his Magnificent Moneymaker.

Unfortunately, Superman, who was to be impersonated by Charles Chandler, a Baptist minister and one of four local men who play the role, was suffering from the flu. So when the time came for the Man of Might to burst out of Westerfield's Dry Cleaning Store, he was too weak to open the door. Then somehow the rumor spread that Superman would fly down to the corner from the 125-foot water tower. When the Reverend Chandler finally did leap onto the platform dressed as Superman, everyone was looking up the other way.

The complete text of his homecoming speech was later printed by *The Planet*. And the Superman project was off to a flying start.

Superman Land, still a dream, had particular appeal because of the steady growth in the nation's leisure time, because of Metropolis's relatively central location, and because one interstate highway runs nearby and another, I-24, will open a mile east of town in February. "It would be foolish," said one merchant, "to let all those travelers go by and not stop and see us." Already Holiday and Ramada inns have bought plots.

Yet the town, which has changed little over many years, seems to be approaching its sudden good fortune with caution. "We want to control our lives and the town's growth," said Mr. Westerfield. "We don't want to get run over by our own success like Orlando, Florida, and Disney World." The town has formed Metropolis Recreation, Inc., which, with Mr. Westerfield as president, is issuing stock and slowly assembling a Superman Center that includes the world's largest mural of Superman flying (25 feet long), Superman souvenirs, a space exhibit, tourist information, and a napping area for tired little Superman zealots. The center, which will soon have a scale model of Superboy's home, is in a former

roller-skating rink. "I keep telling myself Disney started in a garage," says Mr. Westerfield. Eventually the center will be part of the bigger park with a variety of rides and entertainment facilities.

Meanwhile, the tourists are coming—buying gas, food, and souvenirs. The newspaper, where Superman has dominated the front page for 25 weeks, is selling 600 more copies a week. Soon a giant floodlit revolving statue of Superman holding up the planet earth is to rise atop the one-story printshop.

Superman has also united the town's people. Members of the Elks built the center's garden and Garden Club members tend it. Residents of the old folks home sewed 250 foreign flags to line the driveway, including only the second Krypton flag in the galaxy. The first was stolen. The post office is gearing for the expected load of mail orders. Around town many stores enthusiastically erected their own pictorial version of the Man of Might, which resulted in Superman looking oriental, or short and dumpy, or like Senator Edward M. Kennedy. And at least one citizen, never noted for his civic enthusiasm, showed up unannounced one day to cut the center's grass.

"This project is unique," said Mr. Smith. "There has never been one like it built around someone from another world. It's exciting and a lot of fun. But it's no joke for us. Not when you're dealing with the economic life of a community."

*I spend a great deal of time traveling, as my*
*family and* The Times's *expense accountants*
*can attest. "What's it like on the road?"*
*my editor asked.*

# SALT LAKE CITY, UTAH

Near Elk Mound, Wisconsin, a teen-age couple park their bicycles on County Highway H, then stand on the bridge over Interstate 94. There they while away the warm evening hours waving to the hurried and unusually heavy streams of travelers whistling by underneath in their air-conditoned metal cocoons. The friendly pair draw a good response as drivers or riders in practically every car honk their horns, flash their lights, or wave. For there is a special happiness abroad in the land these days and the explanation is simple: It is vacation time.

More than 30 million American families, perhaps half the nation's population, have taken to the road for that hectic but cherished annual summer vacation, when fathers rediscover sons, when daughters moon over boy friends at home, when brothers and sisters fight in the back seat, and when drivers thoroughly tan their left arms. It may displease the rugged ranks of T-shirt-clad professional drivers, as they exchange highway hyperbole over mountains of potatoes at their favorite truck stop, but during this peak vacation month of August, America's endless ribbons of concrete belong to the sedans and coupes and station wagons and campers and boat trailers and bikes.

It is the most deadly driving time of the year. Nearly 6000 persons die on the road during August. But the August vacation is a time when Americans' passionate love affair with their cars is fully consummated.

The American Automobile Association estimates that 90 percent of vacation travel is by car—a stunning 200 billion miles a year. And, with the help of the 42,500-mile Interestate Highway System, more vacationing Americans can travel more miles. A recent survey by the AAA found that 11 percent of automobile travelers took vacation trips of 5000 miles or more in 1970. In 1971, 19 percent did.

Another explanation for the growth of vacation travel by car is longer vacations. Mrs. Janice Hedges, the federal government's statistical expert on vacations, was on vacation recently. But a co-worker found the following figures in her desk: The typical full-time laborer had 1.8 weeks of vacation in 1960 and 2.3 weeks last year. Statistics, however, could never tell the full story of America on the road in the summer of 1973.

It is the sound of rubber tires whining against the pavement, the sight of stockinged feet sticking out of a station wagon's rear window, the sound of a truck's air horn responding to a gaggle of waving youngsters in a passing car. It is the sight of Holiday Inn signs flashing by every other mile, of family dogs wincing in the wind with their ears flapping, of standardized, reflectorized green signs that cryptically proclaim, "Food-Fuel Next Right."

It is the sound of radio signals that fade every 50 miles with announcers who prattle, "If you're in your car on the road, don't go way." It is the sight of a tourist traffic jam near a clump of sage-brush in eastern Wyoming because two mounted cowboys are checking fence lines. It is the sound of excited youngsters at Mount Rushmore in South Dakota. "Hey, Mom? Mom? Mom? Did you hear that, Mom? Huh, Mom? The nose is 20 feet long."

It is the sight of Old Faithful erupting, with its whoosh of steam and water nearly drowned out by the simultaneous click of hundreds of Instamatic cameras. As the crowd disperses, a child runs from the parking lot, yelling, "Hurry up, Dad, or we'll miss it!" It is the sound of a disappointed woman from Connecticut gazing down on the thousands of magnificent, multicolored spires in Utah's Bryce Canyon saying, "Gee, I thought it was a place you could drive your car through."

It is the sight of a line of station wagons dutifully cruising along at 69 miles an hour behind a state trooper's car, and then, when the patrol car turns off, transforming itself into the last lap at the Indianapolis 500. It is the sound of a New York car hurtling through Wyoming's stately Ten Sleep Canyon, honking its way past slower tourists, of a serious South Dakota state employment officer announcing on the radio a sudden summer job opening for "an experienced alligator wrestler."

It is the sight of thousands of screaming signs that order travelers to "See Frontier Fort," "See Reptile Garden," "See the Presidents in Wax," "See Antique Pioneer Cars," "See Live Buffalo," "See the 15-Ton Log," or "See the 40-Foot Icicle Fence." And it is the sound of muttered obscenities among tired travelers.

"Yeah, you bet I'm tired," said Loren Uglow of Atlanta as he sat in his station wagon at a root-beer stand in Mitchell, South Dakota, waiting for his pappaburger (hold the onions). Mr. Uglow was in the middle of his three-week, 4500-mile, $600 camping vacation. And he had just spent an exciting morning watching a mechanic boil out his car's overheated radiator for $17.16. The back of the car was crammed with pillows, magazines, balloons, pennants, lotion, ice chests, paper tissues, balls, plastic robots, a dog named "Bennjie," and Mr. Uglow's three daughters.

The longest time that he and his wife, Peggy, spent in any one place was two days—at his parents' home in Montana. They hoped to stay longer in Colorado, but left after waiting two hours to buy gasoline one morning. "Actually, it doesn't matter what you do on vacation," Mr. Uglow said. "The important thing is getting away from work and the business routine." Then he declared, "We've got to get to Omaha tonight."

Several hundred miles away, Mike Tevault, his wife, Carol, and their two sons, Tony, 8, and Eric, 4, eased their four-year-old station wagon into a parking space at the foot of Mount Rushmore. Tony continued to color in a book. "Let's go," Mr. Tevault said. Tony continued to color. His father, an optometrist from Mount Vernon, Indiana, who had driven through a stampeding herd of antelope during a four-hour search for a motel room early that morning, leaped from the car, jerked his son out, and slammed the door. The keys were inside.

It began to rain. A crowd gathered. The children complained. It rained harder. Mr. Tevault picked up a large rock to break his car window, but a park ranger arrived with a coat hanger. One hour later Mr. Tevault drove off laughing without having seen the carved faces on Mount Rushmore—they were enveloped in a cloud.

Down the highway two teen-age bicyclists, Mark Sontag and Jay Herman of Lake City, Minnesota, were fixing their sixth flat tire in seven miles. "Nice road," said Mark.

Farther west, in Lander, Wyoming, the night attendant in a gasoline station looked up at 11 P.M. as a bug-splattered car zipped up to the pumps. It was the J. D. Newman family of Oklahoma City, nearing the end of their nine-day, 5000-mile vacation. The car doors flew open. Four people jumped out. They raced inside. Toilets flushed. The cash register registered.

"We lost a little time because we stopped off in Yellowstone Park," Mr. Newman explained. "I can't wait to get out of these mountains and back to some flat country." He headed for the car door, then turned to the station attendant. "Can you tell me," he asked, "what city are we in?"

*One night on the road I stayed at
Pearl Hutchinson's Tourist Home. She
was suspicious. We talked.*

# GENESEO, ILLINOIS

Pearl Hutchinson's Tourist Home here has no computerized reservations service, no green glowing message lights, no ice machines, no plastic glasses, no chemically treated shoeshine rags, no vibrating beds, and no souvenir shop selling plastic ice cubes that entomb fake spiders. Her guesthouse also has no air-conditioning, no carpeting, no telephones, no swimming pool, no television, and no food service.

In fact, nowadays Mrs. Hutchinson's Tourist Home has no tourists either.

"Everybody's so rich," says the 74-year-old widow. "Who would want to stay at a crummy old house like mine?" The answer, of course, is very, very few people. Faced with modern competition and tastes, Mrs. Hutchinson's plain, two-story white house at 718 South Oakwood Avenue, and hundreds of other guest homes like it that sprang up along the nation's highways in the 1930s and '40s, are steadily dying off, along with their aging proprietors.

Overlooked by speeding sightseers, neglected by comfort-conscious, affluent automobilists, the tourist home is going the way of other old American roadside institutions like the Burma Shave signs and the two-lane intercity highway. With the exception of some homes in established resort areas, the ranks of the nation's guest homes are dwindling so fast no one even keeps track of them anymore.

"Motel" is the name of the game today for America's highly mobile population. To serve such travelers, there are now more than 52,000 motels in the country with nearly 2.3 million rooms, an increase of about 500,000 in 10 years. Holiday Inn alone opens a new motel every 72 hours.

The tourists still pass by Geneseo—right by. And if they do stop, it's not in town on old U.S. 6. It's out at the 10-year-old Interstate

80 interchange where they can choose from three modern motels, their giant neon signs drawing travelers the way Mrs. Hutchinson's porch lights draw moths.

But in town, just a mile beyond the nearest motel, between East Chestnut and East Locust streets, and just down the porch steps there's a little lighted lawn sign lovingly taped together by shaking hands. Mrs. Hutchinson opened her comfortable, immaculate home to weary travelers back in 1939 when the idea of a $9-billion motel industry and a nationwide system of four-lane highways would have made a good Flash Gordon serial. They were good years then. Almost every night Mrs. Hutchinson's home was full— both rooms upstairs and another one downstairs. And down the street three other ladies rented tourist rooms and Oscar Drayman next door did, too. Even after World War II, when the motels started to blossom, business was good. Of course, more people went to motels then, but the overflow always filled the tourist rooms.

Today, however, the local motels have added restaurants and bars and buffets and dozens of new rooms. One even boards travelers' horses and another offers free breakfasts. So business is very bad at Pearl Hutchinson's place. It's been more than three weeks since anyone stayed at Mrs. Hutchinson's, now the only tourist home in this town of 5800 and the first one on Route 6 west of Chicago, 160 miles away. In fact, this year only six persons have stayed at Mrs. Hutchinson's. And two of those guests were journalists researching guest homes.

It is a quiet house, one Mrs. Hutchinson's grandfather bought more than 80 years ago. The floors are covered with flowered linoleum. The narrow stairway is solid. Each of the two upstairs bedrooms is furnished with a bed, a chair, and a bare light bulb in a wall socket. The white-lace curtains move slowly in an occasional August breeze. A 1969 calendar hangs on the wall next to a faded poem that says:

> Our Home is just a stopping place
> For Friends who come this way.
> We're glad to see each smiling face,
> And wish they All might stay.

The bathtub down the hall, the one with giant knobs that still say "Hot" and "Cold," may be the biggest tub this side of Moline. A crib and folded cot stand ready, but unused, in the hall, while the soft twin beds are the kind that absorb a sleeper between their crisp white sheets. "The ceiling may be cracked," says Mrs. Hutchinson, "but, by golly, my house is clean."

Mrs. Hutchinson says the older she gets the bigger her backyard seems. It is almost overflowing with bright orange tiger lilies, but those two giant elm trees, the ones Mrs. Hutchinson planted as twigs when she was a girl, are slowly dying. "I can't afford to get them trimmed, not on social security," she says. She also cannot afford a daily or weekly newspaper, so in her abundant spare time Mrs. Hutchinson sits on the front porch and sews clothing for the dolls she makes or watches the traffic move slowly by.

"Time was," she recalls, "when the cars were just packed out there. You know old Route 6 was the main east-west highway in these parts." Now it's just a bumpy two-lane local road that links Geneseo with such towns as Atkinson, Annawan, and Sheffield in this corn-producing area. Route 6 is used regularly only by farmers or overloaded trucks dodging the state scales. "Look at all those campers," Mrs. Hutchinson says. "They don't do my business any good. But I can't blame them. Who can afford to pay $20 a night to lodge a family? I charge $8 for a family and I don't think that's out of line."

Mrs. Hutchinson awakens about 5 A.M. each day to tidy her home and work on her dolls and wait for customers. About 5 P.M. she turns on her sign, "Tourist Rooms," and sits on the porch. She stays close to home every day. "Maybe someone will stop," she says. There used to be a few regular customers, but they were elderly and have not been here in more than a year. "I suppose they've passed on, too," Mrs. Hutchinson says. Even when someone does stop Mrs. Hutchinson seems startled and somewhat afraid. "These days you never know about people," she says. So she not so casually tells each guest she is expecting her "companion" home any minute. There is no "companion."

As the evening wears on, the traffic on Route 6 dwindles even more. Occasionally a teen-ager guns his father's car past the front porch and Mrs. Hutchinson smiles. But no one stops. At 10:20 the eastbound freight train rumbles through. Mrs. Hutchinson is still sewing. No one has stopped. By 11 the "No Vacancy" signs are on at the motels down the road where the only sounds are the crickets and the whine of truck tires on the interstate.

Every so often Mrs. Hutchinson gets fed up with waiting. "I know one thing," she says, "this is the last summer I'm doing this. That's for sure!" A few minutes later, though, she muses, "You know if you haven't got something to look forward to, there's no point in living, is there?" Then around 1 A.M. Mrs. Hutchinson closes up her old Singer sewing machine and prepares for bed. The last thing she does is turn off her sign, "Tourist Rooms." No one has stopped.

"Maybe tomorrow," she says, "maybe tomorrow."

*Another night I spent in Sacred Heart. At Earl's Drive-In. Under the light bulb. By the mosquito squadron.*

# SACRED HEART, MINNESOTA

Carla Harried came for an ice-cream cone. Val Jacobson came to show off Chuck Johnson. Palmer Eliason came to talk about crops. Paul McKenzie bought a root beer. But Debbie Reiten didn't come by at all, so Jerry Agre went to see why. Like the residents of thousands of small towns scattered about the country, Sacred Heart's 696 people have a regular summer evening hangout for socializing once the long day's chores are done.

Some of the old folk prefer to play cards at Helen's Pool Hall, so-called because there hasn't been a pool table there for two decades. It is air-conditioned at Helen's and you can buy 3.2 beer. But at some point during these muggy summer evenings, nearly everyone drops by at least briefly at Earl's Drive-In on Main Street, about 120 miles west of Minneapolis.

The regulars stand under the bare light bulb out front or sit on the two picnic tables, chat about things in general or nothing in particular, and offer themselves as living sacrifices to starving swarms of mosquitoes. It is by and large a pleasing pastime, a relaxing change of pace from the long, lonely days in the corn, soybean, and pea fields, or from eight hours at a noisy machine in one of the slowly increasing number of little factories around Sacred Heart.

This town is a small, tidy collection of white homes with china lightning rods that was named by a sick priest who recovered on a heart-shaped river island nearby. In fact it is so small that "if you get lost here," says one resident, "you better not leave."

Downtown at Earl's there is gossip to be shared, impressions to be made, Cokes to be drunk, and dates to be set. Especially for the younger residents of Sacred Heart, dropping in at Earl's has become something of an evening tradition with accompanying ritual.

First, there is dinner at home around 6 P.M. That's when the fire

siren blows every night. No one knows what the 6 o'clock siren means, but no one is about to change it, either. "It's blown as long as I can remember," says Rusty Rustad, the town's police force. There is another siren at 9 P.M. It used to blow at 10 P.M. to mark the actual start of a curfew for young people. However, too many sleepers were awakened then, so it became a 9 o'clock warning instead. But, Mr. Rustad notes, "As long as things are quiet, no one pays any attention to the curfew anyway."

Around 7 P.M., with dinner completed, a few children take to the streets on their bicycles for some ice cream at Earl's. Harlan Sundquist, the new owner who hasn't gotten around to changing the Earl's sign, says he sells 10 to 12 gallons of ice cream a day, depending on the temperature. It was only about 95 degrees here tonight, so sales were not as strong as some days. But the other Sunday it became so warm during a service in one of the town's three Lutheran churches that the sweating congregation got to watch the tall altar candles waver, then melt and droop over in a waxy mass on the floor.

By 8 o'clock, when Rusty Rustad goes on duty, the bikes are giving way to motorbikes and souped-up cars. These are driven by boys. The cars' rear ends are jacked up high. The tires are oversized. The windows are open. The radios or tape decks are on full blast. And the mufflers seem to have broken. To avoid any mix-ups, some cars have their names painted in foot-high white letters on the rear fender. The cars rumble up and down the shady streets, back and forth, around and around, like a chase scene in a Peter Sellers movie or a mating dance by some exotic beasts.

The girls, meanwhile, have dressed in cutoff jeans with halter tops or slacks with pullover jerseys. In pairs they walk up and down the sidewalks, acting surprised and giggling when some boys honk their car horn or "peel" their tires when the stoplight changes.

Peeling is one of the more serious problems for Mr. Rustad, who each evening gets several complaints about young people spinning their tires on some of the town's unpaved streets. The other night, though, a youth was caught riding his bicycle in the graveyard at midnight. Mr. Rustad's other nightly problems are confined to an occasional drunk and some quiet cars out on Parkers' Prairie, the local lovers' lane. "It don't take me long to make my rounds," he says. "Anyone needs me, they just sit down on the curb and I'll be by presently."

There is, however, an occasional chase, and Mr. Rustad boasts that he can get his 9-year-old police car up to 100 miles an hour in second gear, a trick he eagerly shows visitors. He can spot out-of-town cars instantly and watches them closely. As every sheriff since Matt Dillon knows, outsiders usually mean trouble. And Mr. Rustad also keeps close track of just whose car is parked by whose house, embarrassing information for some people.

Whenever Mr. Rustad cruises by the drive-in, the kids all wave. "He's a good guy," says 18-year-old Paul McKenzie. The other night when Milan Skalbeck's dog was run over on the west side of town, Mr. Rustad woke the family with the news and helped bury the beloved animal at 4 A.M. "I know how close you can get to a pet," he says.

By 9 P.M., as if by some coincidence, the girls and boys have gathered at Earl's and the crowd is substantial by Sacred Heart standards. The jukebox is playing. The pinball machine is pinging. And gallons of Coke are flowing. Jerry Agre arrives on his motor-bike to report shyly that Debbie Reiten, his girl friend who stayed home tonight, wasn't mad at him after all. And Mark Erickson

takes Marcia Gunter for a ride on his Suzuki motorbike. The helmet musses his hair. By 10 P.M. things are slowing down.

It wasn't always this sedate in Sacred Heart, where the 12-page telephone book contains 7 pages of instructions. In the 1860s the village's first family, the Enesvedts, had a misunderstanding with the Indians that resulted in several deaths. The railroad came in 1878, but soon after, James McIntyre, the depot agent, died violently. His gun discharged as he climbed over a fence on a rabbit hunt. In 1882 Ole Fjugleskjel opened a lumber yard. Andrew Anderson erected Sacred Heart's first saloon, and two days later the town's good ladies tore it down.

By 11 P.M. the crowd at Earl's has dwindled to a hardy few wearing insect repellent. And the talk centers on the perennial problems of the Sacred Heart Vikings, the football team. As midnight nears, Earl's is closed. The crickets are chirping. A lone paper cup rattles across the cement. And Rusty Rustad is checking the doors on Sacred Heart's one block of stores. Once in a while another heavily laden grain truck blasts through town, sometimes grinding up through four gears in one block. It makes the only breeze in town.

Just after midnight Mr. Rustad walks to the southwest corner of Main Street and another street nobody has bothered to name. He opens a metal box. The town's sole stoplight becomes a yellow blinker.

And one more night has officially come to Sacred Heart.

*What does a nice suburban family do on
a nice summer day? They go to Fantasyland,
of course. So did I.*

# ARLINGTON, TEXAS

Click. Click. Click. Click. Click. Click.

Twelve hours a day and more the shiny silver turnstiles flip over and over and over, each click representing another customer, another vacationing American who has paid $5 or $6 to enter the summer fantasy world of yet another theme amusement park. Once, such fantasy was left to Disneyland, which opened in 1955. But now, what seemed to be a Disney patent is running out. Other giant concerns, with visions of more than sugar plums dancing in their corporate heads, are bankrolling a growing number of theme amusement parks.

Already about 20 such parks in the United States, drawing customers from 500 miles away, annually attract about 25 percent of the nation's estimated 200 million amusement-park patrons, most of them during the busy vacation season. Soon, thanks to interstate highways and the descendants of Tomorrowland, Fantasyland, Frontierland, and Adventureland, it may be possible to drive across the country without setting foot in Realityland. "There sure is a boom," said an official of the International Association of Amusement Parks and Attractions.

"The new parks are a lot better than the junky asphalt amusement parks I went to as a kid," said Wayne Temple as he, his wife, and two children rested their feet in the middle of 10 hours of programmed pleasure here at Six Flags Over Texas. This 12-year-old park, a 145-acre amusementland on Interstate 20, halfway between Dallas and Fort Worth, is, as some immortal public-relations man would put it, the original copier of Disneyland. It is representative of the new generation of such parks. It is carefully planned. It is carefully organized. It is carefully clean, very clean, almost disturbingly clean. It is staffed by clean-cut, well-dressed college students who  say "Hi" and volunteer to take families' pictures.

It is, by nothing resembling chance, on an interstate highway with "E-Z access" for hustling travelers. It is in the suburbs where there is more undeveloped land and where there are more affluent families with growing incomes and leisure time. And it is supposedly out of reach, both geographically and economically, of the urban rowdies whose escapades have given some city amusement parks a bad name in recent years. It is, in short, an escape.

"You've got to have a clean, pleasant atmosphere if people are going to get away from an unclean, unpleasant atmosphere," said Bruce Neal, a spokesman here. "We would like this place to be like you would want the rest of the world to be all the time." That is, presumably, lots of fun.

So there are some 95 separate rides and attractions, none of them of the step-right-up-you-won't-believe-your-eyes variety. There is a five-story slide, a nostalgic musical revue, a puppet show, a petting zoo, and a dolphin show. There are rides on rafts, trains, fiberglass Indian war canoes, cable cars, riverboats, antique cars, outdoor elevators, runaway mine trains, and hollowed-out logs. And like every other amusement park in the world, it has the world's fastest roller coaster. All attractions are under the basic historical theme of the six flags that have ruled over Texas—Spain, Mexico, France, Texas, the Confederacy, and the United States.

For $5.95 ($4.95 for children) 22 million visitors have eased through these local turnstiles. Just like the other new theme parks (but unlike Disney parks), the admission price buys unlimited rides and shows inside. Take Six Flags Over Texas, add a few different rides, vary the historical theme, change a few flags, and you have Six Flags Over Georgia, a seven-year-old, 276-acre park on Interstate 20 not far from Atlanta. Change the rides again and add some more name entertainment and you have Six Flags Over Mid-America, a three-year-old, 200-acre park on a paved-over wheat field on Interstate 44 near Saint Louis. All three Six Flags parks are owned by the Great Southwest Corporation, a Los Angeles-based, mobile-home, land-development, amusement-park concern that, in turn, is largely owned by the Penn Central Railroad.

Take away the flags, raise the price 55 cents and you have Worlds of Fun, a three-month-old, 140-acre park on Interstate 435 near Kansas City. A $20.5-million investment with the world's communities as its theme, the park belongs to Mid-America Enterprises, Inc., whose board chairman is Lamar Hunt, the Texas millionaire.

Take away the rides and substitute trained seals, penguins, dolphins, a killer whale named Shamu, and a water-skiing elephant that all commute by jet from the West Coast, and you have Sea World, a four-year-old, 70-acre park southeast of Cleveland near Interstate 80. "It's a nice change," said one woman. "You don't often see a whale in Ohio."

Take away all the rides, buildings, and attractions and you have a 600-acre plot on Interstate 94 in Gurnee, Illinois, in northwest suburban Chicago, which within a few months will become the construction site of a $40-million historical theme park owned by the Marriott Corporation. And so it goes from Williamsburg, Virginia, to Anaheim, California.

Even the patrons' comments heard among the screams of roller-riders are similar.

"It's a great place," said 12-year-old David Shore as he ended his fifth ride on the Georgia park's rollercoaster.

"The log ride was the best," said Mike Rathgerber at the Saint Louis park.

"I don't like the waiting in line," said Christy Garnett in Kansas City.

"There's always something going on," said Ron Ciancutti at Sea World.

"I like the one-price feature," Jerry Kruse said here at Arlington. Like 40 percent of the visitors, he is from Texas. And like many others, he fit an average eight-hour visit at the park into his regular vacation itinerary, a sort of reward if his child behaved in the car for the rest of the trip.

The park is built with the family in mind. Parking-lot signs advise those not wishing bumper stickers placed on their cars to lower their sun visors. Free strollers are available. Drinking fountains gush real ice water, and the grounds are attractively landscaped. Girls in hot pants whiz by on roller skates to pounce on litter. The lines move quickly and are air-conditioned from overhead. There are many benches and a Lost Parents center. Everything is hosed down every night. The 1750 young summer employees are smiling and polite. Pets are not permitted, but they can stay all day in an air-conditioned kennel for 25 cents.

This summer crowds are flocking to the park's Southern Palace Music Hall, where an enthusiastic, smiling, integrated cast of 16 happy college students presents a musical parade of hit songs from *South Pacific* to Elvis Presley. Frequently, the songs are interrupted by applause from the 1500 members of the audience who recognize a favorite tune. With lights flashing and band booming, the show culminates in a songful plea for world brotherhood. It brings down the air-conditioned house.

Then, 23 minutes later, for the tenth time that day, an enthusiastic, smiling, integrated cast of 16 happy college students presents a musical parade of hit songs from *South Pacific* to Elvis Presley.

*Disneyland it ain't. But Clarence and*
*Dick Hullinger have some plans.*

# AT THE INTERSECTION
# OF INTERSTATE 90 AND
# SOUTH DAKOTA 63

This town is officially nameless. It is unincorporated. It is on no map. But it could be a city of the future. For this is one of hundreds of entirely new little communities growing daily at many of the 13,500 interchanges on the Interstate Highway System.

The permanent population of this new breed of town here is five, not counting the two dogs. But the temporary population—the people who buy gasoline, souvenirs, campground spaces, and "radar range" hamburgers—is somewhere around 1200.

Developments at highway junctions are not brand new, as any driver, lured off the road by the garish gasoline beacons, can attest. Historically, Americans have built most of their towns around transportation intersections. Chicago is, perhaps, the prime example. But the pioneers who arrived by riverboat, covered wagon, and stagecoach built their towns to live in. Today's "new towns" are designed to pass through—as quickly as possible. They are a new form of community: the transient town, whose only lifeblood is the traveler's money or credit card.

Every day 10 times as many people stop at this anonymous town as live in Belvidere, the nearest "old-fashioned town," a few miles down the four lanes of cement. "There's no question," said a federal Highway Administration official, "large-scale development is coming to our interchanges."

There is much to be developed. The $50-billion Interstate System contains 42,500 miles of road, 98 percent of it completed or under way. And 83 percent of the system is in rural areas, where the new town development potential is the greatest. The new communities provide convenient, if rarely attractive, places for rumpled travelers to stretch their legs, fill their tanks, walk their

113

pets, quench their thirst, satisfy their hunger, relieve themselves, and be on their way.

The new towns' money-making potential has not been overlooked by some corporate giants. In addition to their existing facilities on interstates, Holiday Inns, Ramada Inns, and other hostelries and gasoline chains have purchased many parcels of farmland surrounding interchanges yet to be built. Earl Holding, owner of Wyoming's Little America Refinery, has built Little America motels, restaurants, and curio shops at interchanges in Salt Lake City, Utah; Flagstaff, Arizona; and Cheyenne and Little America, Wyoming.

In Wayne, New Jersey, the Union Camp Corporation, a large forest-products company, has created Transtates Properties, Inc., to develop seven interchanges on its woodlands along Interstates 95 and 16 in Georgia and South Carolina. "We aim at taking something that is usually a mess and making a good thing out of it," says Samuel M. Kinney, Jr., Union Camp's president.

The company's own interchanges, called Oasis Villages, will contain integrated facilities from motels, restaurants, and gas stations to campgrounds, golf courses, and picnic areas—all with the same planned architectural and landscaping theme. The concept, which Union Camp expects to franchise, includes leasing the land to motels and gasoline companies for an annual fee plus an income percentage.

One of the plan's first completed projects, a Howard Johnson's motel near Savannah, Georgia, is renting every one of its rooms every night after only 90 days of operation. Two more motels and a gas station will open there this week. For Union Camp the plan is economically quite sound. Development enhances the value of its surrounding woodlands. And, as a corporation spokesman pointed out, an acre of trees grown for paper is worth $5 a year to Union Camp. An acre of gasoline station will bring upward of $15,000 annually.

Out here in South Dakota astride the line dividing the Central and Mountain time zones, Clarence and Richard Hullinger hired no land-use consultants, and they plan no franchises. But their goal is similar. Three years ago, when this section of Interstate 90 was opened, the father-son team decided to build a gas station at what is for the moment called Exit 170. In South Dakota there are 413 miles of Interstate 90, a four-lane, high-speed highway that connects Boston to Seattle and serves as Chicago's Eisenhower Expressway on the way.

Two years ago the men bought 80 acres of wheatland from Andy Blom, a farmer. They decided to construct a new "old Western town" to attract more of the 6000 wallets that pass by daily on the interstate. This naturally led to building a restaurant. A motel may be added later. And a private campground is just down the road. A year ago there were 2 buildings here. Now there are 12. Next month it will become 13 and eventually 30. The telephones go in this week.

"We want to interest as many people as possible," said Clarence Hullinger, the father. So they moved an ancient prairie hill out of the way to give speeding drivers a better view of the old-fashioned, false-fronted Main Street they have built. It includes a marshal's office, a Wells Fargo office, a land office, a barber shop, a blacksmith shed, an impressive collection of Indian and cavalry relics, an array of antique tractors, and, of course, a saloon. A schoolhouse will be the gift shop. There is a reproduction of an old ranch house. A railroad depot will go up soon, followed by a train to tour the grounds. Then the men will move in an old church they bought in Cottonwood, South Dakota, 80 miles away. After that come pretend plots on a fake Boot Hill.

A watering trough and the hitching posts are up now, and already travelers, bleary-eyed from the arid emptiness of much of this vast state, have begun to stop. On this rolling prairie, where the saying is "You can see for three days," any structure is eye-catching. The Hullingers are thinking of calling their new town "Two Strike" for an Indian chief said to have killed two buffaloes with one arrow. But this name may change because many outsiders connect the phrase only with baseball.

Some other new towns do not need new names. Arlington, Wyoming, for example, was once a stop for the Overland Stage. Then it was a ghost town. Now it is an interchange on I-80. It has a gas station, a restaurant, a campground, a planned motel, three cabins, one house, and a highway-department garage. A nearby Elk Mountain interchange, once a void, now has a gas station, three house trailers, and two families.

Even in established communities the economic impact of the

interstate is considerable. One study showed that 185 miles of the superhighway in southwestern Wyoming increased personal income in two counties by $69 million a year. Near here, four acres of interchange land recently sold for $14,000; before I-90, the land went for $100 an acre.

Conversely, interstate bypasses have sometimes hurt old towns, such as Fernley, Nevada, which relied on a steady stream of hungry, tired travelers needing gas. Now drivers whistle by the communities or stop on the edge of town at the modern facilities that advertise "E-Z Off-On."

At the Hullingers' new town, however, the sudden influx of substantial numbers of temporary residents doesn't seem to have changed the life-styles of its five permanent residents, although it sometimes excites Sparky and Snooks, the dogs. Glenn and Lucy Freeman are delighted with the growth. They have seen the number of camper vehicles at their place grow from fewer than 20 to more than 110 a night. Rodney Vollmer, who lives in a house trailer with his wife, Debbie, and their 18-month-old son, Kelly, is away all day at his distant cattle ranch. So he isn't bothered.

And Mrs. Vollmer loves the countryside anyway. "It's so nice," she said, "to live far away from people where you can go outside and holler a while if you want to." If all goes as planned for Exit 170, though, that may not be the case for very long.

*What's it like to run a motel in the*
*summertime? I had no idea—until I stood*
*behind the counter for 24 hours.*

# ALBUQUERQUE, NEW MEXICO

"Do you have a room for tonight?" the rumpled father asks wearily.

Out in the car a rumpled mother, three rumpled children, and a rumpled dog watch intently. When the father reaches for a pen to fill out a form, a soft cheer seeps from the air-conditioned station wagon. Everyone begins gathering up coloring books, dolls, handbags, toy pistols, and swimsuits. And another motel room is rented.

It is a ritual as old as the automobile itself: Americans on the road in search of a night's lodging. On these warm summer evenings during the peak vacation period, it is a ritual performed perhaps two million times a day, about once for every one of the 2,551,007 rooms in the 52,000 motels in the United States.

Here in New Mexico at the intersection of two major interstate highways, I-40 and I-25, the cars begin streaming down the cement exit ramps soon after 2 P.M. For many travelers, a computer has already made their reservation and promised to bill them, even if they do not appear. In fact, the computer based in Omaha or Memphis or Phoenix has determined, in effect, how far each family will drive in a day. The average vacationing family now drives a lot farther than before the high-speed highways stretched a day's travel from an exhausting 300 miles to a fairly easy 500.

It does not matter to these travelers in search of a vacation Valhalla that seven years ago the land around here was a sandy waste beyond Albuquerque's limits. Few people, save the scouts for Holiday Inns, knew that this property was destined to become, in effect, a new "transient town" dedicated to the needs not of those few who live here but of those thousands who pass by here.

On Sept. 2, 1966, the interstates opened here. On Jan. 11, 1967, Holiday Inns bought a parcel of land. On Nov. 27, 1967, they

**117**

began construction of a new motel. The motel opened on Oct. 1, 1968. It was followed by several other motels, truck stops, and restaurants. And now just about anyone driving through this city passes by what the Holidex computer calls H. I. No. 126AB. The result is an average annual occupancy rate of 98 to 99 percent, compared with the national average of 70 percent and the break-even average of 60 percent. "And summertime," a motel official said here, "is family time when you really make your money."

Long before the sun came up one recent day, the innkeeper, Murphy Jenkins, and his assistant, Jim Sanders, knew very well that they would have no vacancies for the coming night and, for that matter, the next night and the next night and the next night. In fact, Frank Cortese, the bellhop, knew he would make close to $30 in tips. And Joe Roloson, the bartender, knew he would sell a case of beer and a quart of vodka every hour. And Bennie Davis, the housekeeper, knew she would lose about 75 ashtrays and 50 towels and two families would forget luggage. And Mr. Sanders knew the morning mail would bring 10 keys that yesterday's guests had carried off. But Mrs. Margaret Parker could not know that there would be no $12-to-$22 room at the inn for her.

The day actually began at 4 A.M. when Steve Dillon, the night clerk, started the wake-up calls for travelers apparently very anxious to get on the road. At 6:30 A.M. Agnes Martinez arrived to handle the remaining guests checking out and, with colored paper slips in numbered slots, to begin plotting which new guests, some of them still asleep hundreds of miles away, would stay in which rooms.

By 8 A.M. almost every guest had hefted his bags into a gaping car trunk or tied them on a rooftop luggage rack. The long hallways were empty, but silently they began to look like narrow, carpeted battle zones. The maids, 18 of the inn's 96 employees, were attacking each of the inn's 192 rooms, tossing the soiled linens and towels out the doors, emptying the trash, vacuuming the shag rugs, and setting the partly used soap bars aside for charity.

The washing machines began to chew on the day's 550 sheets and 970 towels. The swimming pool, out where the construction crews were working on an additional 108 rooms, was little used. Mr. Jenkins was in Phoenix for an emergency regional meeting to update menu prices for this month's inflation. And Gordon Winfield had just left the Holiday Inn in Dallas, heading west. Slowly, the seven ice machines recovered from the onslaught of tourists surreptitiously swiping scoopfuls for their portable coolers. Then, about 2:30 P.M., Connie Brown and Loretta O'Brien, the two receptionists who would handle the brunt of the day's tourist barrage, went on duty.

Minutes later, like clockwork, they begin arriving. Mrs. Rosalie Simon checks into Room 333. George Tarleton checks in with his wife and child. Mrs. Simon returns. Her room faces the highway. "I need my sleep," she says. She gets Room 335. The Tarletons march by in their swimsuits.

"You have to be very patient with people," says Mrs. Brown, who, like many out here, fled from the East.

Charles Garrett of Rockwall, Texas, arrives with his two young sons. "My wife is fighting high blood pressure," he says, "so she stayed at home. Now I know why."

"Families are the messiest guests of all," says Mrs. Davis, the housekeeper. "Businessmen use one towel, one bed, one ashtray and that's it. Not families. And families seem to steal more, too." Mrs. Davis is famous for her store of motel lore, like the story of the man who threw out some holey socks and then wrote to have them returned. Or the story of the housebroken pig who stayed in Room 133. "He had his own bed," she recalls.

About 5 P.M. Ramsay Conyer of Morristown, New Jersey, arrives with a reservation. The motel does not have his name, but he gets one of the few remaining rooms and never learns of the error. Shortly before 6, Mr. Winfield, a Braniff Airlines pilot being transferred from Florida to San Francisco, drives the 652nd mile from Dallas. Next stop: a California Holiday Inn. A young man drives in. He wants a good stationery store. Miss O'Brien directs him. Mrs. Parker, who is driving from Nashville to Los Angeles at 50 miles an hour, arrives. All the rooms are full or reserved. She is sent to another motel. One half hour later she could have had one of the unused 6 P.M. reservations.

And so it goes into the evening, each traveler another face and another room number. Stretching their arms, rubbing their eyes, and sucking their sunglass earpieces, they fill out forms, submit credit cards, get directions, and become numbers on the board.

At 7 P.M. Room 157 calls for more towels. Room 407 has toilet trouble. Then a young couple shuffles to the desk. Mr. and Mrs.

Russell Barnes from Emporia, Kansas. They are ill at ease and smile often. Mrs. Brown looks at them briefly. "You're honeymooners, aren't you?" she says. The newlyweds look stunned. "In that case," Mrs. Brown continues, "let's give you a room with a king-sized bed." The couple blushes. "Aren't they cute?" says Mrs. Brown.

Suddenly a voice from nowhere says, "Is my Daddy here?" Miss O'Brien leans over the counter. A lost boy soon is rejoined with his parents. Room 435, Eric Dickman, checks out. He prefers to sleep by day and drive by night. "Are there some nails in 311?" a woman guest asks. "No ma'am," Miss O'Brien responds and then shrugs.

At 9 P.M., 19 guaranteed reservations are still unclaimed. Mrs. Brown rents out a couple to a lucky few travelers. For the others there is no room. At 10:30 Robert Keats, 13 hours out of Omaha, drags himself to the desk and pleads, "I can't go any farther. Please give me a room." He gets a couch in a meeting room. At midnight there are 13 unclaimed guaranteed reservations. Mr. Dillon, the night man, starts renting them to "walk-ins," travelers without reservations.

Then, at 4 A.M., Katherine Golden checks in and becomes Room 249. As it has been for 10 weeks, the inn is full. There are 343 paying guests in the building. And moments later Mr. Dillon begins the wake-up calls.

*I spent an eternity in Mentone once.*
*And then I wrote about it.*

# MENTONE, TEXAS

For just about everybody, Mentone, Texas, is only a 40-mile-an-hour speed zone on the way to somewhere else. But to a handful of chickens, uncounted cats, a few dogs, a pack of coyotes, and 43 persons, Mentone, Texas, is home. All right, so it is the smallest county seat in this vast state. And the only town on the only paved road in Loving County, where the population works out to one person for every four square miles. So what if there is no bank, no lawyer, no civic club, no newspaper, no hospital, no cemetery, no doctor, and no water.

It's only 32 miles to the grocery store, traffic is not exactly overwhelming, there is ample sand, and, as one resident noted, "You can lie on your belly and see for miles. There may not be anything to see. But if there was, you could see it."

Mentone, to be sure, is just one of thousands of obscure American towns, those tiny clusters of lights that hurried travelers vacantly watch pass under the wing of their plane or outside the closed windows of their speeding car on a family vacation trip. Such towns remain unknown until an outside event—such as a plane crash nearby—thrusts them into the national spotlight. That hasn't happened here yet. So placid, unassuming Mentone (named by a lonesome French surveyor for his hometown, Menton) is, in a way, as unexplored today as it was 100 years ago.

There still isn't much to see in Mentone on these torrid summer days that regularly get up to 110 degrees. The town flashes by so quickly and quietly. Yet if you look sharply, you might see a waitress hopping over the Keen Café counter to hand a beer to someone unseen behind the jukebox. Or you might glimpse Royce Brewer's grimy face peering out the lighted window after a long day in the oil fields. Or maybe you'd see Jack Keen, the town's child, pitching pennies in a corner. "You don't have to make anything up in Mentone," said Mrs. Mary Belle Jones. "It's all true."

It is hard to understand what attracted those three anonymous cowboys who built the first bunkhouse here late last century. The rust-brown water that flows nearby is far too salty for human consumption. Vegetation is so sparse that it takes almost 100 acres to support one cow. And in those olden days the Indians were not a minority here, as Oliver Loving discovered. In 1867 that cattle driver was shot, scalped, and left for dead by a band of Comanches. In five days he crawled 18 miles for help, chewing his glove for nourishment. Then for $250 a band of Mexican traders hauled him to medical help. Mr. Loving, for whom the county was named, died anyway.

The area still retains a frontier atmosphere. The few travelers on State Route 302 wave or flash lights at one another as they whistle along at 90 miles per hour. For miles the road runs straight as a cactus thorn with infrequent road signs the only evidence of man. Most signs are peppered with bullet holes from the rifles that everyone carries slung in the back window of his pickup truck. While in town at Keen's Café, there is the usual warning: "State Law prescribes a maximum penalty of five years imprisonment for carrying weapons where alcoholic beverages are sold, served or consumed." Another sign reads: "Women Will Not Be Served Here. You Have to Bring Your Own."

Keen's is, in fact, the center of the area's social life, not counting the irregular PTA meetings. Just about everyone stops by the café at one time or another. Some people even buy food. For the others, well, the cafe sells about five cases of beer a day. Edna Clayton, the county clerk, wanders over from the courthouse across the street now and then, mostly now. There are, after all, just so many deeds to be recorded. Every few months there may be a trial, so Bill Winston, the judge, is around then. But it has been seven years since the jail was used. Traffic cases do not clog the judicial docket. Loving County had its first traffic fatality only last year.

"It's a nice life here," says Mrs. Anna Loudermilk, the school-marm. Then, she adds, "If you like it quiet."

One of life's bigger events is the regular 32-mile trip into Pecos to get water. The water company there charges 10 cents a barrel for the liquid, which is carried in a trailer tank behind the family car. Each load lasts two to three weeks, depending on how much company you have, says Mrs. Jones, the wife of Sheriff Punk Jones. The water supply usually lasts longer for Mrs. Ellen Goodrich, who is a widow. But sometimes her grandchildren come from Los Angeles. They like to flush toilets for fun, a luxury that people here cannot afford. Sometimes, however, you can't flush the toilets. That's when the exposed pipes are frozen, and everyone reverts to the "two-holers" that each house has out back.

Such inconveniences, however, lead to rampant neighborliness. Everybody lends everybody anything. Mrs. Jones owes Mrs. Goodrich a dozen eggs. And Delores Ligon, the school janitor, still has some borrowed muffin tins. Mrs. Ligon likes the vastness of this southwest Texas region, where the horizons seem so much broader than a city's. "Out here," she says, "the country is close to you. It ain't got no boundaries." It also has no crowds. It has been 13 years since Mrs. Ligon stood in a line. And that was at Disneyland.

There were crowds, and lines, once. That was back in the 'twenties and 'thirties when the oil boom swept through here and the shifting population was somewhere over 2000. There were rows of tar shacks, shanties, and tents, even a hotel and lumberyard then. And 12 sacks of mail came twice a day. Now, Bill Brewer, the combination postmaster–justice of the peace, sorts only two sacks once a day.

As mechanization reduced the jobs for cowhands and oil-field roustabouts, most families left. The few workers who are still here maintain the declining oil wells, whose pumps resemble so many giant praying mantises nodding up and down as their gas-powered engines slowly go puck-puck-puck in the twilight. Of the 17 children of the local families who attend school in Mentone, 16 of them travel long distances over dirt roads from faraway cattle ranches. The lone child in town is 13-year-old Jack Keen, who speaks like the adults who are his only constant companions. Young Jack, a tobacco-chewer for half his life, is a popular companion among workers at the cafe.

At Keen's, Royce Brewer sips a Coors beer as the jukebox plays Hank Thompson's "On Tap, In The Can Or In The Bottle" and, with some amusement, recounts the political feud between the Mooreheads, who were ranchers, and the Hoppers, who were oilmen. Moorehead descendants are currently in power and there has been talk—denied by the Moorehead faction—of political favoritism and vote fraud in local elections, which always seem to be decided by one or two votes. Also, some residents believe there are those who have kept piped water out of the county because that would bring in development and a potential threat to their political dominance.

So Mentone goes its own isolated way. "This town has been dead so long," said McKinley Hopper, "that all you need is a belated funeral." At night the place is so quiet that a pack of coyotes occasionally steals into town to grab a dog and carry it off.

"When I came here as a bride," Mary Belle Jones remembers, "I thought this was the end of the world. But the place grows on you. A body can see forever here. And then, wherever your husband and children are, well, that's home anyway, isn't it."

*Did you ever wonder what a gas-station owner*
*was doing before you drove in and you*
*drove out? Well, I did. So I stayed a*
*while with Jack Neels.*

## LANDER, WYOMING

At 5:30 A.M. the alarm clock goes off at 1295 Goodrich Drive here. Within minutes, Jack Neels is up, shaved, and driving his 1961 Jeep to work. Just before 6 A.M. he opens the door, unlocks the cash register, and turns on the pumps. Another busy summer day has begun for the West Side 66 Service Station, one of 400,000 gasoline outlets gradually opening for the day across the country.

With Americans taking to the highways in record numbers during the peak vacation period, the nation's gas stations have never before pumped so much auto fuel—200 million gallons on a typical summer day, about one gallon for every American every day (versus 175 million in winter). For vacationing Americans, a visit to a gas station with its unkempt bathroom is hardly a memorable experience. But to spend a summer day in a gas station on the road to Yellowstone National Park is to see a little piece of the nation stop by.

On this day Mr. Neels was to pump 1733 of those 200 million gallons. Unlike some gas stations during the current fuel shortage, Mr. Neels has set no limits on purchases. Nor has he reduced his hours. Yet on this typical summer day he was to come close to emptying his cavernous underground storage tanks. And there were to be a few frantic phone calls to obtain fuel. But, of course, he did not know that would happen as his first local customers began to trickle in. It was still too early for the tourist trade that makes up half of his business in the summer.

Mr. Neels spends the first hour "doing the books"—checking the pump readings, the cash register tape, and the oil and tire supply. Years ago such gasoline outlets were simply general stores

126

with a barrel of gas out front. Then the stations became specialized, selling only gas and related automotive products and services.
Now, however, they are diversifying again, broadening the mer-
chandise they offer for sale in an attempt to earn more money. In
addition to gas and oil, for example, Mr. Neels sells bread, work
gloves, tires, milk, batteries, postcards, charcoal lighter fluid, butter, peanuts, cigarettes, Sloppy Joe mix, coffee, dill pickles, lemon
pies, orange juice, napkins, facial tissues, evaporated milk, mufflers,
tape recordings, ice, worms, sunglasses, popsicles, windshield
wipers, pastries, caramel corn, bubble gum, plums, pizza puffs, and
a frightening-looking food, pink popcorn.

By 7 A.M. the 31-year-old Mr. Neels has unlocked the oil-can
dispenser and put the tires out front. At 7:15 Tom Ortman, who is
6, walks in. He wants a can of chewing tobacco, which, he quickly
adds, is for his brother. Then Don Addy, a dairy farmer from
Genoa, New York, pulls in for a tank of regular, which sells here
for 40.9 cents a gallon. Don Holde, owner of the A-1 Trash Co.,
hauls away the station's 400 pounds of daily rubbish, and Earl
McWain, the milkman, arrives on the second of his two weekly
visits. Each time he leaves 10 gallons of milk. "That's pretty good,
considering this is a gas station," he says.

At 8 A.M., as the chill leaves the air here in the Rocky Mountain
foothills, Mr. Neels opens the two work-bay doors and drives in
Jim Gill's '69 Mercury for an oil change. At 8:30 Butch Gunsaul-
lus, a 17-year-old helper, arrives along with Seth Howard, a vacationing truck driver. He wants no gas, just two blocks of ice.
Business picks up. Joe Velehradsky from Nebraska buys a quart of
oil and $6.26 in gas. At 8:45, as usual, eight United States Steel
vans pull in to gas up for a day of hauling workers to a nearby ore
mine.

And so it goes throughout the day—a slow period, then a hectic
time, then slow, then hectic. "Ninety percent of the time," Mr.
Neels says, "as soon as I light a cigarette, someone will come in."
He lights a cigarette. William Mortensen drives in. He wants a $2
lube job on his Chevrolet Camper. "Fill 'er up, too," he says. The
camper takes 68 cents in regular. "That guy does the same thing
every year," Mr. Neels says.

In mid-afternoon Mr. Neels sees his regular gas supply nearing
the 2000-gallon level, about one day's sales "unless we get real

busy." He orders a truckload from Casper, Wyoming, 150 miles away. Delivery tomorrow. "That's cutting it close," he says. "We ran out a couple weeks ago." Norman Day of Westford, Massachusetts, another of the day's 153 customers, buys 35 gallons for his giant motor home. A couple of pickup trucks with extra tanks buy 40 gallons apiece. The bread man comes. Then the used-tire pickup. "We get 40 cents apiece," notes Mr. Neels, who earns $700 a month for his 60-hour weeks, plus 5 percent of sales other than gas and oil. Then he mails the week's credit card slips to Phillips's Denver office.

Another customer tries the old game. He orders $2 in gas and an oil check. While Bob Hill, another helper, checks the oil, the automatic pump passes $2. "I only ordered $2," the customer says. Mr. Hill pays the difference.

"I really like this work," Mr. Neels says, lighting a cigarette and then looking for an anticipated customer. "You get to meet all kinds of people. And most important, you're outdoors a lot."

More travelers stop. Unfolding from their cars and stretching, they wander into the station's rest room or buy an ice-cream bar. "You got any maps of Colorado?" one asks. "Yeah," Mr. Neels says, "but we've got a map shortage, too, this year." About 6 P.M. he goes home for dinner.

The cars keep coming after dark, each one ringing the station's bell seven times. A man buys 50 cents in gas. "How far does he think he'll go on that," Mr. Hill wonders. More travelers gas up as they search for motels. Several couples buy gas on the way to the drive-in. "This is the time of night I hate," Mr. Hill says. "You never know what's gonna happen."

At 9 P.M. Scott Adams, his cowboy hat tipped way back and his rawhide gloves on tight, wheels a tanker into the station with more than 55,000 pounds of fuel—8150 gallons of regular and 2550 gallons of ethyl. "I sure do get tired of that road from Casper," he says as he ends his 550 total miles of driving for the day. In the complex procedures that are the gasoline business, Mr. Adams's load was refined by the Continental Oil Company in Billings, Montana, piped to the Mobil Oil refinery in Casper, loaded on an independent truck, and delivered to a Phillips 66 station. "I can't figure it out," he says. "I just drive the truck."

Minutes later, a happy Mr. Neels arrives to watch the unloading.

"You're early," he says. "Things worked out just right," Mr. Adams says.

Mr. Neels's station will not close until midnight, when final figures show sales of $1,073.25 including $592.11 in regular gas and $40.70 in soda pop. Mr. Neels decides to buy his wife and two daughters a round of ice-cream cones. Another day is over. Sales were "pretty good." And the West Side 66 Service Station did not run out of gas.

# WEST YELLOWSTONE, MONTANA

Most of the time there are no more than 700 persons in this 640-acre town in southwestern Montana. In fact, most of the time townspeople are well outnumbered by the coyotes and bears that roam the surrounding pine forests or inspect the local garbage cans.

But suddenly each summer, as if on a signal from some colossal travel agent, 2,500,000 people drop in to West Yellowstone for a visit.

Now, it may seem strange to some that a mass of humanity equivalent to the entire population of Oklahoma or five Atlantas travels thousands of miles to the most sparsely populated county in the 48 contiguous United States. It is not so strange, however, when that county includes Yellowstone National Park, the country's oldest national park and a traditional mecca for motoring Americans on vacation.

And because it is also an American tradition that that many billfolds not go unnoticed by smiling businessmen, West Yellowstone is thriving. "It is safe to say that this town exists for tourists," says the head of the local chamber of commerce in what, it is also safe to say, can only be described as an understatement.

There are, to begin with, 71 motels in West Yellowstone's 24 blocks. Every last lot here is zoned for commercial use. Just 600 feet from the park's western gate there are 40 souvenir shops, their doors open, their cash registers ringing, and their neon-lighted signs showing horses in a perpetual gallop to somewhere. There are 25 restaurants, 10 trailer parks, and 14 gas stations.

To put it one way, West Yellowstone, Montana, has 4.5 motel rooms for every permanent resident. Or, putting it another way, when every motel room is fully occupied, West Yellowstone's population is multiplied by 10. Robert Schaap, the head of the chamber of commerce, runs a motel. Larry Hultz, the chief of police, runs a motel. So does his deputy. Irv Dellinger does not. He

130

runs a lumberyard that provides materials for the motels to add their new rooms each year.

The town is so full of optimists and so busy with tourists that no one has thought to plan a cemetery. Even traffic regulations here are designed for travelers. There are few stop signs and no stoplights. And there are no parking meters to discourage stopping and shopping. "You can't spend money from a moving car," one merchant noted. So, travelers may leave their campers, vans, station wagons, trucks, motorbikes, motor homes, and boat trailers when and where the spirit moves them, knowing that in West Yellowstone there is no such thing as a parking ticket. "We're pretty easygoing about petty things like that," said Mr. Hultz, who wears a uniform only for special occasions.

West Yellowstone is now at the peak of "The Season," as it is called here. The pizza ovens are belching out pizzas at a record pace. The Dairy Queen ice-cream machine struggles to churn out enough frozen milk for the lines of tourists peering in its windows. And over at the Dude Motel, Vivian Schaap is so busy running credit cards through a machine that she has no time to write her mother. Down at the information booth, a converted railroad car, Susan Prud'Homme is hard put to handle swarms of visitors whose main question deals with leaving town as quickly as possible. "Everybody asks, 'Where can I go to see the bears?' " she says.

Such an attitude among travelers distresses residents like the chamber's Mr. Schaap, a former Boston computer executive who forsook city life two years ago. "This town has great potential," he says. "We're trying to make it a destination in its own right rather than a means to an end—the park." As a result, the town recently added summer-stock theaters, nightly square dances, an impressive Indian and Animal Museum, and regular buffalo barbecues.

And like dozens of other American summer resort communities, West Yellowstone is trying to broaden its appeal and economic base by adding attractions during other seasons—a seemingly formidable task for a town where the airport closes in late September until the following spring. Particularly in the winter, West Yellowstone has seemed like the kind of place where the main local entertainment was a stroll out to the highway to watch the beer cans rust. After Labor Day three-quarters of the stores have closed, along with the park. Those stores that do stay open post signs like:

"Open Thursday Afternoons 1 to 4." The few Roman Catholics and Lutherans who stay for the winter have held joint services. And the town has had only one doctor—on Tuesdays.

Little wonder, too, because the winters here at 6669 feet are not mild. Roads are frequently closed. Temperatures hover below zero. Fires are fought not with water but with snow blowers. And the snowfall, which starts in September and ends in May, is sizable. "We get about 20 feet of snow a year," Mr. Schaap says, "but it's unusual to get over 18 inches at any one time."

Recently, local officials discovered tourism business was growing 1.5 percent annually while the number of motel rooms was growing 7 percent annually. The business solution was obvious: boost the tourism, especially during usually slow periods.

This fall, therefore, West Yellowstone will open a convention center in a former railroad dining hall that is so big, choral groups use the fireplace for a stage. Then there is what one local publication calls "the largest natural indoor skating rink west of the Mississippi." Aware of the nation's increasing leisure time, the town also now sponsors dogsled races, cross-country skiing, snowshoeing, ice fishing, and winter camping.

And like many northern communities, West Yellowstone has felt the impact of the snowmobile revolution. So the town sponsors snowmobile races. The motels have begun renting out snowmobiles, organizing daytime and overnight snowmobile expeditions into the national park, and offering customers heated garages for their machines.

Naturally, West Yellowstone's liberal traffic regulations also apply to tourists' snowmobiles. In fact, Ted Collette, the snowplow driver, has orders to leave several inches of snow on every street so that the buzzing snowmobiles will not damage their treads.

The winter business potential is so good that West Yellowstone, which was not incorporated until 1966, may even leave up its street signs this winter. Normally, they are removed because the snow buries them. It is all a far cry from the winter of 1907 when the Yellowstone Park Railroad opened this virgin forest area for settlement. But even then, Charles Arnet and other early residents opened a store and a stagecoach line for the park's visitors. As Chief Hultz puts it, "Tourism is all there is."

*Matt Dillon would never recognize the place. Neither would Wyatt Earp.*

# DODGE CITY, KANSAS

There was yet another burial up on Dodge City's Boot Hill this weekend. More than 200 mourners gathered around the gaping grave in the warm evening sunshine. The men took off their sweat-stained hats to bow their heads in prayer as the 2700-pound cement vault was lowered slowly into the hard brown prairie soil.

"This is a strange occasion," said the Reverend Rudy Treader. "It is to my knowledge the first time I've ever buried a vault without a deceased." This was, indeed, no normal burial for Dodge City, the rip-roaring railhead where the blazing six-shooters of Wyatt Earp, Bat Masterson, and Doc Holliday sent many a victim to meet his maker. The ceremony was the burial of a time capsule crammed full of 1972 memorabilia, and it was one of the highlights of six days of celebrations marking the 100th birthday of what was once dubbed "the wickedest little city in the world."

Dodge City's centennial, with the theme "Cow Town to Now Town," is one of scores of such celebrations across mid-America this summer in a region that was opened to large-scale development only 100 years ago with the arrival of the railroad, the iron horse that changed the face of the West. Kansas alone has 41 municipal centennial celebrations scheduled this summer in such places as Great Bend, Lyons, and Phillipsburg. Frequently the festivities mark the anniversary of the arrival of the Santa Fe Railroad. For instance, back in June, Hutchinson, Kansas, east of here, celebrated the 100th anniversary of its founding and the railroad's arrival. A century ago the rail gangs worked their way down the line in two months to what was to become Dodge City.

With the help of television and movies, Dodge City has burned its saga into the pages of American history—and into the minds of American viewers—first as the headquarters for the buffalo hunters who ravaged the Plains herds. Then it was the shipping point for thousands of cattle driven hundreds of miles by thirsty cowboys who needed restraining by such famed lawmen as Earp, Masterson,

Errol Flynn, and James Arness. In those days as many as 25 men might die violently in Dodge in one week. That is about as many as die violently on a Friday night now in some cities.

Once there was a scurry of activity here whenever the mile-long dust trails appeared on the horizon, signaling another herd's arrival. Today there might still be dust trails on the horizon, but they would be from herds of tourists in their air-conditioned station wagons coming to rest in Dodge City's shade and to visit Boot Hill and the false-fronted replica of the notorious Front Street, at one time Dodge's only street.

Today Dodge City has tidy thoroughfares like Wyatt Earp Boulevard and Comanche Street and a growing, prosperous population of 17,000 that makes drumheads and agricultural machinery or fattens the cattle for butchering or mans the stores that serve the wheat farmers in a 100-mile radius. This year's crops of agricul-

tural products and tourists are both good. By current estimates almost a half-million tourists will stop by Dodge City this summer. For 50 cents they can ride a real stagecoach or visit old-fashioned stores with new-fashioned prices or witness a phony shoot-out at 8 o'clock every summer night just before the dance hall show at the Long Branch Saloon.

This last week it was the turn of Dodge City's own residents to celebrate. And celebrate they did with a $100,000 series of pageants, parades, picnics, suffragette marches, rope tricks, an air show, revival meetings, and contests in horseshoe pitching, pie eating, beard growing, Frisbee tossing, and watermelon-seed spitting. Many residents wore bonnets, long gingham dresses, string ties, or beards. Those without centennial dresses, beards, mustaches, or "smoothie permits" were subject to immediate "arrest" and dunking by the Brothers of the Brush patrol.

"A centennial celebration," said George Henrichs, the celebration's goateed chairman, "is a great opportunity for a community like ours to take stock of itself and to pull together in a common cause. And it's a lot of fun." Mr. Henrichs presided over the burial of the time capsule, which is to be dug up and opened Aug. 20, 2022. Inside, Dodge City residents then will find empty Pepsi-Cola and Jim Beam bottles, newspapers, an inflated football, a Coors beer can, church membership lists, a centennial scrapbook, a drumhead, a Montgomery Ward catalog, women's shoes, a man's suit, letters addressed to grandchildren now infants, centennial coins, and a wash-and-wear backless minidress. They will also find a dead centennial fly that didn't make it out in time.

After the burial, everyone adjourned to the high school for the nightly performance of an impressive historical pageant titled "Dodge City—Symbol of the West." With the help of the entire football field, two movie screens, a giant stage, lighting effects, covered wagons, old cars, a dozen horses, and many narrators, more than 400 town residents portrayed their city's turbulent, raucous history for about 3000 spectators. In the dramatization, Indians were portrayed sympathetically while the buffalo hunters, Dodge City's first entrepreneurs who have often been treated as heroes, were depicted as smelly, thoughtless killers.

Narrators noted that this city was incorporated in 1875. But Dodge City has never been too concerned with legal niceties. So it celebrated the centennial in 1972, 100 years after people started living here. Also mentioned were the local visits of Charles A. Lindbergh and Bob Hope, as well as the blizzard of 1886, the tornado of 1942, and The Great Tragedy of '02—when the forces of temperance closed the bars.

Heritage Day on Sunday opened with more than 1000 people gathered in a tent on Boot Hill for an old-fashioned church camp meeting, complete with paper fans and some churchgoers praying on horseback. All the town's churches could not agree on a format, so the Methodists went ahead with it on their own. Then there were sack races in Wright Park, followed by group singing and demonstrations of baton tossing, knife juggling, and rope twirling.

"The Centennial," said Mrs. Lola Harper, a longtime resident who planned the day's events, "makes people realize their heritage and take pride in it. This week's activities depict real things. They are so much more interesting than fiction."

*Who gets up at 4:45 A.M., does calisthenics*
*for an hour, and wishes he hadn't? A*
*reporter covering a healthy farm boy.*

# GOOD THUNDER, MINNESOTA

The stark farmyard light stands its silent nighttime vigil over by the toolshed where the farm's six tractors are resting. Then, ever so slowly, a thin band of pink lights eases up into the eastern sky just over the tasseled tops of the mile-long cornfield. As if on a signal, the crickets' chirping gives way to the birds' singing. The stars start to fade. And soon the sun is out, baking the corn and soybeans and anyone not in the shade.

But by then, 16-year-old Dick FitzSimmons has already had his first breakfast and done over an hour of calisthenics for the upcoming football season. The sturdy, young, 5-foot-10-inches tall Fitz-Simmons has long, dark-blond hair billowing over his forehead. His tanned hands are strong and toughened. He is, in fact, the very embodiment of the American Medical Association's latest profile of the healthiest American—a teen-age boy living with moderately affluent parents on a farm in the north-central United States in the summertime. The medical group reached its findings by analyzing the nation's disability days—days when a citizen's normal activity is restricted by illness.

The AMA found that on the average farm folk are healthier than city people, Middle Westerners healthier than any other region's residents, men healthier than women, young healthier than old, affluent healthier than poor, whites healthier than blacks, those living with relatives healthier than those living alone, and July through September the healthiest months.

For Dick FitzSimmons, a soft-spoken farm boy in Good Thunder (population: 468), 1100 miles west of Times Square, and for thousands of other farm residents in towns like Freeborn, Blue Earth, and Blooming Prairie, problems like crime and smog are distant dilemmas indeed. So on these muggy summer days, life

goes on as usual—slowly, physically demanding, fiercely independent, and dictated, as always, by nature and a never-ending list of chores. There is also always something to be repaired. But it would never occur to anyone to call a repairman. If anything is broken, you fix it yourself, plain and simple.

The FitzSimmons place is a sizable spread, 1400 acres farmed in partnership by Robert FitzSimmons and his brother, Michael. They raise more than 600 hogs, as well as corn, soybeans, and oats, and their income brings Robert FitzSimmons—Dick's father—around $17,000 a year. It could all be gone tomorrow in the pelting fury of a hailstorm, however. And it means a lot of six-day workweeks and very long days for everyone in the family.

Dick awakens at 5 A.M., grabs a piece of toast and a pillowcase holding his clean athletic clothes, and heads down the dirt road in his seven-year-old Chevelle, the deep-throated mufflers echoing off the towering corn at roadside. His tape player blares the Grass Roots singing "Walking Through the Country." Twelve miles and 15 minutes later he is in the locker room of the Amboy–Good Thunder High School. By 5:50 A.M. he and 50 other football hopefuls are on the field, where the mosquitoes rise in tribute from the dew-covered grass.

"It's a beautiful morning," barks Rich Bullard, coach of the Chargers. "C'mon, FitzSimmons, move it." And he does, for two hours, until his once-white T-shirt is soaked with perspiration and dirt and grass stains. Then a shower and a quick drive to Larson's Gas Station and Lunch Counter, where he downs 20 ounces of milk and a couple of his favorite caramel rolls.

At home, young FitzSimmons, his father, and some cousins bale straw, expertly stacking more than 300 of the dusty 50-pound bales on wagon after wagon under a cloudless deep blue sky. Very quickly Dick's clean brown shirt shows the stains of perspiration. "I don't know why it's never cool when you're putting up hay or straw," he mutters.

Mrs. FitzSimmons, who is finishing her four daily loads of wash, serves lunch at noon—three pounds of hamburgers, two dozen ears of corn, a salad, cottage cheese, peaches, and pitcher after pitcher of cold milk. In the summer Mrs. FitzSimmons buys at least 14 gallons of milk a week. "But I've never bought any vitamin pills," she says. "We never seemed to need them. We just get lots of fresh air, exercise, and work." To her, good health is something to be expected, like frost in October.

She doesn't recall exactly when anyone in her family was last ill. "I think we had someone down in bed back in the early sixties," she says, "and Dick had a sore throat a few winters ago." Last year's medical bills for the 11 members of the family totaled $203.17, but that included $75 for Paul's broken arm. "I guess we just don't have time to be sick," says Dick FitzSimmons as he buckles on his heavy work boots. His afternoons are spent baling straw, running errands in town, feeding the hogs, overhauling a tractor or his car or turning the soil between crop rows to keep weeds down.

Every so often those tasks are interrupted by one of those awesome, flashing Middle Western thunder storms that come rumbling in off the Western prairie, within minutes soaking Good Thunder's black soil with giant drops before rolling on eastward. Almost immediately, screen doors slam again as area residents emerge from shelter to resume their labors. This summer it has rained more than usual here—and at the right times. The corn is now more than seven feet high and many stalks have two ears. So it looks like a bountiful crop to be sold or ground up to feed the pigs. Feeding the pigs is one of Dick's last chores before an early dinner of pork chops, green beans, carrots, a salad, milk, and, perhaps, a homemade doughnut or two.

By 6 P.M. young Mr. FitzSimmons, who is unsuccessfully cultivating a mustache, is back on the football field in Amboy in search of a likely starting assignment as center or middle linebacker. After another shower he discovers his weight is 159 pounds, a loss of nine pounds in two days.

At home around 8:30 he works on his car, tosses a football around with his brothers, or telephones his girl friend, Julie Shouts, a sophomore cheerleader. On Friday nights they see a movie in Mankato, 13 miles to the north, or sip a soda at the Pioneer House Café in Good Thunder, where Jesse James is reputed to have once shod his horse.

Dick, a junior who gets average grades, has no desire to attend college. "Dad keeps saying this land will be ours someday," he says, "and I reckon he's right. I'll stick to farming. It's all I've ever known, you know. No one's hanging over your shoulder all the time tellin' you what to do. I'd just go up a wall." Besides, he doesn't like cities. He and three friends recently camped in northern Minnesota, visiting a city on the way home. "That Duluth is a mad place," he says. "The people are all over you. And all those hills. . . ."

Around 10, Dick joins his father watching television in the cool basement recreation room that the family dug out and built together. At 11, young FitzSimmons raids the refrigerator for two oranges and a large glass of milk before stiffly climbing the stairs in his boots to bed.

Outside, the yard light—one of thousands sprinkled throughout the rural Midwest—is on again. A falling star streaks overhead. And the only sound is the Jensens' dog barking across the fields. In another six hours it will all begin again.

*Who stays up till 4:45 A.M., couldn't do a
calisthenic if he had to, and isn't sure what
he did? A reporter covering cowboys on a
Saturday night in town.*

# CAMERON, MONTANA

He was called a waddy, a buckaroo, or a ranahan. He lived with cattle for weeks at a time. He had no radio, no television, and no pickup truck. A saddle was his home, his pillow, and his prized possession. He was, of course, the much fabled American cowboy. And while most everything about his lonely life has changed over the decades, one thing has not: Saturday night in town.

Across the West on these summer Saturday nights, thousands of cowhands doff their work duds, shower, shave, put on their clean hats, and maybe even splash on a little cologne. Then they hop in their pickup trucks and take the dirt road to town for what is referred to as "a little partying." It involves bravado, boasting, brawling, telltale telling, and the prodigious consumption of alcohol. It goes on till sunup. It is much beloved. And, the cowboys claim, it is relaxing.

"Whoooeee, ain't this some shindig," Chuck Armitage shouted as he whirled around the dance floor minus his partner. Like many persons here last Saturday night, Mr. Armitage was not quite up to an interview. But friends said he was the owner of the Blue Moon Saloon, the largest structure here in what Doc Holliday might have called a one-cow town.

Six nights a week Cameron is the kind of town where coyote births would be front-page news. If there were a newspaper. Which there isn't.

Cameron is generations away from Deadwood, South Dakota, Tombstone, Arizona, or Dodge City, Kansas, where Marshal Earp took on early-day cowhands on countless Saturday nights. Today, however, the law has the good sense to stay out of this town on Saturday night. Instead, the police sit in their patrol cars outside of town waiting for the cowboys to weave their 300-horsepower buggies down the highway where to this day there is no speed limit.

Saturday evening achieved its prominence in the West because it marks the end of the arduous, six-day workweek with days that can start at 5 A.M. and end around 10 P.M. As Cecil Klatt, head of the nearby Diamond J Ranch put it, "There is only once a week that you don't have to work tomorrow." For some people Sunday is a day of worship or rest. For the cowboys, Sunday is a day of recovery.

The Saturday fun officially begins after dinner at 6 P.M. Madison County's cowhands got a jump on the good times last week because a local car dealer bought the grub—enough beef for a giant barbecue—as a sort of thank you for past business. Word of the festivities had spread throughout the area. There were even posters in the Long Branch Saloon and Mr. Ed's, competing bars in Ennis, 12 miles up the road. Those bars, which were all but deserted the other night, knew their turn would come, perhaps this week. By 8 P.M. the party at the Blue Moon Saloon was well under way. Jeeps, cars, and trucks lined the highway while the crowds spilled out of the false-fronted bar into the night, where thousands of gnats gleefully greeted them.

Young Tim Combs, a wrangler on Mr. Klatt's spread, had his hat tipped way back and a beer can in his hand. He knew it was Saturday because he got to sleep till 5:45 A.M. before feeding the horses. The previous Saturday night Mr. Combs was in Ennis. "But you sort of rover where the partying is," he said.

John Bausch, a brawny rancher who raises 600 head of cattle on 6000 acres 19 miles from here, had just completed baling 1500 bales of hay, the vital crop that will carry his herd through the Montana winter. But first he rose at 4:30 A.M. to move his herd to fresh grass before the heat and flies got bad. "This is our first outing off the ranch all summer," said his wife, Donna. "Out here, you know, work comes before pleasure." She had cooked breakfast, lunch, and dinner for the ranch hands, all 15 of them. "But," she added, "until you ring the bell you never really know how many feet you will have under your table."

Much laughter and the sounds of The Montanans—two electric guitars and a piano—burst through the door. Fifteen couples were dancing a polka in a space the size of a living room. The dancers'

ornate silver belt buckles flashed in the light as some older folk watched from couches along the walls. The women wore long dresses, hot pants, or slacks. The men wore plaid shirts, jeans, and, of course, their hats.

The beer and Scotch were flowing fast. "Do you know what's wrong with this party?" a cowboy asked a visitor for the fifth time. "There's too many foreigners here—like you. That's what's wrong. Why there's even some folk from Californy—damn foreigners."

"In the winter," said Tim Gross, a cowhand for the Castle Mountain Cattle Co., "you can fire a cannon down the street and not hurt anyone. But not on a summer Saturday." It had been two weeks since the 21-year-old Mr. Gross was in town because last week his boss told him to watch the cattle while all the other hands had the night off. "Jeez, did that make me mad," said Mr. Gross, who earns $15 a day plus room and board. He spent this Saturday "doctoring cows"—finding the sick ones and administering a shot for foot rot.

Then Mike Doud, a cowhand on the Bear Creek Ranch, began recalling the Saturday night he had spent at the rodeo in Dillon with Jim Overstreet. "We went to Skeet's Café," he said, "and had a burger and strawberry pie. Ain't that the truth, Jim?" The men nodded. They had heard this story many times before. The women smiled quietly. They knew their place. Encouraged, Mr. Doud continued: "We was leaning on a parking meter, Jim and me and Todd Holland and Larry Poulton, and up walks this long-haired hippie guy and calls me a dirty cowboy. Ain't that right, Jim?" Much laughter. "He grabs me three times," said Mr. Doud, "and then we had a little hassle. I turned to look for Jim, but he was making no offers to help." End of story. Much more laughter.

Inside, sweating couples were dancing what perhaps could be best described as an improvised jitterbug. The whoops were louder, the laughter greater, and the heat overwhelming. The fan had been removed because someone fell into it. On through the early-morning hours the music continued as Jean and Bob Jamieson sang, "Hold your warm and tender body close to mine."

The beer was all gone now. The trash barrel was overflowing with empty cans and bottles. And a cowboy asked a stranger, "Are you still standing?"

*What do Vernon Center, Minnesota,*
*Shillingford, England, and Peebles, Ohio, have*
*in common? For one thing, I had never been*
*to any of them—not until the World*
*Plowing Championships.*

# VERNON CENTER, MINNESOTA

This quiet farming hamlet in southern Minnesota, normally the home of 347 souls, entertained a quarter of a million visitors this week for the 19th World Plowing Championships.

While the town's entire police force (his name is Brian Champlin) tried to direct traffic on the street, everyone gathered in the mud out at Bert Hanson's place for Farmfest U.S.A. There, between 65-cent hot dogs, Bob Hope, beer, Roy Rogers, sales pitches for new tractors, and interminable waits for toilets, they cheered 38 men from 20 counties as they searched for an elusive goal—the perfectly plowed furrow.

It was the Olympics of agriculture and the farmers' Woodstock combined in one, and the doings entered Vernon Center into the annals of world plowing competition, right up there with Shillingford, England, Hönefoss, Norway, and Peebles, Ohio. "This is all just more than people here can comprehend," said Myrtle Harkins, editor of the *Vernon Center News*. It was all designed, according to Nicholas Topitzes, the festival's executive director, as "a salute to the harried, everyday farmer." Here he could be entertained and educated and celebrate his much-maligned "countryness."

On the first three days of the week-long event, which included a brief visit by Senator George McGovern, no rain was predicted. It poured much of the time. Then with clouds forecast, the sun shone brightly on the eight-mile-long traffic jams of cars and pickup trucks headed for the festival from such distant places as Colorado, Ohio, and British Columbia. Area schools closed for the week and Mankato State College postponed fall registration to house hundreds of visitors.

In addition to posing for family pictures next to the latest model combine, complete with air-conditioning and stereo tape deck, Farmfest visitors could find 180 types of corn growing, new silos, antique farm machinery, raffle drawings for free bags of seed corn, a country-western museum featuring Johnny Cash in wax, and Little Irvy, a 38-ton whale. There was a Bugs Bunny show; the country singer Charley Pride was here, as were Bob Hope and Leonard Slye, better known as Roy Rogers. There were also tractor-pulls with souped-up tractors, some of them driven by airplane engines, pulling thousands of pounds of weights before their over-heated engines blew up in much-applauded clouds of smoke.

But the highlight of the week was the championship of world plowing, or ploughing, depending on which side of the Atlantic you farm. Besides promoting quality plowing, an ancient art that is the first step in the growth of food, the competition is designed to further peace and the international brotherhood of farmers.

Thirty-eight men, including two from the United States, had been chosen in national plowing competitions. They brought their own plows but borrowed tractors here. Each man was assigned two plots, 100 meters by 20 meters. One plot was grassland, the other barley stubble. For two days of timed periods, the tense men inched their plows along the plots as thousands watched intensely. "You couldn't do five acres a day that way," commented Earl Zeigler, who farms several hundred acres near Algona, Iowa.

The plowmen's overturned earth was closely analyzed by a corps of judges, awarding points for uniformity of depth, furrow straight-ness, entrance and exit from each slit, and general appearance. Any grass showing, for instance, cost points. "Soil is our most precious asset," said Alfred Hall, the World Ploughing Organization's gen-eral secretary. "It takes 1000 years to make an inch of soil and it can all be lost in one hour's wind. So the earth deserves the best of husbandry, don't you think?"

The night before each contest, the men honed and oiled their plows, which are specially designed and tested like racing cars. Factory team experts, their companies' names emblazoned on coveralls and caps, hovered in the background for instant consulta-tion. "It takes a year to really get to know a plow," said John Kyle, a contestant from Timaru, New Zealand.

In the morning, tension was in the crisp early fall air. "I'm

always a little shaky," said Bill Goettemoeller of Versailles, Ohio, "but once I get up in the tractor seat I feel a lot better." Then, in a parade to the fields, the men eased their chugging machines, some with tiny national flags flapping by the exhaust pipe, single file down the festival's streets. The shiny silver plowshares glinted in the bright sunshine. The bands were playing. The spectators—all of them farmers—applauded each contestant—all of them farmers —equally. "Look, Rob," said one excited mother, "there's someone from Finland." And although neither she nor the contestant spoke the other's language, they exchanged warm smiles and enthusiastic waves as if they had known each other for years.

A few onlookers rushed out for autographs, and one contestant rose from his tractor seat and photographed the crowd cheering him. "Folks," the parade announcer said, "here comes Marton Brenner of Hungary." Many cheered. "Marton," the announcer continued, "is aboard a Ford tractor and he's using a Kverneland plow. He works on a collective farm that grows wheat, maize, and livestock. He is 38 and has two children." More applause.

Later, Willi Flatnitzer, a 28-year-old Austrian, was awarded the gold plow for first place. Norwegians took 2nd and 3rd, while Mr.

Goettemoeller placed 22nd and Alvin Wolf of Odell, Illinois, was 33rd. The United States has never won, not surprisingly because its brand of plowing the most land in the least time conflicts with the standards of European farmers, whose small farms dictate meticulous care. Next year's contest will be in County Wexford, Ireland.

This was probably the biggest week that Vernon Center, where the old rail depot now houses a flock of turkeys, will ever know, though Mr. Hanson, Farmfest's host, may be glad it's all over. "These people are dumb," the 71-year-old farmer said as he waded through the litter on his 1400 acres of corn and soybean fields. "They can carry these beer cans onto my place, but they can't seem to carry them off."

All week long Mr. Hanson was circulating at Farmfest across the road from his house. Alleged acquaintances clamored for his attention. "Hey, Bert," one man shouted, "remember me?" "I sure don't," replied Mr. Hanson, who says the festival is a fitting kickoff for his retirement. "Keyryst, what a way to go!" he said. "As Ed Sullivan says, 'We put on a really big shew.'"

By November 1, the four dozen telephones, 10 miles of fence, six

500-gallon water tanks, 5 miles of wiring, 350 tents, 8 truck-loads of chairs, 12 miles of water pipe, 5 mobile homes, and 150 toilets will be off the fields, which must be readied for next spring's crops. "In a few weeks," said Rex Day, Vernon Center's mayor for somewhere between 12 and 15 years (he can't recall exactly), "you'll hardly ever know Farmfest was here."

*The forest ranger couldn't believe it. He'd*
*been told to help the forest fire burn.*
*I made some calls. He was right.*

## SMOOT, WYOMING

Has Smokey the Bear been fibbing to us all this time? Or was he just repeating what his boss told him to say and now those statements are inoperative?

A furry symbol of everything that is good in the woods, Smokey has for 28 years warned Americans of the dangers of forest fires. But now Smokey's superiors have decided that forest fires are good—at least some of them. This is a new line of thinking among those who govern the country's 187 million acres of national forest lands.

Following an aging Smokey's advice, squads of forest rangers and other determined fire fighters until recently pounced on every forest fire and quenched it as quickly as possible. The teams were especially busy in recent days as 53 major fires crackled across more than 200,000 acres in a half-dozen states, causing $100 million in damage.

Today, however, a growing number of Forest Service officials are beginning to question seriously that total strategy, particularly in vast wilderness areas infrequently visited by man.

Such wilderness areas, the new thinking goes, are not true wilderness areas if helicopter-borne, goggled gangs of chemical-toting smoke-jumpers swarm over fires started by natural causes such as lightning.

So now federal forest officials allow some fires to burn themselves out on thousands of isolated acres. "We've decided," said Philip L. Thornton, deputy chief of the Forest Service, "to let Mother Nature do her whole thing when it doesn't threaten inhabited private areas. We simply won't go all out to put the fires out." To a generation of adults reared on Golden Books full of Smokey's admonitions and his life story (he was found after a New Mexico forest fire and now suffers from arthritis in the National Zoological Park in the capital) this policy may sound like sacrilege.

150

Yet the friendly old animal notwithstanding, natural wildfires caused by lightning have a definite role in nature's scheme of things. True, they account for 15 percent of the nation's forest fires and almost 50 percent of forest-fire damages. But for eons such blazes, frightening as they may be to living creatures, have cleared away ancient forests as well as accumulated dead underbrush and diseased areas of growth, leaving a clear vista for new grass growths to feed wildlife and, eventually, new generations of timber.

Some trees, in fact, cannot grow without a fire. The pine cones of the jack pine, for instance, will not release their seed for a new tree until after exposure to the intense heat of a forest fire. It is nature's ingenious way of insuring the growth of something living following a fire. Fires also wipe out epidemics of insects that kill trees over wide areas, and fires permit the natural ecological successions in forests from, for example, aspen to hemlock and eventually a "climax forest" of firs. Many species of trees, such as the majestic Douglas fir and grand Sequoias, would never grow if the soil was shaded by other trees. To stop automatically any fire, therefore, is to halt unnaturally the natural evolution of some woods, the new thinking goes. Which is not to say that the woods must be burned to be saved.

State and federal governments spend millions of dollars annually to extinguish thousands of forest fires set by arsonists or careless picnickers and campers. The Forest Service is now seeding grass by plane over much of the woodlands and range country recently burned. The grass will halt erosion until new tree seedlings can be planted, perhaps next spring.

The Forest Service has for years used fire as a limited forestry tool, especially in the South and Southeast. Called "prescribed burning," the practice permits the burning of small forest plots under the most advantageous fire-control and weather conditions. A special manual advises foresters, "Plan your burns to start about 10 A.M. and conclude by 4 P.M." Constantly monitored, the fast-moving fires scorch a section of land, burning off the undergrowth but not the trees. This eliminates unwanted plants that compete with trees for precious moisture and sunlight, and it reduces the future fire hazard when conditions might not be so conducive to control. Mr. Thornton estimated that private interests similarly burn 2 million acres.

But to let natural fires burn is new. In Montana's 1,580,000-acre Bitterroot National Forest not far from here there were at least two naturally caused forest fires in recent weeks. Both were started by lightning. Both were kept under control. But both were allowed to burn. The Snake Creek fire died out at 1680 acres. The Fritzcreek fire consumed more than 1000 acres.

Mr. Thornton expects decisions on letting natural forest fires burn to become a regular part of management in the national forest wilderness areas. Such a policy can lead to some strange scenes, however. Rangers near here tell stories of flying into natural-fire sites in recent months and, instead of dousing the flames, experimentally tossing dry branches on the blaze and fanning the flames with their coats.

As an updated Smokey the Bear might say, "Burn, baby, burn!"

*I was returning from a late-summer swing through the West. There was a fork in the road. One went toward the interstate; the other toward Evening Shade, Arkansas. That's not much of a choice in my book.*

# EVENING SHADE, ARKANSAS

"It's back-to-school time time time time," the radio announcer blabbers from his echo chamber, "so come on down to the Modern Sewing Center, the people who keep you in stitches stitches stitches stitches." It may not put the children in stitches stitches stitches, but the end has come to another summer-vacation period—that orgy of highway hassles and good family times squeezed between school sessions.

"Folks is heading home nowadays," says Jimmie Kunkel. "That's for sure." Mr. Kunkel, who is 1/359th of this town's total population, was standing outside his service station watching dusk fall on Evening Shade and its summer.

This tiny northern Arkansas town is not well known. It is 10 miles from Ash Flat, 22 miles from Strawberry, and a little farther from Needmore. But it does give Jimmie Kunkel and Billy Sharp and some of the other local people a good vantage point these days to watch Americans fleeing from their vacations in cars covered with souvenir stickers like so many battle ribbons. "They come in here tired and grouchy," says Mr. Kunkel, whose service-station sales drop by a third with the end of summer vacations. "They're all heading north now and they ain't stopping for nothing but gas."

Every summer about this time Mr. Kunkel and others note a subtle change on America's roadways. A few weeks ago, with air-conditioners set at "Max Cool," the station wagons left their well-kept homes with happy people in clean clothes eagerly beginning a new adventure, this year's long-awaited vacation. Way back then there were new sights to see, pictures to take, postcards to send, money to spend, and motel swimming pools to try. J. W. Faul of Beaumont, Texas, captured the spirit. "We don't know exactly where we're going," he said then. "But we've got to be on the way."

But now the sights are seen, the pictures are taken, the postcards are sent, the money is spent, and the swimming pools are tried. And sometime after the first flat tire or the 43rd antelope or the 97th game of license-plate bingo, the charm wore off the adventure. "It's like a new toy," said one traveler. "It's not new very long."

The cornfields, once refreshing to the eye, are now dull. The giant, growling trucks that gave good-natured blasts on their air horns for the children are now in the way. The Western hats, boots, and jackets bought in Wyoming are now packed away, probably forever. The marvelous local radio newscasts that reported four murders and then broadcast a jingle for a funeral home are now tiresome. And the announcers' long list of emergency messages for families believed traveling in the area are now giving way again to serious discussions of the problems of aphids on delphiniums. The motorist is tired of the 97-cent fried-chicken snack, the tiny motel soap bars that crumble in water, and the kamikaze bugs that somehow know a driver's exact eye level on the windshield.

Gone for many is that delicious sense of exploration that accompanies travel through highway mirages on unknown roads in new countrysides. Back now is that drowsy ennui that comes with droning drives on well-known, well-worn roads close to home.

Now that blue Indiana car in front, the dented one that was in the motel parking lot last night, that was passed after breakfast today and again after the first gas stop, now that driver is no longer a fellow member of the summer freeway fraternity whose temporary highway companionship was worthy of a friendly wave. Now he has become another urban competitor, one of those faceless thousands who conspire to hog the road and otherwise cause delays for hurried commuters.

In short, the vacation is over.

"All good things must come to an end—thank goodness," says Harold Smith, a Phoenix postal worker, as he checks into his last motel. "I've got to get back to work to rest up."

At an interchange on Interstate 90 in South Dakota, Dave Newman of Minneapolis pauses at 1 P.M. after the day's first six hours of travel. He is 19 years old and spent the last year as a bellhop earning money for a four-week trip to the West Coast on his motorcycle. The odyssey was everything he had ever dreamed of as he waited, heavily laden, for the hotel elevators at work last winter. But Dave Newman is tired now and often mumbles into the kerchief he wears over his face for wind protection. "I said I should be home by midnight." And with a roar he is back on the interstate. But now the mountains are in his rearview mirror.

This vacation was also the "trip of a lifetime" for Bernie Fuller and his wife. In 21 days they drove 6000 miles from their Toronto home to Los Angeles and back. "It was marvelous," he says. "We've just lost all track of time. You know, we saw Disneyland, Universal Studios, and three secondary Hollywood movie stars."

In Wyoming's wilds, Joe Velehradsky eases his car onto the dusty road shoulder. He has driven 150 miles and it is time for his wife, Ina, to take the wheel. They are nearing the end of their one-week, 2200-mile vacation and must return to work near Omaha. "What I really hate," Mr. Velehradsky says with fervor, "is driving across Nebraska and all those fields. How many times have I seen those same fields? How many?" And, shaking his head, he crawls into the passenger seat for the next 150 miles. Then the window rolls down. "We've got to get home tomorrow," he adds. "I've got golf league at night."

He is not alone in his thoughts. While motel owners prepare for the off-season when, wonder of wonders, some travelers stay more than one night, millions of returning vacationers in recent days have found themselves thinking not about tomorrow's boat ride, fishing expedition, or hike, but about the overgrown lawn at home, the laundry to be done, the mounting bill at the dog kennel, and the back-to-school shopping.

On the way home there's also that shopping stop to restock the refrigerator with eggs and bread and milk. And the chores waiting at work. And restarting the newspaper and the mail delivery. And, of course, the bills for the trip.

"This little junket will cost me about $900," says Bob Williams as he signs for another $5.68 in gas. A vacationing truck driver, Mr. Williams is returning his family to Pasadena, Maryland. "We'll skip any trip next year. It takes a while to save up this much," he said. Then, with his hands in his pockets, he nudges a pebble with his foot. "Sure has been nice though," he says. "Sure has." Suddenly, a little girl screams from the car. "Come on, Daddy. We gotta get back on the road."

*When I got home, a nearby community was*
*up in arms—both human and lethal—over*
*some sneaky snake in the grass.*

# BUFFALO GROVE, ILLINOIS

Roman emperors had their deadly pet lions. Cleopatra had her deadly pet asp. And David Pearson had his deadly pet cobra. At least, he thought he did. But then David went out to his garage on Maple Drive here and—the snake was gone!

That discovery touched off a serious summer suburban serpent search and a bizarre four-day chain of events that probably could only have happened in America during the final week of summer vacations. But the incident, which affected the lives of thousands of residents in this normally sedate suburb 32 miles northwest of Chicago's Loop, perhaps taught a lot of people here what the combined powers of suggestion, fear, a summer heat wave, and a platoon of television camera crews can do to normally rational people.

"I still can't believe it," said Police Chief Harry J. Walsh of Buffalo Grove, who has a fresh bottle of aspirin on his desk. Neither could Buffalo Grove's 19,200 residents. And, as it turns out, they should not have, either. Because now, it seems, after all the panic, all the armed searches, all the police overtime, all the crank calls, and all the television newsclips, Seymour, the deadly cobra, who could slither into bedrooms at night, is really Seymour, the mild-mannered rat snake, who cannot even bite a field mouse to death. He must squeeze it.

The stage for the great cobra caper was set weeks ago when David, who is 18 years old, agreed to keep the snake for a vacationing teen-age friend. The friend, Eugene Bowling, said he wanted to raise snakes and was assured by the person who sold him the snake—whose identity has not been determined—that Seymour was a valuable though deadly Egyptian cobra worth more than $4,000. So when young Pearson saw Seymour's empty cage, he pictured a dangerous snake loose in the grass near neighborhood tykes on tricycles and families out barbecueing burgers in the area's 90 percent humidity wave. He ran to the telephone. And, the police department's log dutifully notes, he filed a "missing cobra" report at 3:22 p.m. last Saturday.

The call was somewhat unusual, even for a mushrooming, four-square-mile suburb that until recent years was largely a collection of cornfields. The police, of course, treated the call as seriously as any other. Who wanted the responsibility of discounting it if someone was bitten? Initially, officials had to rely on the "expert opinions" of some local park workers who said the snake's description sure sounded like a cobra.

The 21-man police force was mustered and joined by more than 50 firemen, Civil Defense workers, and volunteers. Patrol cars with loudspeakers cruised the streets, ordering frightened families indoors for their own safety. Some hastily complied. Others flocked to watch. Playgrounds were abandoned. Swimming pools emptied. And squads of searchers—armed with pistols, shotguns, hockey sticks, and golf clubs—beat the bushes and fields. One team even waded several blocks through sewers. "This was the first cobra hunt I'd ever been on," Sergeant Arthur Voigt said with a straight face, "and I kept asking myself why would someone want to keep such a snake in my town on such a hot day on my day off."

Then, they came. By the carload the television-camera crews, otherwise idle on a slow summer weekend, swarmed over the town like vultures, eager to chronicle the snake hunt—in color—for millions of presumably concerned viewers. The police were busy, so the crews interviewed neighbors, most of whom knew less about the situation than the reporters. In some accounts the 5-foot cobra grew to 17 feet. "And he can travel 35 miles an hour," someone said.

Zoo and police switchboards miles away lit up with anxious callers seeking information on the trio of boa constrictors they heard was heading their way. Tourists flocked to watch. Some said the snake was aggressive and could climb; some it could not. Everyone agreed that the snake hunted at night and was very deadly.

Special antivenom serum was rushed to a nearby hospital and Monica Kulikowski, a nurse, was pictured holding the vital medicine. Penni Poremski locked herself in her bedroom, and Mrs.

James Kerr carried a crowbar whenever she went outdoors. Some children cut up garden hoses and tossed them on lawns to scare adults. The police set enticing mice free in the Pearson garage to lure Seymour out. Then they tried gas. Someone suggested a dish of milk for bait. Another person suggested renting a snake flute or a mongoose.

"The television people made a carnival out of the whole thing," a village official said. "The only danger during the entire snake scare was that some TV crew would run over a policeman."

On Monday Ray Pawley, reptile-house curator at Brookfield Zoo, examined some skin that the snake owner said Seymour recently shed. Mr. Pawley said the skin did not come from a cobra but from a common rat snake. As Chief Walsh prepared to announce that there was no cobra after all, a sergeant ran up to him.

"Chief," the sergeant said, "did you hear about the dog?"

"What dog, sergeant?"

"The dead dog, sir."

"What dead dog?"

"The dead dog with the fang marks on its leg."

"Oh, no!"

It seems that Joe Misicka, a neighbor of the Pearsons, returned from shopping to find King, his 60-pound dog, dead on its tether just eight feet from a muddy creek where a cobra could cool itself during the midday heat. The report soon flashed over the airwaves, although an autopsy quickly revealed the dog died of heat prostration when it caught its leg in the chain.

The search was called off. And the town began assessing damages, which included $641 in overtime pay for the police. The incident kept the prowler calls down for a few days, but David Pearson, who has gone into seclusion, was charged with disorderly conduct. And a policeman was treated for injuries received when he was struck in the mouth with a television microphone.

So far, Seymour, the center of all the fuss, has not returned. If he is a cobra, which snake experts value at perhaps $50, he will be dead after the first fall frost. But in Buffalo Grove his memory will linger on.

# F A L L

*I saw a line in an obscure government
report saying some 2000 one-room schools
were still in operation. How? I wondered.*


# SPARKS, NEBRASKA

Vernon L. Brill is 38 years old and a part-time garage mechanic,
campground operator, and insurance salesman. He is also part of a
much-revered but dying American institution—the one-room
schoolhouse. As the lone teacher in this tiny town's school, which
began fall classes today, he is responsible for the basic education of
the children in School District 71, a remote 48-square-mile area in
northern Nebraska.

On school days when howling blizzards don't block the dirt
roads, he drives 23 miles to this crumbling crossroads community
(population: 3) to instruct 15 children in kindergarten through
the eighth grade. For this, Mr. Brill, who is working on his bache-
lor's degree in education at Chadron State College, receives $6,000
a year and an occasional meal at a pupil's home. He is among 42
such teachers in Cherry County and less than 2000 others in similar
schools across the country.

These one-room schoolhouses are the remnants of the nation's
first education institution, an institution that taught the three R's
to millions of Americans from George Washington to Chet
Huntley, with Abraham Lincoln, Bat Masterson, Thomas Edison,
and Herbert Hoover in between. Until the mid-1800s the one-room
school taught the majority of Americans. But, like many aspects of
a simpler America, it is vanishing.

In 1966 a federal survey found 6491 such schools in the nation,
1413 of them in Nebraska, which has the most. By 1968, the latest
year for which nationwide figures are available, only 4146 were left,
with 1033 of them here. And Washington officials estimate that
the decline has quickened.

Faced with decreasing and older farm populations, rising costs,
and greater educational demands, thousands of smaller school
districts throughout the country have merged in recent years, some

161

after long, bitter feuds. Larger schools, their proponents argue, will offer children a better education and preparation for college, a preparation they want but which their parents never had. "Those one-rooms are a pain in the neck," said Melvin Olson, a state education official in Lincoln. "They just don't provide the best education." As a result, the state's one-room schools have now been whittled down to 744, with about 125 closing each year.

For the moment, however, Sparks has avoided that fate. Its 15 students, tanned from their summer's work, jumped from their parents' cars and trucks about 9 A.M. today and scrambled into the three-year-old school building—the district's third since 1885 and the first with an inside toilet. They helped Mr. Brill adjust desks to their new heights. After the Pledge of Allegiance, the books, which come from a county library in Valentine, 20 miles southwest, were distributed amid much whispering and giggling.

Mr. Brill, in his 12th year of teaching, asked the older children to note what they wanted to improve in their handwriting this year. While the eighth graders—Shirley Bruecklander and Rose Ann Foster—dashed off a few sentences, Mr. Brill helped the five second graders practice printing letters. Fred Copeland and Billy Foster, the kindergartners, played in the corner on the floor. Then Mr. Brill read the responses ("I'm not going to slant letters every which way") while the youngsters practiced at the blackboard.

"I probably don't explain as much to the whole class as in other schools," Mr. Brill told a visitor, "but I more than make up for it in individual instruction." He teaches arithmetic, reading, spelling, English, science, and social studies. There are two recesses, and 30 minutes for lunch brought from home. At 3:30 today after cleaning up the school, the children, who come from six families, all piled out the door and went home to help with the evening chores.

There are 180 school days. The youngsters will be off at Thanksgiving and Christmas and, if it's an average winter, maybe five days when the school and the roads are buried in eight-foot snowdrifts. Classes end in mid-May and next year Shirley and Rose Ann will attend the 880-student high school in Valentine, the county seat.

"I think our kids get everything in school that others get," said Lawrence E. Turner, the local board president, "except maybe all the competition and social life. But they'll get that soon enough." "We like having our children at school close to home," added Mrs. Martha Foster, who has three boys at the school. "We have more local control over their education this way and they get practically individual tutoring." It is also less expensive. Area landowners pay a 15-mill school-tax levy—that is, $15 for every $1,000 of assessed valuation. In Valentine, the area's largest town, they pay 72 mills.

The Sparks school was founded in 1885 by a hardy band of homesteaders (including the Sparks brothers, Eldon, James, Charles, and Levi) whose great-grandchildren now run much of the cornland and cattle ranches sprawling across this sandy range where electricity arrived only 21 years ago. Here, the faraway problems of desegregation and decentralization seem unreal. More important is the weather forecast—given at the beginning, not the end, of each local newscast—and the fact that most boys now forsake the farm for the city.

It is a friendly area where a 3000-acre ranch is not unusual, where the farm family is dependent only on itself, and where the nearest neighbor is several miles down your driveway, several miles along the unpaved road, and several miles up his driveway. It is a place, in short, where independence is prized greatly and threats to it are fought fiercely.

And so the Sparks area, whose 38 landowners decide most school issues, has resisted any consolidation attempt, including an abortive one-year trial with a neighboring district three years ago. That ended in a bitter dispute that saw old family feuds resurface and several ranchers secede from the school district.

But independence has its problems, too. The total annual school budget has climbed from last year's $7,176.49 to $8,240. And teachers, a mobile group, are increasingly hard to find and keep here. "It's just not feasible any more to train any one person to teach so many subjects in that many grades," says Mr. Olson in Lincoln. Mr. Turner of the Sparks board adds: "If they're trained in the big city, they don't come back to the country." So, Mr. Turner says he himself may go to a big city next spring, but only to look for a country teacher.

*Fall, to the true fan, does not mean the opening of school. It means the opening of something else.*

# PHILADELPHIA, PENNSYLVANIA

When the financially hard-pressed board of education here announced a range of serious spending cuts last May, including an end to 600 teaching jobs and all extracurricular activities this year, the statement was met with a citywide chorus of cynical yawns. It was, after all, the fourth consecutive year the board had warned of financial disaster.

But when September came and the city suddenly realized these economies also meant the end of varsity football, the uproar rivaled the screams of a Super Bowl crowd. The threat to high-school football touched off dozens of protest meetings, talk of a mass march, and a lawsuit against the school board by teen-age football players. But now, under the prodding of a mayoralty candidate, Frank L. Rizzo, the Philadelphia Eagles have rushed in with enough money to save the season, and football practice has begun.

Philadelphia's angry football fans seem placated. The 600 teaching jobs, though, have not been restored and school officials still face a $30-million budget gap. "What this says," remarked Dr. Mark R. Shedd, the Philadelphia school superintendent, "is that the people who make the noise have a distorted sense of values."

The sometimes bizarre series of events began last May when the board—faced with increased costs and staggering debt payments—drew up what one member called "a baloney budget" of $360 million, although it knew it would receive only $330 million in revenues and needed $394 million just to maintain last year's level of operation. Among the items slashed from the budget was $4.5 million for all extracurricular activities, including $79,000 for varsity football. The rest covered other sports, drama, art, music, school yearbooks, and student newspapers.

On September 1, when football training was to begin, the

165

coaches and teams were physically barred from the fields and Philadelphia became the first major city in the nation to eliminate high-school sports—at least temporarily. "My God," said one aroused parent, "they just can't do that." Similar feelings were expressed throughout the city. Bob Caesar, Lincoln High's football coach, asked, "When a student gets to high school, are reading, writing, and mathematics more important than extracurricular activities?"

The Philadelphia Federation of Teachers had already threatened a strike and had gone to court in an attempt to halt the cuts. Mayor James Tate said the board should not have "a prevalence of stuffy people who are antisports."

On September 3, Dr. Shedd told the schools' 22,000 employees that the academic year would end four weeks early next May 24. The teachers' union urged the mayor to remove any board member who failed to support a full sports program.

C. Carson Conrad, head of the President's Council on Physical Fitness, arrived in town, found the situation "deplorable," and vowed to do everything possible to help, short of providing money. Then four football players and a cheerleader sought an injunction in United States District Court to halt the board's cutbacks. And Jack McKinney, a local college coach, reported: "Everywhere I travel, people are laughing at us. They can't believe this is happening."

Most speakers expressed concern over the possible effect of the cutback on the city's 285,000 public-school students, 60 percent of whom are black. The lack of activities would encourage drug use, dropouts, and juvenile gangs, contended the Public League Coaches Association, whose members each stood to lose up to $1,800 a year in supplementary income. Sports, on the other hand, teach teen-agers leadership, team spirit, self-sacrifice, and "the give-and-take of life," the coaches said. Coach Caesar added that 94 percent of the 2000 seniors in varsity sports stayed in school last year to graduate, and 57 percent went on to college, many on athletic scholarships.

On September 8, 500 persons attended a rally sponsored by parents, coaches, students, the Veterans of Foreign Wars, and the Philadelphia Labor Committee, a Socialist group. The group decided to march downtown two days later. But events were moving swiftly as the cuts became a political issue. Both mayoral candidates were on record as favoring restoration of all extracurricular activities.

Thacher Longstreth, the Republican candidate and a former football player at Princeton, said the schools could close even earlier in May to save money. He also suggested closing the city's Civil Defense Office, thus freeing those funds for sports. Mr. Rizzo, the Democratic candidate and former police commissioner, demanded more economies by school officials. He was particularly angered by the purchase of a $900 desk for Dr. Shedd.

According to current versions, on September 7—two days before classes resumed—Mr. Rizzo telephoned Leonard Tose, the owner of the Philadelphia Eagles, who had donated $55,000 to the school system from the proceeds of the August 16 game against the Buffalo Bills. Mr. Rizzo asked Mr. Tose to donate another $24,000. At a news conference the next day, Mr. Tose produced a check and said: "Mr. Rizzo has told me $79,000 will get the kids back on the [football] field. Let's start the game!"

The school board's acting president, however, the Reverend Henry H. Nichols, said he would accept the money and restore all extracurricular activities, including football, only if Mr. Rizzo would guarantee that, if elected, he would provide whatever funds the schools needed to finish the full year. Mr. Rizzo agreed, providing he could audit the board's books first. Mr. Longstreth agreed, too, and last Monday the board ratified the deal. Football practice began after the next day's classes, two weeks later than usual. The first games were pushed back to September 30.

For Central High's star halfback, Kenny Anderson, the decision to restore extracurricular activities had a special significance. He lives for football practice, he said, adding: "I love the game and I want to play it." He has received feelers from a half-dozen colleges about a scholarship, which he says is the only way his family could afford higher education for their children.

For Dr. Shedd, the larger issue "is whether the urban schools will survive or not." "I object," he said, "to people who get hysterical just because the great American pastime isn't going to happen here, but don't say a single word about the 600 teaching positions wiped out. It's a question of priorities." He remained skeptical, too, of the entire football deal. "We are operating on the political promises of two mayoral candidates," he said, "and that's a lot of fluff. I want to see the color of the cash."

"Even though campaign promises are tenuous," one school official said, "at least one of these guys will be mayor when our annual spring crisis comes up, and we'll have someone to go to. It's not money in the bank, but it's a lot more than we've had in the past."

*A friend got an invitation to an unusual convention. I thought beer cans were trash.*

# LAKE GENEVA, WISCONSIN

Doctors and mechanics and housewives and teen-agers—about 600 persons in all—gathered here this weekend to share a common passion: empty beer cans. These men and women are the Beer Can Collectors of America and over the weekend they met at the Playboy Club in this resort community, 75 miles north of Chicago, for their annual "canvention," a three-day orgy of trading that saw grown men sweat profusely in hard bargaining for an empty beer can. "This is the fastest growing collecting hobby in the country," said one of the group's officers as he rushed off to make a deal.

The BCCA, as it is affectionately known to members, has its own emblem (a hand reaching for a beer can rampant on a map of the United States), its own button, newsletter, mug, and windshield sticker, as well as some voluntary beer-can trading guidelines to combat inflation, which has pushed the value of a 1930s beer can all the way up to 10 or more newer cans. Soon the group will publish a complete listing of all 12,000 American beer cans, including forgotten brews like Jaguar, Buccaneer, Bullfrog, and Olde Frothingslosh.

The collectors came from Colorado, Canada, and Connecticut and big and small towns in between. They came in campers, Cadillacs, and Camaros. But they had one thing in common: every single car was packed tight with empty beer cans. These were the "traders," the duplicate or expendable cans used to barter for other cans, the missing links in an individual's cherished collection. The idea is to get as many different beer cans as possible in the best possible condition without duplication or giving up rare cans.

Some members arrived here two days early, anxious to get first crack at any good trade. Even before registering, swarms of collectors gathered around a new arrival's car trunk to haggle good-naturedly. "You must be kidding," said one collector. "One current can for an obsolete? I can get three for this one easy." They settled on two, but not before each man said he was being taken.

Beer-can collecting probably began Jan. 25, 1935, the day after the Gottfriend Krueger Brewing Company in Newark turned out the first can. For years collecting was done only by isolated individuals. Then, in 1970—the year after beer cans began outselling beer bottles—two Saint Louis brothers discovered they had the same hobby. They formed the BCCA (P.O. Box 9104, Saint Louis, Missouri 63117), whose membership rose like a fine head of brew. And thus began the latest chapter in the American mania for collecting. There are now 609 members, not counting tolerant spouses, in 35 states and 5 countries. Last year about 225 people met in Saint Louis. Next year's canvention will be in Cincinnati.

Like this year's, it will have a special commemorative beer can (empty) and many different types of free beer in cans (full). Meticulously, each can will be opened on the bottom to preserve its appearance on the display shelves that line countless collectors' basements, which are dehumidified to combat that dreaded enemy —rust. There will also be another Miss Beer Can, another bus tour of local taverns, and a goodly supply of Beer Can Collector shirts, jackets, cuff links, and charms. Most important, however, will be the constant trading that continues into the wee hours of each morning when, if one man has emptied a few too many beer cans, a sober collector can make some good trades.

"There is no real value in the cans," noted Roger Johnson of Buffalo Grove, Illinois. "The value is in the bartering and the friends you make while trading." Mr. Johnson stood next to Herb Elliott, a toolmaker from Danielson, Connecticut, who was phoning his employer in Hartford daily to report sick. Mr. Johnson and Mr. Elliott have traded by mail for two years but had met only moments before. They seemed to be lifelong friends already. Like most collectors, both men spend about five hours a week and $200 a year on their hobby.

"It's just a deviation from the regular grind," said Duane Hack of Hartford, Connecticut. He collects beer cans to relax after a hard day's work—collecting stamps and coins.

At some risk, Kenneth Heistand even waded into his flooded basement in York, Pennsylvania, recently to rescue his cans. He later spent many hours washing and drying each one of the 1200. One man's trash is another man's treasure. So, many collectors walk along country roads or visit municipal dumps or recycling centers looking for cans. Mr. Heistand, a truck driver, takes his coffee breaks by rummaging through roadside rubbish barrels. "Interstate highways are the best," he said.

"Everybody has his own thrill," said Bob Hurst, 18 years old, of Elwood, Indiana. "Beer cans are better than dead butterflies." They are, that is, unless they set off anti-skyjacking metal detectors, as John Zembo's collection did at a Texas airport. Mr. Zembo explained to the officer that his bag was full of empty beer cans. "Sure thing," said the sky marshal.

Mrs. Tobi Harms of Peoria, Illinois, is a new collector, despite her husband's protests. "Have you ever looked closely at a beer can?" she asked. "They really are beautiful, so colorful and shiny. And no two brands look alike." She was excited because she had just traded one Sheridan and one Fabacher Brau to John Vettzer for one Malt Duck, undented, unrusted, and unscratched.

However, because Mrs. Harms has just 200 cans, she only ranks as a "brewery worker" on the BCCA's membership list. That means a lone star by her name. Depending on a collector's can count, he or she is an "apprentice brewer" (two stars), "journeyman brewer" (three), "brewmaster" (four), or "grand brewmaster" (five stars).

Ernie Oest of Port Jefferson, Long Island, New York, who was chosen this year's top collector at last night's banquet, is a "grand brewmaster" with more than 5000 cans. So is Larry Wright of Saint Louis, the outgoing president and a co-founder with his brother, Denver. Larry has more than 1800 cans in his basement, which has become a tourist attraction for neighborhood repairmen.

Recently, Mr. Wright, who runs a vinyl-plastics company, achieved the dream of every beer-can collector. He got an empty can of Soul Malt Liquor, which was made for only a few weeks in Watts, California. He got the can in exchange for 25 others from an elderly California can collector known only as Cacti Pete, who travels with his wife in search of beer cans. On a recent trip east his car was full of beer cans when he got to Indianapolis. So Cacti Pete did the only logical thing. He shipped his wife home by plane to get the extra front seat space in his car.

Such dedication to old metal cans was repeated here. "Dan," said Doris Heideischeit of Cedar Rapids, Iowa, to her husband, "Dan, do you want something to eat? Dan? Honey? Are you hungry, dear?" But Mr. Heideischeit was disappearing across the aisle to barter. Another man here computerized his entire can inventory and carries a stack of computer cards with him for ready reference.

The collectors' eagerness gave rise today to rumors that one member was selling cans for money, an incredible breach of etiquette. "I suppose," said Mr. Wright, "that with our rapid growth it is inevitable that money will turn a hobby with a personal touch into a regular business. Then, anyone with a lot of money can buy the best collection. We can only postpone that as long as possible."

*. . . But then I also thought*
*turkeys were to eat.*

# MONTGOMERY, INDIANA

"OK now, are we ready?" the announcer asked the turkey jockeys. Bang! And they were off—well, sort of off. And the Second Annual Daviess County Turkey Trot Festival was sort of under way.

The festival last weekend was a four-day frolic for thousands. Like dozens of similar local festivals springing up around the Middle West these days, it had rides, races, beer, tractor pulls, amateur shows, and bands. And like the countless corn, dairy, pumpkin, and gladiola festivals elsewhere, the Second Annual Daviess County Turkey Trot Festival was a combined farewell to summer and a hello to fall, heavily flavored with civic boosterism.

Such festivals, which have mushroomed in the last two years, according to experts on fairs, seem in part to be compulsive attempts by small counties and communities to put themselves on the map like the big cities, which keep drawing their rural young folk away. The fairs also attract valuable tourist dollars. Perhaps they make rural life more fun. And if the festival makes some corporation aware of a potential site for a satellite plant with a few jobs, well, that's just fine in this economically undeveloped area of declining population.

Generally, festivals have a local theme. Since Daviess County, here in southwestern Indiana, contains roughly 40 turkeys for every human being, the theme was somewhat ready-made. "We considered a festival for hogs," said Ron Meyers, a chamber of commerce officer who helped originate the fair, "but what can they do? Then we said, 'What can turkeys do?' Well, they can run. So we have turkey races." In fact, Daviess County has the only turkey races in the world sanctioned by the National Turkey Federation.

The turkey, which Benjamin Franklin wanted as the national bird, is not exactly bred for racing. It is bred to die. And as the peak slaughter season now approaches, most of the nation's 132 million turkeys are making their way to their doom on some holiday

platter. Here at Montgomery's Ruritan Park, however, 30 birds got a reprieve. They went into training for the festival races, a series of elimination heats over a 213-foot, feather-littered course leading up to today's finals.

"I've been working with Snoopy here for three weeks," said 13-year-old Alan Wininger, the eventual grand champion, who was sponsored by the Washington (Indiana) Airport. Snoopy, who weighed in at 25 pounds, strained at his collar, which was borrowed from a neighbor's cat, and his leash, on loan from a dog. His 18-second heat today set a world record.

Larry Brawley, a loan agent who piloted Dollar Helper, also trained his turkey, although he knew it was useless. "This is one dumb bird," he said after a poor 37.8-second showing. "Maybe the harness was too tight."

Chris Beckett even mowed his lawn into practice lanes for

Turkey Lurkey, a bird entered by the A to Z Pet Shop. But Turkey Lurkey blew the race when he wandered off the track to check on a shiny piece of litter.

If there was a prize for most elaborate preparation, however, it would have to go to the Chicken City Special, a turkey entered by Chicken City, a club of 12 young boys, all self-avowed cowards, who meet in a converted chicken coop. "We have bicycle demolition derbies and we camp out, and for initiation we smear peanut butter all over your hair," said Tony Murphy. "You wanna join?"

For three weeks their bird stayed in the secret clubhouse, along with another turkey "just for company." Brian Traylor's dad donated some feed. Mrs. Sue Showalter, Timmy's mom, sewed a red and white warm-up jacket to keep the evening chill off an exercising turkey. But the youngsters did not train the bird.

"We wanted him to stay wild so he'd run from ya," explained Tony Ward. "We're rookies at racing," he continued, "so we decided if the turkey lost, we would eat him. On the other hand, if he won, we would eat him. We can't keep him. Our allowances won't cover the feed costs." And a murmured chorus of "that's rights" came from his pals.

Other birds in the race stared at the crowd, ran the wrong way, or pecked at the dust. "I won't tell you folks what's happening," the announcer said. "I'll just let you figure it out."

Originally, chamber officials decided the grand winner should survive. Last year's victor, Firebird, did—for a while. But his sizzling 23-second race time didn't impress a pack of neighborhood dogs a few weeks later.

After each day's turkey heats, the crowds wandered to the rides or the food stands, where, in apparent deference to the turkey contestants, humans could gobble up only beef, pork, and chicken. An 800-million-candlepower searchlight, which could be seen hundreds of acres away, pierced the sky, drawing millions of insects from nearby counties.

Ralph Brumett sat precariously on a plank over a tub of water. Fun seekers with 25 cents threw baseballs at a lever, trying to dump him. "It wasn't bad," he said, "until the Little League team came by."

"Attention, Tom Draper," the loudspeaker said, "report to your tractor immediately. You're up next in the tractor pull, Tom." Clouds of black smoke gushed into the air as each tractor strained for the furthest distance under the load's increasing weights. (Don Padgett and Jarit Perkins won.)

At the stage, Jim Wampler, an off-duty state trooper, was master of ceremonies for an amateur show complete with applause meter. Claire Ann Queen sang "Sam, You Made the Pants Too Long," the Sons of the Pioneers sang "Dead Skunk in the Middle of the Road," and Emily Fern played the piano. (The Fairchild Sisters won.) "We have no losers here," Mr. Wampler told the crowd seated on blankets. "We just have seven nonwinners."

Suddenly, the night air was filled with the sounds of two electric guitars, four drums, two cymbals, and an electric organ. It was the four men and six amplifiers of Heavy Duty, the United States Army's "rock band" clad in undershirts. "Hi, folks," said the leader, "we're the groovy guys from Fort Knox." And like moths, the young people swarmed toward the pavilion's lights. "They were a big hit here last year," a festival spokesman explained. "I guess you could say they're back by popular demand. And besides, they're free."

Dozens of teen-agers were moving and nodding and gyrating to Heavy Duty's sounds. Every once in a while an adult sneaked into the crowd to drag away their offspring. Into the night the sounds blasted out over the town of Montgomery. After one particularly strong song, the band's leader was elated.

"Heavy. Heavy," he said. "How was that one, Morgantown?"

Then, someone leaned over and told him where he was.

*Where station wagons go, can baby-sitters be far behind? Even in Sin City West?*

# LAS VEGAS, NEVADA

Giant neon signs touting all-new, all-nude revues. Gambling dens that never close. Chorus girls in see-through feathers. Gaming tables where runaway dads drop family savings. Prostitutes. Discothèque dancers who move body parts most people never knew existed. Loud bands. And baby-sitters.

Baby-sitters? In Las Vegas?

Yup.

It's all part of the city's new image. No longer content with the high-rolling, late-night Frank Sinatra crowd, Las Vegas—that garish green Gomorrah that turned the desert into a tourist attraction—is out now to earn the families' funds. After all, a dollar bill from Sac City, Iowa, or Maple Shade, New Jersey, makes the one-armed bandits whirl just as fast as a buck from some Big Daddy in New York City. So now there are asphalt campgrounds, tame midway attractions for the junior set, and family-type restaurants.

And following right along behind the constant caravans of suburban station wagons are those ubiquitous female family followers—the baby-sitters. Once long ago in the fifties, baby-sitting was a part-time hobby for dateless teen-agers who sat with family friends for 35 cents an hour and a Coke. In Las Vegas until recent years baby-sitting was a limited business whose clientele consisted largely of divorced working waitresses or careless chorus girls.

But now, like everything else in this 24-hour city where sunrises and sunsets seem irrelevant to life, baby-sitting is big business. So big that accredited sitters are checked by the sheriff's department, examined by health officials, and licensed by the county and city. Today when Mom and Dad come to Sin City West, they can drop their children in the hotel room and their bundle in the casino. "The Las Vegas family trade is growing tremendously," said Miss Jerri Vigliani, a former Mrs. who a year ago bought out her employer, the Reliable Babysitting Agency ("Mature Women With Transportation").

Families visiting here have their choice of eight licensed baby-sitting agencies with a battalion of several hundred smiling sitters standing by on alert status with traveling bags of toys in hand. The sitters range in age from 21 to 70 (many of them look like every-body's neighbor's grandmother). Often they are widowed or di-vorced. Long ago they fled places like Clinton, Iowa, and Colum-bus, Ohio, and they love the climate here, where summer temperatures hover around 111 in the daytime—when most sitters sleep.

For some, baby-sitting is a profession or second job. For some, it's a hobby. For others, it's a dodge for boredom. But for each it can be fairly remunerative. Some full-time sitters, working long hours, seven days a week, earn more than $150 a week, ample in a city where nice apartments go for $160 a month. For tourists the standard charge is $2 an hour for one to three children with a four-hour minimum. The agencies, which match the tourist with the sitter, get about 20 percent of everything earned.

The oldest service is the Las Vegas Babysitting Agency. It was founded 21 years ago by Mrs. Marie Birch, who said, "I would never bring my children out here. I'm from Philadelphia." None-theless, Mrs. Birch has noticed a substantial jump in business—and competition—in the last two years. Her service, like the casinos and neon wedding chapels, is open 24 hours a day, so the telephone often rings at 2 A.M. with some late-arriving vacationer.

"It doesn't bother me," Mrs. Birch said. "I need the money more than I do the sleep. But I can never understand some people. They can't get a sitter fast enough to get down to the tables and throw their money away." Her 200 "girls" work almost every night. So, too, do the 50 women who work for Mrs. Sandra Detzer at Sandy's Sitter Service, a three-year-old agency where, in these increasingly liberal times, a number of couples have hired a baby-sitter while they got married. Most of the parents, though, want a sitter while they take in a dinner show, gamble a bit, and catch a late show. Some, however, stay out past dawn or linger at the tables so long that they gamble away everything except their watches, which they leave with the sitters as collateral.

Meanwhile, back in the motel room, the sitters, who provide their own transportation, may not drink or sleep on duty or drive the children anywhere. Some baby-sitting services require uniforms,

but not white ones. "That reminds a kid of the dentist's," one sitter explained.

All the sitters seem to be women. "We're not against men," Mrs. Detzer said. "It's just that generally parents don't want them for sitters, especially with their little girls." Mrs. Detzer keeps detailed files on the sitter preferences of regular customers who gamble and gambol here several times a year. Some of Miss Vigliani's customers are local people, casino workers who sometimes hire sitters for a week at a time. "I guess they don't want to take care of their children," she says.

Children are not always the customers. For $2 an hour an elderly woman whose husband travels a lot regularly hires Mrs. Laverne

Cleary to visit with her. And for 16 hours over a two-day period Sally Lindberg baby-sat with a lonely poodle in a motel room. "I'm saving up for a trip to Hawaii," she said. Mrs. Lindberg is one of the steadier sitters for Miss Vigliani, who has 65 women registered as sitters. "I work seven nights a week," Mrs. Lindberg said, "but I had a night off in July." With summer vacations over, most of her customers now are vacationing parents with preschool toddlers.

Like many sitters here she can spot a child from New York City two motel rooms away ("Often they are brash and ruder"). But most of the children enthusiastically recount their afternoon's activities in the pool, their parents' latest fight, or the day's happenings on the road. "I hear about the Grand Canyon every single night," she said.

Mrs. Alice Akerberg, a 56-year-old woman who works for Reliable and can remember children's names and ages from months back, takes along a mysterious looking sack on each job. "There's never been a child yet who hasn't asked what's in it," Mrs. Akerberg said. "It's a great little icebreaker." It's a sack of toys—marbles, crayons, jacks, dolls, cars. "Children in motel rooms are so bored," she added. But what with the toys, the chatter, the TV, and jumping from bed to bed, the youngsters seem to have a good time.

"The first night the parents hire you," Miss Vigliani observed. "The second night the children do." Miss Vigliani, who operates from her mobile home, says she interviews each of her 65 "girls" to insure they like children and are willing to entertain them properly, not simply watch them. "I ask myself if I'd want each applicant to sit with my son," she said. "Of course, he's 30 now. But I'm very serious about this job."

Mrs. Agnes Ryden is one of those who passed the interview. A divorcee, she lives in a trailer near the Tropicana Hotel. Like other serious sitters, whenever she leaves home, she checks out with the service by phone and reports in when she returns. She likes the unsettled working hours and meeting different people, including one seven-year-old who taught her to play poker. "I'm available any night," says Mrs. Ryden, "but never in the daytime. It bothers my dog Tommy too much when I'm gone too long."

*In college I laughed so hard at Chickenman
on the radio. Then in the phone book the
other day I saw his creator had an office one
block from mine.*

# CHICAGO, ILLINOIS

It was lunchtime and three businessmen sat around the restaurant table at Mr. Kelly's sipping coffee and talking shop. Around them a few dozen other men in business suits were finishing their buffet meal in the carpeted elegance of the big dining room where hushed conversations mingled with silverware clinking on plates.

Suddenly, an employee brushed the loudspeaker controls, flooding the dining room with the loud dance-band sounds of another era. In an impromptu instant one of the businessmen was on his feet like a bandleader. "We'd like to thank you folks for coming to Mrs. Kelly's," he said, "and we hope you enjoyed yourselves as much as we did."

The diners, stunned for a moment, broke into laughter.

"But before you go," another of the trio said, "we'd like to express our appreciation to the chopped steak here. May we have a warm thank you please for the chopped steak?" The audience responded.

"Please, no whistling," said the third man. "It upsets our applause meter. Can we hear it now for the lovely Mongolian barbecue dish?" More applause and laughter.

Minutes later as the men left to return to work, restaurant employees lined up to shake their hands. "Thank you for coming," said one waitress. "We enjoyed you."

On the surface these businessmen may seem unusual. But actually they are not. Like many around the world they spend their lunch hour discussing business and sales and profits. They worry over accounts. And they seek new clients. It's just that their business is unusual. It is the business of humor.

Engaged in this funny business are Dick Orkin, B. Ziggy Stone, and Bert Berdis, the creative end of Dick Orkin Creative Services, a five-year-old Chicago-based concern that makes humorous radio programs and commercials heard by millions of Americans daily. Theirs is a highly demanding business that requires a product to be sold professionally with no visual aids and yet humorously, all within 30 or 60 seconds. Yet for a handful of little-known American companies it is a growing business these days, as more manufacturers turn to comedy to sell their wares in a marketplace cluttered with similar-sounding commercials and jingles.

"Doing comedy is a very serious business," said Mr. Orkin, a 37-year-old former disc jockey and Shakespearean actor with a bushy mustache. "You have to work hard at comedy to be truly funny." You can't prove it, however, by watching these sometimes zany men at work. They simply have too much fun.

The trio heads for a downtown advertising agency here, which they hope will consult them on some comedy work. The men enter an elevator, one of those automatic boxes with nondescript music seeping softly from the ceiling. Mr. Stone cocks his head. "I've heard this elevator before," he says. And they take another.

Upstairs an agency representative ushers them toward a small room where the men are to make a presentation to agency officers. "By the way," Mr. Stone whispers to the woman, "did they deliver the buffalo yet?"

The phone rings in the company offices at 2 East Oak Street. The secretaries are busy, so Mr. Orkin answers:

"Good morning. Dick Orkin Creative Services."

"Is Dick Orkin there, please?"

"I'm sorry. He's no longer with the firm."

Later, Mr. Berdis calls a client in Fort Wayne, Indiana.

"May I speak with Mr. Shannon, please?"

"He's not here right now."

"I see. Well, would you check the men's room, third stall from the left. I know it's his favorite."

Such good times seem spontaneous, and they are practically nonstop. Mr. Orkin's wife, Bunny, is so used to the jokes that she suspects every phone call at home is a friend playing a high-pressure salesman.

At the office Mr. Stone is introduced to a reporter. "I'm sorry," he says, "we already get a newspaper." Then he begins to explain his job seriously. "I've been training a parrot for four years now for an appearance on the Ed Sullivan Show."

The men constantly break into accents or skits, even while hailing a taxi. They can never describe an incident; they must act it out. And their business meetings and phone calls are punctuated frequently by the sounds of a revival meeting, a man coughing continuously, an angry crowd, or a machine-gun battle—all piped from a battery of sound effects in an adjoining studio. There, a plaque proclaims the company motto: *Illegitimi Non Carborundum.* ("That's 'Don't Let the Bastards Get You Down,'" says Mr. Orkin.)

Yet besides fun, the shenanigans have a real corporate purpose. They keep the men sharp humorously and they often prompt a funny line or spark a humorous situation that Mr. Orkin jots down in a little black book for future use. "I've always viewed life as a very serious mess," he says, "and the only way to solve that is to be funny."

As a high-school student in Lancaster, Pennsylvania, he wrote funny radio commercials for his father's gift shop. Then he was a local disc jockey, but tired of always playing songs like "The Theme from Moulin Rouge." So with sound effects he pretended to broadcast from an elevator where strange characters kept coming and going. He was fired.

But in the mid-1960s his comedy work brought him to Chicago's WCFL, a little-known radio station newly determined to capture the lucrative youth market. The station climbed to No. 1 locally, thanks in part to a chicken. As a spoof of Batman, Mr. Orkin created and played Chickenman, a daily radio serial that saw Benton Harbor, a mild-mannered shoe salesman, turn into the Crusading Capon, the Wonderful White-Winged Warrior who ventured from his secret Chickencave to "fight crime and/or evil." His misadventures were so popular that other stations leased the tapes. Ultimately it led to Mr. Orkin's own company, a $600,000-a-year business that has now syndicated the series to more than 600 stations from Boston and Philadelphia to Los Angeles, Australia, and beyond (but curiously not to any stations in New York City, which seem to favor their own creations).

The show's success spawned other serials. They included the Tooth Fairy—"exciting true-to-life stories about dentistry and teeth" in which Newton Snookers, a dental assistant by day for Dr. Nelson Armadingo ("Put your money where your mouth is") becomes the Midnight Molar Marauder by night. Mr. Snookers feels he is carrying on the family tradition. As a child he saw his father put a coin under his pillow one night.

Perhaps Mr. Orkin's favorite character is RaMonde LaRue, a helpless, seedy emcee from another era who hosts some late-night television movies here. Mr. LaRue, who is played by Mr. Orkin, is totally baffled by the wonders of "eclectronics," but he presses on with his "gala frilovities." One of them is "The Revolving Tumble Raffle of Fate," a giant wire barrel from which Mr. LaRue draws prizewinners. The barrel, however, contains but one postcard. And when Mr. LaRue cheerily telephones news of the winner's good fortune, the prizewinner hangs up.

The most recent Orkin creation is the Fame Game, a musical radio contest awarding winners an all-expense-paid ego trip including their picture on billboards and a hired mob of screaming fans to greet the winner after work each night.

Recently, the company (seven people, including Mr. Orkin's brother Sandy) has concentrated on comedy commercials for Middle Western companies and a scattering of national clients, including Rogers Paints, Coleman camping equipment, and General Finance (Mr. Orkin is the voice of "Friendly Bob Adams," who keeps getting strange phone calls). The Orkin style differs from the old John and Marcia radio routines. Instead of a couple discussing a dishwasher, a dishwasher will speak to a woman. For Rogers Paints' Great Discovery Sweepstakes one stage mother after another brings her tap-dancing daughter to the paint store to be discovered, instead of discovering the paint.

For the Minnesota Milk Federation they created Warren Floogle High School, where a cast of characters discovers the values of milk, "a tempting drink that comes from touching cows in certain places." To meet the American Medical Association's concern over nationally declining interest in disease inoculations, they created "Where Are They Now?" a panel show featuring, among others, a newly rejuvenated Anthony Polio and Louella Rubella.

One of Mr. Orkin's better-known commercial campaigns was for Martin Oil, a local gas-station chain trying to set itself apart from the competition. Mr. Orkin's firm dressed all station attendants in purple ballet tights. The advertising ploy worked. Business increased, if only out of curiosity. But the campaign was dropped some months later when the union representing the burly attendants threatened a strike over what they called the "purple fag tights."

The men realize, however, that not every product lends itself to humor. An Ohio cemetery once approached them for an ad. The men were stumped—briefly. Then they produced a tape full of soft organ and violin music and an announcer extolling the peaceful virtues of the park. At the end he intoned, "And Forest Gardens is conveniently located just six feet under Cleveland."

"We didn't get that job," notes Mr. Stone, "but the violin music was awfully good."

*My editors in New York City wanted to know:
What are people doing in suburbia these
days? "Well, they shop a lot," I said. And at
Woodfield Mall there is a lot to be shopped.*

# SCHAUMBURG, ILLINOIS

It has been nigh on to 72 months now since old Ed Oehlerking donned his coveralls and cap, clambered up on his big green combine, and rode out in his field here to harvest the corn and beans for the last time. Farmer Oehlerking has spent a lot of time in Florida since then. You see, he suddenly came into a lot of money. He sold his soil for $5,000 an acre so that some of the best cropland in western Cook County could become some of the site for the world's largest enclosed shopping center, Woodfield Mall.

This tribute to a merchandising mania, which is one and a half times bigger than Vatican City, may be larger in scale, but in essence it is much like any of the 14,500 shopping centers from Orlando to Oahu. Such centers, often built in tiny towns whose biggest structure was once a feed store, have become American suburbia's answer to the cities' declining central business districts. Except that in modern suburbia, nothing is central. And nothing is permanent.

Mr. Oehlerking's farm is now covered by a J. C. Penney store and a parking lot. Eddie Freise's old place is a furniture store and a parking lot. Bill Rohlwing's farm is a twin movie theater and a parking lot. And the Clausings' land is a parking lot. "I never shop over there," said Marian Oehlerking, whose husband is now a real-estate investor. "It's too big for me."

But it is not too big for 197,000 other people who on some days jam the 191-acre shopping center, driving more miles looking for a parking space than they did getting to the center. Woodfield (named for the late Robert E. Wood of Sears, Roebuck and Marshall Field of Marshall Field's, two mall tenants) is big. It has its own newspaper. One man spends his entire working life cleaning railings. Another, Art Dern, cleans litter from miles of carpeting. "I hate chewing gum," he says.

The 2-year-old, X-shaped mall is a $90 million, trilevel collection of 177 stores with 6000 employees selling everything from skirts, shoes, and snakes to baby-sitting, bratwurst, and bras. The stores include Lord & Taylor, Marshall Field's, Sears, I. Miller, Wurlitzer, Puppy Palace, Maternity Modes, and Granny's Donuts. And Alex Dipietropaolo will sew up any split pants.

The management does not disclose rents, but tenants call them "ridiculous" and "astronomical." "It's unarmed robbery," said one who, like the others, had to decorate from the cement up. A number of store areas are boarded up.

It is not too hard to find Woodfield though. It has one of the few 128-foot, 750,000-gallon, yellow-and-orange-striped water towers in the neighborhood. On the outside the mall resembles your typical Pentagon Building minus most windows. The multicolored enclosed interior (kept at a constant 72 degrees) reminds many of a freeway interchange—decorated with carpeting, sculptures, and a waterfall. At peak weekend travel times the lanes of shuffling shoppers creep along the marble or carpeted walkways, some taking exit ramps to other levels to avoid being tied up around spilled ice-cream cones and overturned baby carriages. "We try to clean up those messes as quickly as possible," says Gerard

Dempsey, whose responsibilities include maintenance. "All my men are radio operated."

The sounds of Muzak seep from the ceiling. "It's soothing if you've just been on the expressway," said one employee, "but after eight hours of soothing, you go home babbling." Generally, though, the acoustics are as good as those in any high-school gymnasium.

Woodfield is owned jointly by A. Alfred Taubman and Richard Kughn, mall developers from Michigan, and Homart, a Sears subsidiary. It is managed by Stanley Jaffe, one of a corps of shopping-center managers in the nation who work their way up from small malls to the big time. Whatever their league, these commercial collections exert powerful economic and social influences on suburban life. New Jersey's Delaware Township even changed its name to Cherry Hill to match a new mall's name. Attractive centers can sap the economic vitality of many surrounding suburbs. And in recent years centers have also attracted increasing numbers of politicians. Governor George Wallace, for instance, was not shot on a visit to a Maryland central business district.

Shopping centers also offer many uses in one place. Without fear of being mugged or questioned by police, a shopping-center patron can sit at a central mall, read a book, watch the girls, snooze, or meet a mistress in anonymity safe from the fall rains, as some do at Woodfield. One Cleveland shopping center even has a cemetery next door.

But like practically everything else in suburban American life, the shopping center requires a car. There is only one way a shopper can reach Woodfield alive—inside a private motor vehicle. And sometimes here on the edge of Interstate 90, even that is a little risky. So Schaumburg officials made the mall into its own police precinct.

The mall even has become a tourist attraction and a place for tired housewives or tourists to drive for a walk. For instance, the other day when the Peder Boes and Klaus Haugs of Norway came to visit their cousin, Mrs. Marie Rasmussen-Hengels, everybody walked through Woodfield. "We have nothing like it in Sarpsborg," said Mrs. Haugs as she stared at the cavernous center and walked close to the mall wall.

Every day charter buses from places like Des Moines or Grand Rapids park in their special lot here. For many foreign tourists,

mostly Japanese and German, Woodfield is a half-day stop, like the Statue of Liberty or San Francisco's Fishermen's Wharf. As a convenience for those tourists unanxious to visit the city of Chicago, 32 miles southeast, one suburban store here sells city souvenirs and postcards. And when WBBM, a downtown Chicago radio station, wanted a nice place this fall to stage its 50th anniversary celebration with a 780-pound cake, it chose suburban Woodfield "where the weather is always perfect," as the mall ads say.

Being indoors was one attraction the other morning for Mrs. Jill Plaza. Like most morning mall customers Mrs. Plaza was a white suburban housewife wearing slacks and pushing a toddler in a fold-up stroller that fits in the car trunk. She had gotten her husband off to work, done the dishes, and driven to the mall on an errand (to buy mittens for 2-year-old Julie). Then she decided to stroll until lunchtime. Hers was an impulsive trip. Julie will not need the mittens for weeks yet, but it was an outing and a chance to visit briefly what serves today as suburbia's indoor Main Street.

Mrs. Plaza's 10-minute journey to the mall illustrates the attraction of such facilities where one free parking of the car leads to the conclusion of every family errand imaginable. And so between 11

A.M. and 1 P.M. workers on lunch breaks race to the mall to shop. Then business slows, except for the elderly and those playing hooky to ice-skate on the new rink.

Around 4, teen-agers not out for football strut and sprawl in the mall, buying records, making dates, and postponing homework. About 5 P.M. the fathers drop by with wives to purchase furniture or men's suits. There's a pause during dinner, followed by more families, many out for ice-cream cones. The toddlers are long home in bed. At 9:30 generally the mall closes and becomes like any city's downtown—dead.

At 2 A.M., though, the cleaning crews arrive. It is then that Barnani Hirdeza can start the night's floor waxing. It takes him one month of nights to wax the entire floor from one end of Mr. Oehlerking's cornfield clear over to Mr. Freise's bean patch.

*I came upon a little Indiana town on a map one summer day. "I ought to go down there some fall day," I said. So I did.*

# PUMPKIN CENTER, INDIANA

"Pumpkin Center?" the old farmer said. "Sure 'nuff. You go down this here road a piece to Millersburg. Keep a-goin'. Then you'll come to Tater Road."

Tater Road?

"Yep, Tater Road. It ain't marked but you can't hardly miss it. You go north a piece, over the big hill, down the holler to Stompers Creek. There's Pumpkin Center."

And sure enough, there it is. One house, one barn, one general store, three burros, six chickens, one parakeet, one dog, and five and one-third people (counting a mother-in-law who visits one-third of the time). Pumpkin (pronounced Punkin) Center is a living nugget of nostalgia tucked into the brightly colored, rolling, rural countryside of southern Indiana.

The name reeks of Halloween, and that fall holiday was once a big occasion here for farmers battening down their lands for winter. But the advent of television, radio, and mechanical cornpickers, which squashed the pumpkins during the corn harvest, have brought many changes. They do not grow pumpkins here anymore, except a couple for homemade pies. And Halloween night now means that a few rowdies from Salem will drive through town and toss some apples at windows. Still, a wood-burning, pot-bellied stove can warm a chilled visitor as he sips hot chocolate and munches crackers to the tales of a bygone era.

Presiding over it all is Add Gray, an energetic, yarn-spinning memorabilia collector who also happens to be the self-appointed mayor, general-store manager, and Mabel's husband. Brother Bert Gray, his wife, Evelyn, and their daughter, Arlene, live in the farmhouse just spitting distance across Tater Road. "I guess it ain't much to look at," said Add Gray, "but my Daddy come here in 18 and 98, so it's home."

**191**

It is a combination home, general store, and barn tastefully cluttered with a horde of old relics lovingly collected during 50 years of "general storing" and 38 years of marriage. There's a spoon collection ("We're up to 684 now"), a pencil collection ("Land knows how many"), old kettles, hubcaps, meat grinders, bird feeders, refrigerators, lanterns, barrels, loveseats, side saddles, plows, an old soda fountain, a milk churning tub, a wooden leg, a roulette wheel, a wooden beam from the old covered bridge, a clump of tumbleweed, some pretty stones, scarecrows, oddly shaped tree limbs, foot warmers, seashells, some Spanish moss, and a cast-iron chandelier from Pearson's Funeral Home in Louisville, 65 miles southeast.

One slow day years ago Mr. Gray rigged up an electric motor, a long string, a series of sleigh bells, a wooden figure of Santa Claus, and a bass drum, all hanging from the barn roof. Now when he wants to startle visitors, Mr. Gray throws a switch. Suddenly, the dark cavern of the barn's ceiling is filled with "ching, ching, ching, ching, boom, boom" and Santa Claus waves his hand.

Add Gray picked his way through his "trash and treasure" with the skilled hands and memory of a man who has done it a thousand times. Once in a while he got so excited recounting the memories attached to each treasure that he did a quick little soft-shoe shuffle. "Oh, lookee here, boys!" he said. "See that there green bottle yonder? It come over from England in 18 and 16. Full of vanilla beans it was. And this here stove. The Dyhuff sisters in Paoli gived it to me. I don't know why I collect all this. I reckon I just . . . oh, see that barber chair? That was old Sal Boone's. He died a while back. Hundred and two he was. Oh, he loafered many a day around my old stove."

That old stove has been the social center for this area of Orange County ever since Halloween, 1922, when Add Gray opened the general store with $327.28 worth of groceries from Wheeler Foutch Wholesalers in Orleans. Mr. Gray still has the receipt. "I'm my own man," he said proudly. "I've never askt no one for a job."

The store's opening, a big occasion here, was celebrated by hiring a "five-piece jug band and novelty orchestra." However, a dispute developed over what to name this place. "Now old schoolmaster Burgess," Add said, his eyes sparkling, "he wanted to call it Midway a-cause it was midway between Syria and Bromer. But Delmont Cornwell, he comes across the field one night and says he recollects that big pumpkin harvest my Daddy had in 19 and 13 when we had pumpkins clear up that wall. Cornwell says nothing will do him but what we got to call this Pumpkin Center or else he'll fit all week. Well, I don't want no one fittin' in my new store, so we called it Pumpkin Center."

The store did a good business. "We never had no open or close hours," Mr. Gray said. "A farmer knowd someone would be here whenever he needed somethin'. At times we stayed open all night if the boys had been out a-sparkin' and come in with some music." Some nights, he said, Mildred Dillard, Elbert Taggert, Myrtle Riester, and Effie Hunter would drop by for a nickel bag of crackers and play canasta or rook or watch Bob McCoy spit on the stove from clear across the room. Mr. McCoy was the fellow who coined the expression, "I got me enough money to burn a wet mule."

Then there was the biggest night in Pumpkin Center's history. That was in 19 and 26 when Ray Trinkle dropped by to talk with Add's dad about some soybean seeds. It seems Mr. Trinkle was carrying a lantern and walked a little too close to the gas tank. The fire lit up the sky and brought Alvie Boone and Ninevah Strange and even old Ma Hollis to help put it out.

Now Ma was a tough old lady who could dance all night and lived down Mud Lane. Ma specialized in making her own wine and beer for local farmers. Sometimes she, too, would take a few swigs. Then one night old Pa Hollis up and died. Ma said he fell and hit his head on the floor. But everybody hereabouts has wondered ever since how come they found hickory bark in Pa's forehead when the floor was made of pine.

Rough Tedrow was no sissy either. He used to go up a tree and catch a coon bare-handed. In the Depression he charged traveling salesmen 10 cents to watch him catch big snapping turtles by the head. That was over at Round Pond, but you could also find him skinny-dipping off the bridge in Stompers Creek.

Those days are gone now, almost. Ray Wilson, who is said to be the only Democrat in the area, and some other farmers drop by occasionally to suck a toothpick or eat a little cheese around the stove. But others use the 10-party line to chat or listen in. "It seems the young folk ain't got time to socialize no more," said Bert

Gray. His 16-year-old daughter muttered, "Oh, Daddy, not again." "It's true," Mr. Gray continued. "These kids think nothing of driving up to Indianapolis or down to Louisville of an evening. I tell you."

Then shortly before 10 o'clock these nights, Add Gray walks across the road to his store.

The wind is starting to whistle in the wires. And the only other sound is the soft rustling of the dried cornstalks in the next field.

"People ask me why I don't sell all these things," Mr. Gray mused as he stoked the dying fire while one by one the six clocks chimed 10. "My friends gived me all these things. I remember L. D. Hall—he died t'other day—a-lugging those books in here. I didn't pay nothin' for 'em. Now how could I sell them for money?

"Besides, Mabel and I, why we like to live with it all. It's our home. The Lord has given me a wonderful woman like Mabel and good health. What more can I want? It's a simple life, I know. But we have a good time, and we've got things nobody else ain't got."

*I saw a squib in a downstate Illinois newspaper about a strange creature causing considerable commotion there. I couldn't resist a visit. (But then I didn't try too hard.)*

# MURPHYSBORO, ILLINOIS

Mrs. Nedra Green was preparing for bed in her isolated farmhouse near here the other night when a shrill, piercing scream came from out by the shed. "It's it again," she said.

Four-year-old Christian Baril was in his backyard chasing fireflies with a glass jar. He ran in the house. "Daddy, Daddy," he said, "there's a big ghost out back."

Randy Creath and Cheryl Ray were talking on her darkened porch when something moved in the brush near by. Cheryl went to turn on a light; Randy went to investigate. At that moment it stepped from the bushes. Towering over the wide-eyed, teen-age couple was a creature resembling a gorilla. It was eight feet tall. It had long, shaggy, matted hair colored a dirty white. It smelled foul like river slime. Silently, the couple stared at the creature and the creature stared at the couple, 15 feet apart. Then, after an eternity of perhaps 30 seconds, the creature turned slowly and crashed off through the brush back toward the river.

It was the Murphysboro Monster, a strange creature that has baffled and frightened police and residents for weeks now in this southern Illinois town on the sluggish Big Muddy River. It is a creature that has brought a real kind of Halloween to Murphysboro's 10,000 citizens. And although the hobgoblin is so far benevolent, no one here is taking any chances. Many have armed themselves and a good number of God-fearing families decided to curtail traditional Halloween trick-or-treating rounds.

Such monster sightings are bizarre indeed for an old farm county seat where brightly colored leaves fall on brick streets and high-school majorettes practice baton twirling for the Red Devils' upcoming football game with Jonesboro's Wildcats. "A lot of things in life are unexplained," said Toby Berger, the police chief, "and

this is another one. We don't know what the creature is. But we do believe what these people saw was real. We have tracked it. And the dogs got a definite scent."

It all began shortly before midnight, June 25. Randy Needham and Judy Johnson were conferring in a parked car on the town's boat ramp down by the Big Muddy. At one point the couple heard a loud cry from the woods next to the car. Many were to describe the sound as that of a greatly amplified eagle shriek. Mr. Needham looked up from the front seat. There, lumbering toward the open window, was a light-colored, hairy, eight-foot creature matted with mud.

At that point, the police report calmly notes, "Complainant left the area." He proceeded to the police station and filed an "unknown creature" report. Judy Johnson was married at the time, according to the police, but not to Mr. Needham. So when the two reported the monster, the authorities took it seriously. "They wouldn't risk all that if they weren't really scared," said one.

Officer Jimmie Nash was patrolling the north side of town when the radio dispatch came in. "Ten-four, the monster call," he replied. He knew it was a joke. But later as he inspected some peculiar footprints fast disappearing in the oozing mud left by the receding river, Mr. Nash was to become a believer. "I was leaning over when there was the most incredible shriek I've ever heard," he said. "It was in those bushes. That was no bobcat or screech owl and we hightailed it out of there." Later, with reinforcements, officers searched the riverbank for hours, following an elusive splashing sound like something floundering through knee-deep water. They found nothing.

Plains folk here do not excite easily. So the next day on page three *The Southern Illinoisan* published a 200-word account of the "critter," omitting the embarrassed couple's names. That presumably was the end of the case. But the next night came young Christian Baril's encounter and the experience of Cheryl Ray and Randy Creath, the 17-year-old son of a state trooper, who drew a picture of the creature.

That did it for Chief Berger. He ordered his entire 14-man force out for a nightlong search. And Jerry Nellis, a dog trainer, brought Reb, an 80-pound German shepherd renowned for his zealous tracking. With floodlights officers discovered a rough trail in the brush. Grass was crushed. Broken branches dangled. Small trees were snapped. On the grass Reb found gobs of black slime, much like that of sewage sludge in settling tanks, on a direct line between the river and the Ray house.

Reb led Mr. Nellis and Officer Nash to an abandoned barn on the old Bullar farm. Then, at the door, the dog yelped and backed off in panic. Mr. Nellis threw it into the doorway. The dog crawled out whining. The men radioed for help. Fourteen area police cars responded, but the barn, it turned out, was empty.

Ten days later the Miller Carnival was set up in the town's Riverside Park, not far from the boat ramp. At 2 A.M., July 7, the day's festivities had stopped and the ponies that walk around in circles with youngsters on their backs were tied to bushes.

Suddenly they shied. They rolled their eyes. They raised their heads. They tried to pull free. Attracted by the commotion, three carnival workers—Otis Norris, Ray Adkerson, and Wesley Lavander—walked around the truck and there, standing upright in the darkness was a 300- to 400-pound creature, hairy and light colored, and about eight feet tall. Without menace, but with intent curiosity, the creature was watching the animals. The men ran for help. The creature left. But an hour later Charles Kimbal saw it again peering over the bushes, its head cocked, watching the ponies.

That creature report, which carnival operators delayed filing to avoid hurting business, was the last official note of the Murphysboro Monster. However, there have been many unreported incidents. For instance, Charlie Etherton, the caretaker at Riverside Park, has found some unusual footprints in the morning dew recently. The park trash cans, especially those near the river, are regularly overturned as if something was looking for someone. And his son Lawrence has heard screams down by the water. "I don't know as how I believe in it," Mr. Etherton said, "but when it gets dark now, I don't get out much."

Then, two of Mrs. Green's sons, Wayne and Richard, were setting out fishing lines a few nights ago not far from the Bullar barn when that now familiar cry came from the other side of the pond. But Mrs. Green and the others are reluctant to report the incidents for fear, not of the monster, but of the hundreds of humans who flock to each sighting with rifles and shotguns.

Somehow, no one has shot anyone else yet, but the police had to close the park one night. It was crammed full of hunters and curious campers. "This is no hoax," said Tony Stevens, the newspaper editor. "This is hunting country, you know, and anyone who goes around in an animal costume is going to get his butt shot off."

Local officials are not really sure what to do. They invited Harlan Sorkin, a Saint Louis expert on such creatures, down for a spell. Mr. Sorkin said the descriptions matched those of over 300 similar sightings in North America in the last decade, one of them on an Ohio River levee not far from here. There has even been a movie, *The Legend of Boggy Creek*, made about a similar creature in Arkansas.

Mr. Sorkin says the creature is probably a Sasquatch, believed to be a gene deviation in a large ape that has produced a creature that Tibetans call the Yeti, or Abominable Snowman, and Rocky Mountain Indians call Big Foot. Typically, he said, these creatures are very shy and favor river bottoms for their ample vegetation. Even in winter here in southern Illinois, which is further south than almost all of Virginia, plenty of plant life is available, especially in the vast Shawnee National Forest, which straddles the state 400 miles south of Chicago. Mr. Sorkin speculates that this year's flooding forced the creature from its natural home, perhaps a cave down river.

Generally a placid creature, the Sasquatch is said to have killed some hunting dogs during chases. And there are stories of wilderness loggers in the Northwest found crushed next to their emptied rifles. "These creatures have the strength of five men," Mr. Sorkin said, "and when frightened, they take five-foot strides." To skeptics Mr. Sorkin replies, "You know the gorilla as we know it today was not discovered until the early 1800s. Can you imagine what people thought when they first saw it?"

Whatever it is called, the exotic new inhabitant here is real to residents of Murphysboro, a "hospitable" town which, the chamber of commerce says, "welcomes newcomers in a way that makes them happy to be living here." "These are good, honest people," said Chief Berger. "They are seeing something. And who would walk through sewage tanks for a joke?"

"I know it's out there," said young Randy Creath. "It would be fascinating to see it again and study it. But, you know, I kinda hope he doesn't come back. With everyone running around with guns and sticks, he really wouldn't have much of a chance, would he?"

*Every day I watched a new football field
and stadium grow out of a cornfield like
some weird new hybrid crop. Then, suddenly,
there was a school there, too.*

# BUFFALO GROVE, ILLINOIS

Buffalo Grove High School had a homecoming with no alumni. It will have a prom with no seniors. And there will be no graduation at all. Other than that, though, it is a fairly typical high school—for suburbia.

For out here on the fast-growing fringes of Greater Chicago, last year's cornfield has become this year's football stadium, parking lot, gymnasium, cafeteria, classrooms, lockers, and theater—$10.5 million worth to serve the shifting citizenry of these little-known suburbs. To put it mildly, Buffalo Grove High School is new, like most everything else in Buffalo Grove and Wheeling and Palatine and Schaumburg, and all the other exploding, increasingly self-sufficient suburbs that circle Chicago and many other American metropolitan areas.

Buffalo Grove High School is, in fact, so new that the new trophy case is empty, the new library shelves have ample space, the new walls are graffiti-free, and the locker rooms smell strangely clean. Stretches of lush, new green sod end abruptly in old mud. Some new administrators have new-construction hard hats by their desks. And a new poster advertises, "Last Chance To Order Buffalo Grove's First and Best Yearbook."

The sprawling, two-story school opened September 4 just 27 months after the voters of Illinois High School District 214 narrowly approved the expenditure by 584 out of 9240 ballots cast. It became the eighth high school in this once suburban high-school district, a 68-square-mile area that is bigger than Saint Louis and has more people than Atlantic City. On opening day, when they handed out two-page maps to guide everyone through the labyrinths of BGHS's winding halls, there were 76 teachers, 10 administrators, 18 custodians, 20 secretaries, and 1385 students.

The students are juniors, sophomores, and freshmen drawn from

200

overcrowded schools nearby. (Seniors, it was felt, had too many academic, social, and extracurricular ties to transfer for their final year.) They come from middle-class families in the legions of well-kept new homes that spring up here faster than you can say back yard barbecue. The teen-agers wear neatly pressed clothes. Their fathers are sales directors or office managers or field representatives. And they have lived in two or three similar suburbs around the country as a corporate whim and their fathers' careers dictate.

The district's students, 60 percent of whom will go on to college, are almost entirely white. "I think there's a black at Wheeling High," said one teacher. The high-school district's enrollment stands at 19,175 and is rising. There is no talk of declining population here 32 miles northwest of Chicago. There can be, it sometimes seems here, only expansion, and like everything else in these new suburbs, the new school was built to grow. Next year the students will number 2000 and the year after 2500. By the fourth year, it is reckoned, the wave of development will have rolled on past Buffalo Grove toward Mundelein, Wauconda, Crystal Lake, and other largely unknown towns that highway planners and housing developers decide will become new northwest Chicago suburbs.

"But right now," Dr. Clarence Miller, the principal, said enthusiastically, "this is the growing area." Dr. Miller, a 45-year-old former mathematics instructor who has worked in suburban schools for 16 years, spoke as he toured his new air-conditioned school where room walls adjust to class size. Windows and blackboards run from floor to ceiling. Bold swaths of color slash across walls. "There's no reason why a school must be a dull tan or gray," the principal said.

Classes end not with bells but electronic tones. Students smile and say "Hi" to strangers, and rest rooms are marked, not with "Boys" and "Girls," but with brightly colored, 10-foot-high male and female symbols. "For those who get confused," Dr. Miller said, "I tell them it's blue for boys and red for girls."

There are, however, still some wrinkles in the new building. The 2600-seat folding bleachers in the gymnasium had to be adjusted recently. The mud wreaks havoc on bell-bottoms, and the headsets in the foreign-language laboratory pick up only a local FM radio station.

Nonetheless, the students have adjusted and have easily ignited instant loyalties for the Buffalo Grove Bisons, the senior-less football squad with an 8–0 record this fall. "Not bad for an expansion team," said one player. At the age of six weeks the school could wait no longer and had its first homecoming celebration complete with a queen (Lynn Andrews), a king (Jim McGowan), and an automobile-decorating contest (Volkswagen).

Like generations of teen-agers before them, Buffalo Grove High students hang around their hall lockers impressing each other and gossiping until the last possible moment before class. They complain about cafeteria food. They draw posters announcing the junior-class hayride. And the school's new student newspaper, *The Charger*, has editorially endorsed automobile seat belts as a good thing.

Fads today are infrequent, though (wild-colored socks were the latest). There is no official dress code at school, so bare midriffs and slacks are common. Students say any drug taking is secretive and generally regarded as "uncool," the same as couples going steady. Unlike their older brothers and sisters, today's students mingle socially in groups, not pairs, gathering at a predetermined house on a Friday night to listen to tapes, dance, decide where else to go, and, if parents are absent, sip some wine or beer.

For transportation most must still borrow Dad's car. Scott

Michaelson, for instance, borrowed his family's Chevrolet Impala the other weekend and took Terry Orton, the student council president, and some other friends to a nearby movie, one of the growing number of first-run theaters in the suburbs. (Popular movies in recent months included *American Graffiti* and *Billy Jack.*)

A few students hang around the shopping center opposite the school. Few can remember their last time in Chicago. But most, like Miss Orton and Gail Lehmann, work after school, earning money for odds and ends and clothing with a few hours' work a week at a supermarket checkout counter, a hamburger stand, or a dry-cleaning store.

For Miss Andrews, the homecoming queen, such work combined with studies and dance club leaves little time for reading nonschool books or magazines or watching television. Nor has she found much time to consider her future. For her father, Chester, a sales manager with Georgia-Pacific's paper-plate division, is frequently transferred. At age 16 Miss Andrews has already lived in the sub-urbs of four states.

"We're near Chicago now," she recalled. "We lived near Detroit once, and near Memphis, and, let's see, where did we live in Wisconsin? Oh, yes, a suburb of Milwaukee."

*How does someone convince 460,000 people*
*that he should live in Washington, D.C.?*

# SAULT SAINTE MARIE, MICHIGAN

"Hi! I'm Congressman Philip Ruppe," the man said for the 250th time that day. "I wonder if we've met."

"Yes," the machinist said, shaking the outstretched hand, "you helped my mother with her social security."

"Well, fine," the 46-year-old Republican incumbent replied, eyeing another approaching pack of workers. "Good to see you again. Hi! I'm Congressman Philip Ruppe. I wonder if we've met. . . ."

It was no time for substantive discussion of serious issues. It was 6 A.M. and 32 degrees at the plant gate, and the sun would not rise on Iron Mountain, Michigan, for another hour. Representative Philip E. Ruppe (pronounced REW-pee) was starting another campaign day in search of his fourth two-year term representing Michigan's mammoth 11th Congressional District. Seventeen hours, five factories, seven speeches, countless handshakes, and 350 miles later he went to bed in Marquette, Michigan, a very tired representative.

"You never really know if you sell anybody," Mr. Ruppe mused, "and I don't openly ask for their vote. But at least they see you are up and about like they are. That you care enough."

Probably, Mr. Ruppe need not run so hard. His opponent, James E. McNamara, a Democrat and member of the John Birch Society, is little known in the district, which includes Michigan's Upper Peninsula and a sizable chunk of the lower peninsula as well. Mr. McNamara, a 42-year-old political neophyte and father of 11, co-owns a charter airline in Marquette. He has made some campaign appearances but has relied heavily on radio and television. In several dozen interviews over three days here a reporter could not find one voter who knew the name of Mr. Ruppe's opponent. "Is there one?" asked an Iron Mountain housewife.

204

Local observers, recalling Mr. Ruppe's frequent visits and conscientious handling of constituent queries, see no way the congressman can lose on November 7. In 1970, even against a Democratic challenger who had the full support of his party, Mr. Ruppe got 62 percent of 138,000 ballots. Since then, five heavily Republican counties have been added to his district. The district, one of 19 in Michigan, is an immense area, although the population of some 460,000 is about typical for a Michigan district. Its 23,000 square miles, many of them rolling, deserted woods, include 27 counties, or 40 percent of the entire state, making this single district twice as big as Belgium.

For all its size the largely isolated area seems aroused over few issues this year. Voters most frequently mention the weather (three inches of snow already), poor deer hunting, and high gasoline prices, none of which are exactly under Mr. Ruppe's control. And here in "the Soo" (population 15,134) life goes on as usual with little significant involvement with its bigger Canadian sister city. Except for an occasional dinner in Canada, most residents leave the $1.50 bridge crossing to tourists who come to see the giant ore boats ease through the locks.

Mr. Ruppe, a wealthy, former brewery president in Houghton, Michigan, has studied the needs and desires of his district. As befits a Republican representative from a traditionally Democratic area, he has cultivated a moderate to liberal image. But, as the 6-foot 4-inch representative noted between campaign stops, "At election time people remember what you've done for them more than how you've voted in the House."

Mr. Ruppe visits his district about once a month, appearing at a flurry of functions during a four-day weekend. Or he borrows an office in a city hall and receives constituents for 10 or 12 hours. Or he fires back quick replies to letters or phone calls. During an appearance on a radio talk show in Ishpeming, the congressman had an energetic 23-year-old aide, Paul Hillegonds, on the phone next to him getting immediate answers from Washington as constituents phoned in. "Phil always seems to be where you need him when you need him," said John O'Donnell, the Democratic mayor of Iron Mountain.

But recognition and name identification are important, too. So Mr. Ruppe's 15,000 red, white, and blue campaign pamphlets contain no less than 13 pictures of the congressman on two pages. When he visits a county, he buys 30-second radio ads that say he is in town and "looking forward to meeting as many of you as possible." "I mean how many voters can you possibly see in a day?" Mr. Ruppe said. "Maybe 1000. That leaves 21,000 others you miss in this county alone. So you reach them any way you can."

His favorite way is face to face. But unlike hectic Presidential campaigns with their advance men, newsmen, cameramen, and Secret Servicemen, Mr. Ruppe's race, like many other congressional contests, is an informal, slightly organized, and easily amended affair.

"Okay," Mr. Ruppe said to two aides as he hopped into his family's Pontiac station wagon in Iron Mountain the other morning, "what's first?"

"The day shift at Lake Shore, Inc.," said Mr. Hillegonds, consulting a schedule telephoned from Mr. Ruppe's office in Houghton.

After the first factory Mr. Ruppe stopped at a state highway garage ("These fellows talk to a lot of people around the county") and a café. "See," he told the sleepy-eyed diners, "you can't even eat breakfast without some politician sticking a pamphlet in your hand." This year with an unsleepy eye on the 18-year-old vote, present and near future, Mr. Ruppe added a generous sprinkling of high schools to his schedule. Then there are the senior-citizen home, grocery stores, and the chamber of commerce luncheon.

"I suppose," Mr. Ruppe said, "this time I'm running more for the next election than anything else. If you beat the hell out of your opponent now, they're going to have a hard time finding someone—and some money—to run against you next time. And if next time is a bad year for Republicans," he continued, "maybe the voters will remember you were there listening when you didn't have to be."

*What happens, I wondered, to a little*
*Illinois town when a not-so-little corporation*
*decides to spend $40 million locally?*

# GURNEE, ILLINOIS

"It won't," said Mayor Richard Welton. "It will," said Kenneth Miller. "It won't," said Robert Sheridan. "Oh, it will, too," said Grace Smith. And so it goes here these days as little Gurnee—30 square miles of farmland splattered halfway between Chicago and Milwaukee—approaches a historic election to determine much of its future.

The issue on Saturday's ballot is: Should the Village of Gurnee (pronounced gur-KNEE) annex 600 unincorporated acres that the Marriott Corporation bought for a $40-million amusement park? But the real issue, the issue that arouses Dick and Ken and Bob and Grace, is: Will a giant amusement park annually attracting 3 million people (the population of six Atlantas) change the treasured rural life and values of Gurnee, a town of 3300 people in country where "Deer Xing" signs are still valid?

It is the kind of economic and emotional question facing hundreds of tiny towns near the nation's sprawling metropolitan areas. Through no fault of their own, these collections of cornfields, bean patches, and Main Streets find themselves in the path of platoons of ruthless earth-movers, cement trucks, and suburban-bound city dwellers determined to carve their own place out of the smog, if only for an afternoon at an amusement park.

The issue is one being fought far from the city lights and glare of urban publicity. But the movement is a relentless outward migration that raises some provocative and very divisive questions.

Can a community like Gurnee stop the development? Should it? What gives Gurnee residents the right to block others from the countryside? What gives some well-known Maryland developers the right to change the life-style of a little-known village in Illinois? No one, at least in Gurnee, has any definitive answers. But this week, at least, they have some definite feelings.

The park, said Mr. Welton, "will be a wonderful thing for all of us living here."

"Now," said Mr. Miller, "you know something that big just has to affect the town's personality."

"The park benefits," said Mr. Sheridan, "far outweigh the problems."

"The Marriott proposal," said Mrs. Smith, "is just another step down the road to traffic jams and pollution."

The Marriott Great America park proposal, the latest corporate attempt to out-Disney Disneyland and tap the increasingly lucrative leisure-time market, is an ambitious project even for a village that once supported three blacksmiths. The park would be an elaborate array of fantasy attractions, including a daily Mardi Gras parade, all based on old-time life in New Orleans, the Southwest, the Yukon, New England, and, ironically, a small American town.

A Marriott hotel, Marriott industrial park, and Marriott shopping center would follow on the 600 acres, which are on both sides of the Interstate 94 interchange just west of Gurnee's village limits. The park itself would cover 80 acres, 5 acres less than its parking lot. Construction crews, shooting for a 1976 opening, want to start relocating 1.4 million cubic yards of farmland next spring. Another task involves Pine Street, a quiet, one-lane, dead-end street of ruts that serves 12 homes. Within months, according to Marriott's plans, all homes must go and Pine Street will become a six-lane grand entrance to Great America decorated with dozens of smiling college kids taking tolls.

But first comes Saturday's election, which will set the town back about $300 in costs. The election, which is nonbinding on the Village Board's final vote on the development, was called after a petition drive drew 381 signatures from residents who agreed with Ken Miller, a 34-year-old tool and die maker.

"Mayor Welton kept saying, 'The people of Gurnee want Marriott,'" Mr. Miller recalled, "but I knew I didn't want Marriott. And my friends didn't want Marriott. So I figured let's have an election to see how many do want Marriott."

Many of the petitioners, like Mrs. Miller, were longtime residents who remembered what Gurnee was for them and their ancestors. It was a quiet little burg first named Wentworth, then O'Plaine, then Gurnee (allegedly after a railroad surveyor). They

remember a Gurnee where runaway slaves slept overnight, where Elmer Wirth and Willis Appleyard went frog hunting or skinny-dipping in the Des Plaines River and where Birdella Williams and Dr. Hiram Orson Biddlecome Young led the summer singalongs that began with "Annie Laurie" and ended with "Abide With Me." And they remember the school play when Norton Flood tucked Arthur Howard's coattail into the rising auditorium curtain.

When a farmer moved in those days, he took his well-built home with him. "I know Gurnee can't stay one big farm," said Nancy Miller, "but there must be a happy medium." As the developers followed the interstate through this fast-growing Chicago–Milwaukee corridor, Mrs. Miller saw the Mohrmans' woods turn into a trailer court, the Ficker pasture became a housing development, and the Wilson place is now a shopping center.

And today the Millers' village seems threatened. So they are on a committee to organize Marriott's opposition. But it is one tough job. "They come in here with their millions and their big lawyers and their studies and graphs and charts and all those officials who are good public speakers," says Mr. Miller, "and they say a park wouldn't hurt Gurnee. And we get off work at 4:30 and we're tired and we go to the meeting when we should fix up the house and we say, 'You're going to ruin our town?' and they say, 'Prove it.' It's so hard."

Marriott paid the town board's way to Atlanta to study Marriott's theme park there. Mayor Welton became convinced that Gurnee could keep its curbless streets, its roadside ditches and mailboxes and avoid the fast-food strip development that some here fear. He doesn't like to threaten, he says, but if Gurnee doesn't annex the park site, some other town might. Then it would get the $7-million payroll and the more than $200,000 in property taxes while Gurnee got only the problems.

He scoffs at fear of increased crime, pollution, and traffic congestion on the streets called Depot, Darline, and Grand. "Marriott says 85 percent of the traffic will use the tollway, not local streets," he says, "and the park will be open only 125 days a year. That's better than a housing development." So the mayor is confident of the outcome, in part because many opponents live outside Gurnee and cannot vote.

But his opponents are unconvinced. They wonder who will run their village when one-half the property valuation is owned by a corporation 762 miles away. "I don't know," sighed Mrs. Miller. "Things are changing so fast now. Why is everything suddenly so big, so rushy, and got to be done overnight?"

The annexation was approved and construction is underway.

*She peddles gas, ham, and passion—*
*not necessarily in that order.*

# HILAND, WYOMING

The pretty young woman sat at her desk. She was confused. As she stared out the window, something stirred within her, something strange, something she had never before experienced. Was it her feelings for Jack? And that wonderful moonlight swim in the park? Or was it, yes, of course, that was it. Suddenly she began to type, her fingers passionately caressing the keys as the words of love flowed like a flooding river.

And so 30 years ago Betty realized for the first time that she was meant to write. That she would write true-confession stories like no one before her. And thousands of women would read them and cry and suffer right along with Brad and Pam and Ted and Sally. And all those other pretend people who populate the pulpy pages of *Real Confessions, Daring Romances, My Confessions,* and *Revealing Romances*. Stories like "Doing Without Sex Did Her In," "He Gave Me Melt-in-Your-Mouth Kisses," "At 14 I Already Had a Past," and "His Looks Raped Me."

Few readers would suspect that the author of stories such as these is a 63-year-old widow who runs a Chevron gasoline station, a post office, a ham-sandwich stand and is the entire population of this microdot of a town in the vast void that is central Wyoming. But she is.

She is Betty Evenson, a fast-talking, loud-laughing, friendly woman who gets most of her soapy story ideas from the truck drivers who stop to use the store's bathroom and gulp down the "sagebrush ham sandwiches" that have made The Bright Spot (one long and two short rings on the telephone) famous in this area. "Everybody who stops here is automatically a good friend, not just a visitor," she said as she buttered the 297th ham sandwich of the week. "Here, have a kiwi berry. I just got them from the Fruit of the Month Club."

For every ham sandwich she makes, Mrs. Evenson (pronounced

EVE-ensign, as she quickly pointed out) awards herself a hunk of ham, a habit that over the years added many pounds to her 5-foot 1-inch frame. "I went to a California fat farm a couple years ago," she said. "I didn't lose any weight there, but I lost six pounds on the bus ride out."

"We don't have much cash with us," a customer interrupted. "Can we put the food on a credit card?"

"Send me the money when you get home," Mrs. Evenson said. "Who's next?"

"What are you going to call this story?" she asked a reporter and then answered, "I know. 'I Sell Gas by Day and Sex by Night' or 'She Peddles Gas, Ham, and Passion.'" And then Mrs. Evenson broke into the jolliest cackle this side of Midville. "I always put my characters in fictional places like that," she said. "Otherwise, people would know who they were."

Not likely. For starters, the sheep far outnumber the humans on this arid, rolling rangeland 1940 miles west of Times Square where a "big town" has 3000 people. Unencumbered by wires, billboards, or houses, the two-lane highway stretches straight to the horizon. Here, travelers do not drive their cars; they aim them. "In the old days when the road was gravel," Mrs. Evenson said, "you stopped everywhere. But nowadays people don't stop so much at the little places."

Which, in a way, is all right with Mrs. Evenson because it gives her more time to write. "I get up at 7," she said. "The store is open at 7:02 and I'm writing by 7:05. But I don't suppose I've ever written longer than an hour at a time. There are always interruptions and my customers like to be talked to, not waited on. You know, I made ham sandwiches for some of them when they were children. Now they bring their kids here. Yes, sir, I make really good ham sandwiches." She is right.

Mrs. Evenson's first story, written when she was 6 years old, was called "Lydia and Her Little Sister Hazel." "It was terrible," Mrs Evenson recalled. "When I was young," she added, "nothing could officially happen to me until I wrote it down in my diary or somewhere. Writing puts things in order, makes things valid." Today, though, Mrs. Evenson finds writing harder. "You have to feel things to write them," she explained, "and when you get older, you don't feel things so strongly any more. Sometimes when it's minus

42 outside and my knee hurts, I think about retiring. Then I'd never ever have to make another ice-cream cone. But what I do here is not work. It's my whole way of life. I couldn't stop."

Most of her stories, punched out on an ancient typewriter in her apartment behind the restaurant counter, run between 3500 and 5000 words, for which she might earn $400. "Confession stories are very moral. Today they let sinners enjoy it, but sin is never triumphant. So I use the old sin, suffer, and repent routine," she said as she adjusted her doorstop, a can of green beans. "I used a can of pineapples for years," she chuckled, "but I got hungry one night. How many people can say they ate their doorstop?"

Most of her ideas come from such drivers as Buster Harnden, who has stopped his bus here for 34 years. Many of the drivers talk more openly with Mrs. Evenson than they would in their hometowns. One told of a married man who got a neighbor woman pregnant. Mrs. Evenson wrote a similar story, except the woman was single and the married man childless. He adopted the baby.

Two neighboring ranch families were feuding here years ago. Then one of the men was injured on the range and was rescued by his antagonist. That led to a similar story. Mrs. Evenson is now working on a nonfiction account of the 50 years of the store, which her father founded. There was the blizzard of '49 (that led to a story about a couple trapped by snow) and the time she was robbed and the time the sheriff chained a prisoner to her stove and the annual Christmas Carol Sings.

But her writing is interrupted frequently because of her latest boy friend, Cliff Gitthens, a retired pipe fitter. Sometimes the couple goes dancing till 3 or 4 A.M. "People think the only reason old folks get married is for companionship," Mrs. Evenson said fiercely. "Me, I enjoy falling in love. It's a wonderful feeling. You know, you're never too old to fall in love.

"Hey," she said, grabbing a piece of paper, "that's a good story title."

*For years I'd wondered how those*
*delicious morsels got to my plate each*
*Thanksgiving. In a way now, I wish I hadn't.*

## CUMBACK, INDIANA

From early May until mid-November every year Merle Lucas's life is for the birds—literally. He feeds them. He talks to them. He doctors them. He guards them. He even sleeps with them. But he doesn't do these things because he necessarily loves them. It is because his business is birds. Mr. Lucas is a turkey farmer, one of a band of little-known men with computers, corn, and shotguns who help shepherd turkeys from little feathered balls of fluff to steaming juicy mouthfuls on holiday platters.

And there is no busier time in this risky, $550-million-a-year industry than right now in the last few hectic weeks before Thanksgiving and Christmas as the last of this year's 129 million befuddled birds move toward their delicious doom. Thanks to freezers, aggressive advertising, and rising costs of other meats and poultry, turkey growing has become a big business year-round, complete with its own lobbying group, flock insurance, and *Turkey World* magazine, with a column entitled "Gobbles from the Editor's Perch."

Here in southwestern Indiana's Daviess County, temporary home for 3 million turkeys that will eventually stuff the stomachs of diners in the Northeast, turkeys are a way of life for hundreds of farmers like Mr. Lucas. The turkeys line the feather-littered roadside. Millions of beady eyes follow every movement from behind fence slats. The birds gorge themselves on vitamin-enriched corn, soybean, and fish meal, and then, five months after hatching, they are trucked away to the slaughterhouse in town.

Once, the turkeys' wild ancestors had to dodge only Indian arrows. Then turkeys became a backyard business for a farmer's wife with an ax to grind and pin money to be earned. No longer. Today the birds are genetically engineered by a dozen giant breed-

214

ing firms that computerize bloodlines and desirable characteristics of dozens of turkey generations crossbred for big breasts, strong legs, tender meat, and white feathers (which, after plucking, produce a bird more attractive to the shopper's eye).

Even the hens' ovulation is controlled by lights. And the birds are artificially inseminated. "Natural mating isn't efficient enough," said one grower. Artificial breeding brings 75 percent more meat, two-thirds of it white. But it also overloads the birds' old-fashioned, naturally engineered wings, effectively eliminating their ability to fly more than a few short hops toward the feed trough. Turkey eggs are still laid naturally. But they are immediately placed in specially controlled incubators where, according to scientifically prepared forecasts, they must hatch in 28 days. The poults—baby turkeys—are sorted by sex and then shipped in air-conditioned trucks resembling school buses to turkey growers like Mr. Lucas.

Mr. Lucas, a gruff, 64-year-old corn farmer given to blunt comments on the state of the now highly organized turkey industry, knows the turkey poults better than their mother, whom the babies never see. He knows, for instance, that the yolk from each egg gives a poult enough nourishment for three days. So last summer Mr.

Lucas knew he had only 72 hours to teach 6000 little creatures how to live.

It was a formidable task since the turkey, with a brain the size of a man's thumb, is not the brightest beast. For example, with no mother around to teach by example, turkey poults know nothing about eating. No one told them that those little grains on the floor under the warm lights of the turkey shed were for eating. So Mr. Lucas had to sprinkle the feed with sparkling grit or marbles to attract the bird's eye.

"From the beginning," said David Graham, a veteran turkey grower and an official here with Armour & Co., a Greyhound subsidiary, "turkeys seem to try to kill themselves." They forget to eat. They drown in their water dish. Or they never master drinking. In fact, turkey growers expect 2 percent of each new flock to die within 10 days. In 20 weeks Mr. Lucas lost more than 325 of his first 6000 turkeys.

But the turkeys' stupidity is not the only problem. For they can kill each other in blind efforts to establish their flock pecking order. This may be natural, but with poults worth about $1 at birth, the loss of birds to tribal excitement is not what Armour, Swift & Co., and the other major turkey producers have in mind. So at age 14 days the birds' beaks are trimmed.

Then there is the feed problem, a costly necessity in these days when corn, soybean, and fish-meal supplies are tight and prices are high. Soybean meal, for instance, is up to $400 a ton now from $100 a ton last year. A turkey consumes about 2 3/4 pounds of feed for each pound of finished bird. The average bird weighs 20 pounds. As a result, the price of turkeys has risen, too.

A small, but growing, number of turkeys spend their entire life indoors. Most turkeys, however, go out into the world after eight weeks to slightly shaded, well-drained fields called ranges where they encounter a new set of dangers. There are foxes and owls and skunks and dogs, some of which kill turkeys for sport. Then, with eight air sacs, the turkey is four times more susceptible to colds than humans. Not to mention cholera, blue comb, blackhead, and other fatal, foul fowl diseases that, with thousands of birds living just a wing away, can flash through a flock with devastating efficiency in a few hours.

Thus, Mr. Lucas walks through each flock at least three times a

day. If he isn't gaily greeted with gobbles or if the birds' heads are drooping or their droppings seem suspicious or they are coughing, Mr. Lucas rushes some over to Wendell Bond, an Armour pathologist nearby. Mr. Bond diagnoses any trouble, prescribes immediate medication, and enters the details in each flock's computerized history like a class yearbook.

"I like the work. I like the birds," says Mr. Lucas, "and I like to see them do good." So from spring until late fall Mr. Lucas forsakes his own house to sleep on a cot near the flock. If he hears a disturbance or his dogs bark, he is quickly outdoors, shotgun at the ready. Sometimes, though, he is fooled by a few insomniac turkeys raiding the trough for a late-night snack.

Years ago Mr. Lucas's work was concentrated in a much shorter period. That was because 90 percent of the turkeys were eaten in November and December, originally because cooler weather preserved the meat better then. During World War II, however, the Army needed a plentiful supply of low-fat, high-protein food and frozen turkey became widespread. Today, thanks to an advertising campaign by the National Turkey Federation in Reston, Virginia, an eager trade group founded at the Seventh World Poultry

Congress in 1939, and by turkey processors eager to use costly plants year-round, only 45 percent of each year's 2 billion pounds of turkey is consumed at Thanksgiving and Christmas.

In 1973 that meant about 9 pounds of turkey a person, twice the 1951 rate, compared with 115 pounds of beef. In 1972, for the first time in the United States, less whole turkey was consumed (48 percent) than turkey parts in turkey loaves, ground turkey, and ready-to-serve turkey TV dinners.

However they are to be served, Mr. Lucas's turkeys have only a short time to live. Soon the computers will say they are ready and the calendar will say people are buying. On the fateful day, according to Mr. Lucas's contract with Armour, six trucks will haul the protesting birds to Washington, Indiana. There, a conveyor belt will carry them past an electrical device that knocks them unconscious, then past the knife-wielding executioner, and finally into a plucking and washing machine.

As the hooked belt moves along like a disassembly-line, workers clean, grade, and inspect each bird. The intestines are ground for fertilizer, livestock feed, or shipped abroad as a delicacy. The turkeys then pass through cooling machines, past women with odd pistols that inject butter for self-basting birds, and into automatic wrapping machines that entomb the turkey in form-fitting plastic sacks that carry cooking instructions.

About two hours after they leave Mr. Lucas's field, the birds are bundled, boxed, and buried in freezers where the temperature hovers around minus 40 degrees. Twenty-four hours later, frozen so solid that they have broken the toes of butter-fingered buyers, the turkeys are ready for the truck ride to the stomachs of the Northeast.

# WINTER

*No turkeys in Harlan. Just a*
*lot of unlit Christmas lights.*

# HARLAN, IOWA

In a show of civic solidarity perhaps unrivaled since the Indian threat, this western Iowa community—the self-proclaimed "Christmas City"—has pulled the plug on all outdoor Christmas lighting this year because of the nation's so-called energy shortage. It is a step occurring with varying degrees of compliance, sincerity, cynicism, and grumbling in villages, cities, and homes throughout America these days, the start of the traditional holiday decorating time. From New York City to Portland, from Houston to Phoenix, and from Los Angeles to Ludlow Falls, store owners, municipal officials, and neighborhood leaders are pitching in to save electricity, just as President Nixon urged in his energy-conservation plea.

Sometimes this means using smaller Christmas bulbs, lighting them for shorter periods, or storing lights away altogether and substituting nonelectrical decorations. In some places, the conservation moves have aroused strong feelings of participatory patriotism. In others, the feelings were not so strong. "It really doesn't matter to me one way or the other," said Pete Nelson, a lineman with Harlan's utilities company, "but I guess it does save some electricity and me some work." Mr. Nelson is a member of the city crew here that for six years has decorated almost everything that stood motionless for any period of time during Thanksgiving week.

In past years area farmers, their corn and soybeans safely stored away, drove scores of miles to see the lighted plastic bells on Chatburn Avenue and the illuminated garlands on Cyclone Avenue and the colored bulbs on the radio tower and the strings of lights that ran from the Shelby County Courthouse roof to every light pole in the square. In past years thousands of people crammed into town for the annual lighting ceremony, when Mayor Kenneth L. Mueller, a chiropractor, threw the dummy switch that signaled Elmer Potter to signal the powerhouse to turn on the lights.

There were ooohs and aaahs then, and the crowning of Miss Merry Christmas. Santa Claus arrived in a convertible, *The Harlan News-Advertiser* ran its annual Christmas house-decorating contest, and the 35-foot lighted cross atop the grain elevator could be seen as far away as Avoca. The festivities, the biggest event of the year, were a boon to local merchants, a lot of fun for residents, and a genuine focus of civic pride. In fact, Harlan residents boast that their decorations are so renowned regionally that an Omaha television station once filmed them.

So it was no small sacrifice last week when Mayor Mueller and Spence Vanderlinden, chairman of the utilities board, decided Harlan (population: 5049) would lead the way in energy conservation. The decorations would go up, they ruled, but none would be plugged in. "We've got plenty of electricity here," said Mr. Vanderlinden, "and you'd really have to stretch it to think that our savings would have any effect elsewhere. But we wanted to make a symbolic gesture and do our part."

It was a gesture repeated in varying forms throughout the country. In New York City, Macy's, Saks, and Lord & Taylor will not light outdoor decorations. The Rockefeller Center tree will be on for 25 percent less time with 25 percent fewer bulbs. And the Roy Daigle family in Yonkers will trim its tree with tinsel and family pictures—not lights.

The usual 100,000 white lights on Chicago's Michigan Avenue are lit. But at the White House, the Nixon family tree will use no lights, just tinsel. The national Christmas tree across the street will have five spotlights instead of 9000 individual bulbs. The Washington Cathedral has darkened its floodlights. "I can't turn them on again unless I go down in the crypt," said John Baylis, the curator.

Atlanta's landmarks are unlighted now and the Forest Hills Baptist Church, the past scene of huge nativity tableaux and tree decorations, will have a single, unlighted tree. In Langeloth, Pennsylvania, Gus Barbush, the small community's stellar attraction, whose Christmas house decorations annually prompt 40,000 motorists to stop in his driveway, will reduce his lights by 25 percent—to only 9000 bulbs. There will be no official decorations in Saint Paul and in downtown Minneapolis merchants offered to turn their Christmas lights off January 1 instead of the usual March 15.

Ordinarily, the 80 families in Ludlow Falls, Ohio, have a modest Christmas display of 30,000 lights on 30 miles of wire strung over, under, and around a local gorge. Donations from sightseers finance the volunteer fire department. This year, however, as a result of the energy crisis, Ludlow Falls will not expand its display and will extinguish the lights one hour earlier. The Dayton, Ohio, Power and Light Company decided against a special power plea. "If we hit this too hard," a spokesman said, "the people may become too disturbed and won't listen to what we've got to say on the really big things like air-conditioners."

In Hollywood, California, Capitol Records dismantled its 75-foot, tree-shaped light display. But because Beverly Hills installed its lighted Christmas silver garlands in August, they will stay up, though they will go out at 9 P.M. instead of 1 A.M. "The influential people in this community think we've done our share," said Bob Burns of the chamber of commerce. And though the city of Los Angeles dropped all holiday lighting, Disneyland, with more than 20 trees and several miles of illuminated holly boughs, will light up as usual. "We don't want to disappoint thousands of visitors," a spokesman explained.

In Utah the Mormon Church drastically cut its holiday display. But the isolated ski resorts took no special steps. "So far," said the mayor of Alta, Utah, "there's no cutback in flares that I'm aware of."

Conservation compliance was high in the Northwest, where droughts have hampered hydroelectric power plants. Seattle is extinguishing every other streetlight. Downtown merchants shunned lavish lights for plastic candles and a 40-foot, talking, papier-mâché Santa Claus. In parts of Kansas it was different. "There is no electrical crisis in Kansas City," said Don Landes, a power official, so shopping centers went ahead with their plans. People who reduce Christmas lights, Mr. Landes said, "have been duped into a false reaction to a significant problem." Said Bill Webb of Merriam, Kansas: "If the President can fly to his three retreats here and there, I can use my Christmas lights." "It's just a Nixon ploy to get our minds off Watergate," said Yulanda Stephens, of Roxbury, Massachusetts. Diana Edgecomb of Detroit's Central Business District Association fears too much conservation and is horrified by talk of closing stores early to save power. "There is such a thing as going wild," she said.

Here in Harlan the advertising theme is: "We may be dark, but we still have bargains. The inner Christmas spirit is still with us." Even Pete Nelson will do without holiday lights. But not for conservation's sake. "By the time we put all the city decorations up," he said, "I'm so sick of decorating we don't bother at home. You know, if you put them up, then you gotta take 'em down."

*I stopped here on vacation once. There were proud parents, drunk cowboys, giggling youngsters, amazed tourists, and stuffed bears—all having a pretty good time. "You should do a story on this place sometime," my wife said.*

# DATIL, NEW MEXICO

Ninety miles away at the Adobe Ranch, Tom Wagner, Catron County's livestock inspector, finished the day's work about dusk, then clambered into his car and headed here. About the same time, Merle Burns switched off the throbbing rumble of his bulldozer some 50 miles up in the mountains where he is gouging out a new road for uranium prospectors. He, too, pointed his car toward Datil (rhymes with "cattle"). And Jess Allison, the weathered wood-cutter, silenced his blatting chain saw and with his two sons began the 32-mile dirt-road journey here.

There was nothing planned about their get-together. It was simply Friday night. Like thousands of other workers, ranchers, cowboys, girl friends, and families in the rural West, it was only natural that they should drop in for a bite, a drink, or a chat at the nearest roadhouse, which, like as not in these remote parts, is not very near at all. The roadhouse is this region's version of the neighborhood bar, except out here the neighborhood covers hundreds of square miles, often spilling into another state. And when the county's population works out to 0.3 person per square mile, there is not quite enough business to support separate singles bars, gay bars, family bars, and other enterprises.

So Datil's roadhouse, the Eagle Guest Ranch, serves many purposes. It is a combination saloon, community center, restaurant, gas station, grocery store, dance hall, motel, bulletin board, museum, meat market, barber shop, toy department, pseudo-drug store, general hangout, and message center. "This is where everybody comes since I can remember," said Mr. Allison. And he is right. For Datil (population: 100) has been a watering hole, for

225

humans as well as livestock, ever since 1885, when the area's ranchers began driving their sheep and cattle through here.

Like many American towns, Datil owes its existence to its well. It was one of 15 spaced one day's drive apart between Springerville, Arizona, and the railhead in Magdalena, New Mexico, a trek of 132 miles. The last big drive came through about five years ago when the Eagle Guest was already 35 years old.

The inn now dispenses more gasoline than water. But the heart of the business for owner Lee Coker and his wife, Lorraine, is the local trade, the area residents who come and go from 6 A.M., when Mrs. Coker begins frying up the eggs, sausages, and steaks, until closing time, which is a flexible affair. "We try to close at 10 P.M.," Mrs. Coker said. "But closing really depends on how good a time everyone is having."

"You better not close early 'cause we've got a lot of partying to do yet," said Mr. Allison as he ordered another round of Coors beer for all those near him at the bar's end of the room, where a giant buffalo head looks down from atop the stone fireplace. Someone in a jovial mood, probably on some long ago Friday night, installed a pair of Texas longhorns on the buffalo's head.

At the other end of the room, near the general store, Mr. Wagner was just arriving after driving more than 500 miles on his inspection rounds. "If I don't get me a drink right quick" he told the entire room, "I ain't gonna make it." Then he nodded an acknowledgment to waves from the other regulars and took a seat in his usual booth under the mounted deer heads bagged by local hunters. "I buy all my gas here, most of my groceries, and lots of my meals," he said. "Why, everybody in New Mexico and eastern Arizona knows about the good, cheap steaks here." Herman Sanchez, a cattle rancher, and his wife, Margaret, agree. Every Friday night for many a year they have come here for the big, tender T-bone steak with potatoes, salad, and toast that costs $3.

In the general store James Jackson, an employee better known for some reason as J.B., was sawing up 300 pounds of frozen beef that Wayne Hickey, another rancher, recently butchered and had just brought in. A bell sounded as a car entered the gas station and J.B. ran outside in his white apron to pump some gas and change a pair of license plates.

While waiting, Mr. Hickey walked by the store's shelves, which are informally organized and lined with everything from bananas, batteries, and beef jerky to sardines, soap, and a mysterious bottle labeled McLean's Tar Wine Compound. The toys are displayed in a meat freezer case. Mr. Hickey also checked the store's bulletin board where if notices of an event are not posted, then it might as well not happen. The telephone rang and Mrs. Annetta Blood, a waitress who lives in a log cabin where she cooks on a wood-burning stove, took a message for a forest ranger who does not have a phone but was expected to do some shopping here the next day.

Then Mrs. Coker, the cook, addressed her restaurant patrons collectively. "You all hurry up and order," she said, " 'cause I've got to help J.B. cut up that beef." Mr. Burns, the bulldozer driver who has not yet earned designation as a regular here, was finishing a steak. For $5 a night he stays in one of the Eagle Guest's spartan motel rooms. "I heard about this place when I was up in the northern part of the state," he said. "The food sure is fine."

A few minutes later he strolled over to the bar. "Howdy. I'm Merle Burns," he said.

"Well, howdy," said Mr. Allison. "Set yourself down here and make yourself to home. Hey, sweetie," he called to Helen Sickles, a waitress, as he leaned over the counter, "you gonna get us some more Coors or do I hafta climb over and get 'em myself?" Then he gave her 50 cents to feed the jukebox.

Mr. Allison, who makes a living chopping wood for the fireplaces of El Paso, Texas, 243 miles southeast, savored his beer as he looked back over his day, one of seven he works each week. "We got up before 6," he said, "and were out cutting till sundown, whenever that was. Sometimes I hate to come in. It gets so pretty out there it hurts your eyes. But when you're working that hard that late that long, you sure do appreciate a place like this to come to and have a beer and relax." Then, clutching a fistful of change, Mr. Allison, who doesn't have his own phone at home, walked outside to the pay-phone booth to call some wood dealers.

The sparse traffic on U.S. 60 had disappeared. The sweet-smelling smoke of a wood fire was hanging in the chill mountain air. And seeping into the night out of the warm roadhouse came the sounds of Johnny Cash singing "Sunday Morning Coming Down."

*Two girls from one town won half the United States's Winter Olympics medals. What kind of place could do that?*

# NORTHBROOK, ILLINOIS

It was a bright, beautiful day here today. But the sunshine didn't go over too well with some. "The sun," groused one of the village's 27,000 residents, "is killing the ice. It'll be rotten skating."

Bad ice and bad skating are bad news most any time in this northern Chicago suburb, but it was singularly inappropriate today as the town laid out a heroines' welcome for the two hometown skaters, Dianne Holum and Anne Henning, who together won half of the United States's eight Winter Olympics medals. The two medal winners shared honors with three other Northbrook skaters who also were on the 17-member Olympic skating team coached by Ed Rudolph, the energetic Northbrook resident who is generally credited with developing ice sports here to the point that the town can now call itself the "Speed Skating Capital of the World."

The melting ice didn't dampen spirits though. The two Olympic gold-medal winners and their teammates arrived from Japan late this afternoon to a noisy welcome by 300 fans and Mayor Richard J. Daley of Chicago at nearby O'Hare International Airport. They then rode in a horn-hooting motorcade to Northbrook, where they were greeted by fireworks and a crowd estimated by the police at about 8000. And in the Meadow Hill Ice Rink, the scene of local triumphs, the young skaters were showered with flowers and praise while the ice melted around the chilly feet of their admirers.

Miss Henning, 16 years old, and Miss Holum, 20, appeared tired and a bit overwhelmed as they left the airplane. But within moments Miss Henning, the 500-meter sprint-skating winner, and Miss Holum, the 1500-meter skating winner, gave way to laughter and excitement among their young friends. In downtown Northbrook, every store flashed a congratulatory sign. All 14 schools were shut tight and some businesses hooded their registers and closed their doors. But one thing that didn't shut down was the village's $940,000 indoor ice rink. "The people here just wouldn't stand for it," said Frances Plummer, the head skating teacher.

In fact, the skating rink, which was approved in a special bond referendum, is rarely closed at all. Weekdays it runs at least 20 hours a day. On weekends the ice is busy around the clock. There are beginners' skating lessons (more than 1400 enroll in each 10-week session), figure skating (the rink opens at 5 A.M. for practice), ice hockey (eight leagues, beginning at age 5), and the annual ice show—with, of course, a cast of a thousand.

Though Northbrook provides the coach and 5 of the United States team's 17 members, skating is not the town's only passion. "This is just a nutty sports town," said Mrs. Genny Adsit. On that sad day in May when the indoor ice goes away, the tennis courts fill up, traffic grows heavy on the Olympic bike track, and the 1100 boys in Little League scamper to floodlit diamonds. Northbrook is, in short, an affluent sports-minded suburb where almost everyone believes that the family that plays together stays together. Even the Book Bin, the local bookstore, sells more sports books than any other kind.

It is a far cry from the wee village of Shermerville that a band of industrious German farmers founded in the mid-1880s. It's also a far cry from the village of Northbrook that many residents knew only 12 years ago. Since then it has doubled in population and, like dozens of other Chicago suburbs such as Wheeling, Buffalo Grove, and Lombard, has found its 1970 census already woefully outdated.

Housing developers are quickly buying up the remaining farm lands and golf courses. Property that once sold for $1.50 an acre now goes for upward of $40,000.

And the local welcoming hostess, Mrs. Carol Bergey, makes at least a dozen calls a week now at the brightly colored, two-story, two-garage homes springing up in Northbrook's 11.5 square miles.

One survey put the median home value here at $50,000 and median income at more than $16,000, ranking Northbrook among Chicago's 10 wealthiest suburbs.

There is some friction here between a minority of longtime residents, who want the village (Northbrookians do not use the word city or town) to stay the same, and the overwhelming majority of later arrivals, who are bringing change. "Change is inevitable," said John C. Williams, the village president, "even if you don't like it."

But there is no friction over skating.

"We come out as often as possible," said Jack Lofstrom as he stood in a long line at the indoor rink. His daughter Becky, 3, and son Jeff, 4, tugged at his sleeves to get on the ice. Another, Mark, 8, was at home with a banged knee suffered in hockey practice. "Like all our friends," Mr. Lofstrom said, "we carry our skating stuff to church on Sunday. We're out of there at 10:30 and on the ice by 11. It's a great family sport." Suddenly 9-year-old James Dickman smashed into the ice, breaking his left arm. "You mean we have to go home?" he asked his father.

One resident said, "Northbrook is still very friendly and very child-oriented. You don't see parents dropping their children off to skate; they come, too. We may have grown into a big suburb, but we've kept a lot of the friendly qualities and pride in youth that you don't see in the big city." Many such families were attracted to Northbrook by its reputation for good schools and athletic facilities. The athletics are overseen by the Park District, an elected board that can levy its own taxes. One recent study found that 75 percent of Northbrook's population was involved with at least one Park District activity.

For many years Ed Rudolph, the active skating-team coach, has been a Park District commissioner and is generally credited here with pushing development of the ice rink, bike track, and other facilities. "Rudolph was the driving force behind the skating growth," said Chip Maze, a park district official, "but he was operating in mighty fertile sports ground. These parents really believe in sports for their children. Sports teach them discipline, self-confidence, and teamwork. And if you're out ice skating, you're not getting into any other trouble."

These days it seems everyone in town knows the two skating stars. "I used to see them at 7 in the morning out running," said Steve Meyer. Another youth added, "They're always training. I don't think they know what a boy looks like." Their Olympic success has already boosted the rink's waiting list for skating lessons to more than 500. "When I was little, I wanted to be like Sonja Henie," said Mrs. Gisella Pulf as she picked up skating application forms. "Now my daughter has to be like Anne and Dianne."

Tomorrow everything should be back to normal in Northbrook. That is, the stores will reopen, the schools will be back in session, and the ice rink will still be crowded. And, oh yes, the skating team leaves for Europe for another round of tournaments.

*Nebraska, someone said, is a good place to be from. But somebody had to stay here. And they should outlive us all.*

# FRANKLIN, NEBRASKA

Hanna Sanger should have died 7.05 years ago, according to statistics. She has always been stubborn and independent minded, though, so she didn't. And in living a long time here (she's working on her 80th year now), Mrs. Sanger is carrying on a local longevity tradition. For Nebraskans, according to the federal government, can expect to live longer than the residents of any other state, an average of 71.95 years.

Here in Franklin County, just 20 miles northwest of the geographical center of the continental United States, the spunky Hanna Sanger and several hundred other senior citizens have clustered together to give this 1320-square-mile area the highest median age of any Nebraska county, 43.5 years compared with 28.1 nationally. "We've got more than our share of elderly," said Edward Wolf, the city clerk, who is 62 years old.

In town, some old folks gather around the recreation hall, playing pitch or pool. Some shuffle along the sidewalks on errands, grasping their canes with gnarled hands that saw many a harvest. And some ease their bodies into chairs on the porch out at the senior-citizens homes, watching the sun set on another of the 26,279.75 days that statisticians have allotted their lives—on the average.

Such a lifetime is 5.54 years longer than the one a South Carolinian can expect to have in Beaufort County, the opposite end of the nation's longevity scale. And there are almost as many explanations for such long lives as there are social security checks here.

"People is happy here," said Herb Diener, who is 72.

"It's the air," said Asa Chalfon, who is 79.

"I think it's 'cause of the water," said his wife, Grace, also 79.

"I reckon it's 'cause we work so hard," said Fremont Goings, who is 72 and sometimes sleeps as late as 6 A.M. now. That's one hour before the town's 7 A.M. siren awakens all other sleepyheads.

"If you can stand our climate that goes from 23 below zero to 120 in the shade, then you're ready to live a long time," said Mrs. Thyra Sindt, who is 69.

"It's probably a combination of all these," said Dr. Harmon Denham, who is president of the American Aging Association. "Historically, rural residents live longer than urban ones," he said, "and Midwesterners live longer than coastal residents. They have lower food intake. The pace of life is slower. Most importantly, people seem to keep busier in retirement. They don't sit around, worry about their health, and lose a reason for living. And there's probably a selective factor: the hardiest residents stay on while the others move out."

Even Jesse James, who is said to have dickered for property here, left town. And since then, many residents have pulled up stakes. "Our farm population has been cut to beat the dickens," said Mr. Wolf, the town clerk. "There's not too many young folks what stays." The last census found only 4566 persons in Franklin County and its seven towns. That is fewer white residents than there were in 1879, only 10 years after General Carr's Republican River expedition shouldered the Pawnee Indians off their buffalo range here. And every year now for the last decade Franklin County has had more deaths than births.

That keeps old Doc Doering and the Hutchins Funeral Home and the Greenwood Cemetery busy. But it does somewhat limit the scope of life on these vast, rolling plains whose broad expanse is broken only occasionally by the 10-story, white-cement grain elevators that loom up eerily on the horizon like some prairie cathedrals. For many decades the area's aging farmers have labored to fill those elevators and to fatten the cattle that poke through the muddy cornfields. Actually, many farmers have never stopped working, which Dr. Denham says may have contributed to their longevity. Many elderly here are simply too busy working to think about retirement or how poorly they sometimes think they feel.

"And anyway," said Mrs. Sindt, "farming isn't work. It's a way of life. Now, how can you retire from a way of life?" Her husband, Will, for instance, is 72. But he didn't have time to talk one recent day. He was too busy tending his cattle in some distant pasture.

Milo Hill is only 82 years old, but he's slowed down somewhat anyway. He sold his farm-implement dealership and only cares for 100 cattle and 1640 acres of land now. Harry Wistrand is 80, so he's confined his activities to overhauling his tractor, digging out old tree stumps on his son's farm, and rebuilding some back roads. Herb Diener, who is 72, lost his farm in the "dirty thirties." So he works full-time in the pool hall, where he earns 2.5 cents for each hand of cards each farmer plays. "Sometimes I make $2 or $3 a day," he said. "I like it here."

Of course, not everyone is so active. Many elderly just fish or follow the bingo circuit—Minden, Nebraska, on Tuesday nights, Naponee on Thursdays, and Franklin on Fridays. Asa and Grace Chalfon like to travel, something they could not do when their cattle needed feeding daily. Now, however, their journeys are local because Mr. Chalfon says his heart is weak. "I'm all right as long as I don't do anything," he said.

But then there's Hanna Sanger. At 9 sharp every morning she and a squad of senior ladies meet downtown for exercise class with Betty Wistrand, the local Office of Economic Opportunity worker, who organizes parties, outings, and free bus rides for Franklin County's elderly. Exercise class hardly seems necessary for Mrs. Sanger, whose husband, David, died in 1957, a long-lingering victim of shell shock "from the first war."

"They took the farm away from us in the thirties," she said, "but I earned it back myself." She still grows her own garden, bakes countless pies for benefits, and regularly cans dozens of jars of peaches, apricots, onions, cherries, and tomatoes. Recently, she sewed 88 dresses for local less fortunate girls and women, not to mention the boxes of knickknacks she makes from egg crates and glitter.

A while back, though, the 79-year-old Mrs. Sanger felt she needed more living space. So she got out her tools, knocked down a living-room wall, extended the room through the front porch, and, for good measure, tacked on another bedroom. Then she plastered and painted the walls. "I try to keep busy," she says. "There's just so much to be done."

*Another town turns out bombs for the U.S. war machine. So, after donning special static-electricity conductors, I dropped in for a visit—very softly.*

# CRANE, INDIANA

Every weekday morning for the last several years, Mrs. Patricia Ash has awakened around 5, fed and sent her two teen-aged children off to school, and driven 26 miles to work here. Her earnings of $3.84 an hour, combined with her husband's income from a gas station, mean that the Ash family can have new clothes more often and live considerably better than it expected to a few years ago. Peace in Vietnam, however, may end all that. For like several thousand other workers here in southwestern Indiana, Mrs. Ash's income depends on war. She makes bombs.

A cease-fire will mean that the United States will no longer be dropping 3326 tons of bombs a day on Southeast Asia. That means the Air Force and Navy will not be ordering as many 500- and 1000-pound bombs from the Crane Naval Ammunition Depot. And that means each shift will not need to turn out 2200 bombs every eight hours. Which means there will probably not be three shifts anymore. And if that happens, Mrs. Ash, and a few thousand others in the 5800-member work force, will probably be unemployed.

"A cease-fire worries me," Mrs. Ash said the other day as she paused from lining up empty bomb casings to be filled with molten TNT. "I'd just as soon have a cease-fire, like anyone would. I mean, I've got a son and he'd have to go to war some day. But I'd hate to lose my job. But I can always find another one, I guess."

Unknown to her, perhaps, work began more than six months ago to insure jobs for Mrs. Ash and Renalda Nicholson and James Lechner and any other displaced defense worker at Crane. Spurred by local initiative and aided by a flock of federal agencies, the four counties of Greene, Lawrence, Martin, and Daviess have estab-

235

lished a Center for Economic Development to attract new industry and tourism, to help old industry expand, and to ease generally the transition to a peacetime economy. Already the center, which is funded jointly by federal, state, and local governments, has attracted two plastics companies, a recreational-vehicle manufacturer, and a new pork-processing plant. "All of a sudden," said Stan Barkley, a local banker, "we realized we're poor, we know we're poor, and we want all the help we can get."

This gently rolling area of marginal farms and chronically high unemployment has lived with the peaks and valleys of defense employment for decades. "We've learned," said one resident, "that what goes up must come down, including defense employment and ammunition." It is a predicament that has been faced by dozens of American communities and will be faced by others. But the Crane Naval Ammunition Depot is the biggest of 11 such naval facilities. It was opened in 1941 in this isolated section of Indiana largely because the area was beyond the reach then of enemy bombers.

The depot's 62,600 acres, many of them wooded, contain almost 500 miles of road and 175 miles of railroad, the Navy's largest individual rail installation. By road, the depot resembles a national forest. But from the air an observer can see more than 2000 earth-covered ammunition storage bunkers laced throughout the base and spaced to avoid catastrophe should one explode. Slow-moving trucks, marked "EXPLOSIVES," ease their way from building to building where 61 naval personnel and 5800 civilians (1400 of them women) make bombs, flares, and five-inch shells for the destroyers' big guns.

Each building contains only enough explosive for the immediate job at hand. Long conveyer belts connect the structures, carrying tubs of the explosive's components, which are dumped by hand into large vats according to a precise recipe, then mixed and heated to the consistency of pancake batter. Mrs. Nicholson and her co-workers pour 190 pounds of the explosive into each 500-pound bomb, which is then sealed, allowed to cool 24 hours, and shipped by truck or train to waiting ships or stored in a nearby bunker.

The workers commute from such towns as Odon, Bedford, Loogootee, Bushrod, and Mineral City. In World War II, peak employment was 10,000. There were 4700 here during the Korean conflict, about 2000 ten years ago, and more than 7000 four years ago, according to Captain Richard L. McArthy, the depot com-mander. But the handwriting is on the bomb casing: there will be fewer employees here soon. No one expects sudden, drastic layoffs as a result of a Vietnam peace. After all, substantial munitions stockpiles are to be rebuilt and the depot has in recent years diversified its activities. For instance, engineers here are also deeply involved in weapons research and development as well as testing Polaris missile parts.

"But it's pretty clear," said William Sheehan, director of the Pentagon's Office of Economic Adjustment, "that if you're no longer dropping a tremendous number of bombs, you don't need to make a tremendous number of bombs. So there will be cutbacks." It is the responsibility of Mr. Sheehan's office to "cushion the impact of an action taken in the national interest so that the reper-cussions don't fall solely on a little town like Crane." Four years ago the office was helping 28 communities where big defense installations had closed. Today it is involved in 51 such projects, including Crane. Mr. Sheehan's staff helped to fund the Center for Economic Development here and helped it thread its way through

the federal bureaucracy in search of small-business loans or grants.

So far, the biggest problem has been a local reluctance to think regionally in terms of economic development. "There are mayors in the same county who won't speak to each other over basketball and band rivalries," said Joe A. Lackey, the energetic 26-year-old executive director of the Daviess County Chamber of Commerce, in Washington, Indiana. Slowly, he said, this is being overcome, if only in the face of some hard economic realities.

Between 1960 and 1970, 4800 young people aged 17 to 24 left this area for lack of jobs—"at a cost of $10,000 each for their education through high school," said Duane L. Sorensen, director of the Center for Economic Development. "That represents an economic drain of $48 million. And now these young people are earning money and paying taxes elsewhere. That can't go on. We've got to get work here for them. So we're seeking broad-based industrial development. It's not an overnight thing. But we're getting there. We're getting there."

*Christmastime and a correspondent's
thoughts turn to . . . Santa Claus, Indiana.
Little did I know I'd meet the real McCoy.*

# S A N T A   C L A U S ,   I N D I A N A

Even Santa Claus has a zip code. It is 47579. Now some people
may think that is the North Pole, which shows how much they
know. Because Santa Claus is a town in southwestern Indiana,
where Christmas is not just a holiday to celebrate but a business
and a way of life.

The so-called energy crisis has doused the elaborate outdoor
Christmas-light displays, as it has in many cities. In a town called
Santa Claus such measures cannot be taken lightly, so to speak.
Yet even without colored lights here, there is still Lake Rudolph,
Lake Holly, and Lake Noel. There is Herald Circle, Silver Bell
Terrace, Sled Run, and Donder Lane. There is the St. Nicholas
Inn, the Christmas Lake Village housing development, the news-
paper *Santa's Country*, and the Snowflake Drive-in. Not to men-
tion the Santa Claus Land Amusement Park. And presiding over it
all is a special Santa Claus, a jolly 80-year-old man who some
people say is Jim Yellig. But most people know in their hearts that
Yellig is just a pseudonym Santa uses when he is not cuddling
youngsters on his well-worn knee.

This rural crossroads community is not much to look at or work
in or drive through. One of the few things that sets it apart from
the surrounding rolling pastures and woodlands is the candy-striped
water tower with a picture of guess who on top. Another distinctive
structure is the post office, a stone building that looks like a fairytale fortress. Every year at this time the post office receives about
five million pieces of mail—79,365.08 pieces for each of Santa
Claus's 63 residents. The mail is mostly corporate Christmas
mailings and personal Christmas cards that are trucked here from
the post office in Washington, Indiana, canceled with the famous
Santa Claus postmark, and trucked back to the neighboring town's
post office for further distribution. It is enough labor to add 11

239

extra workers to the normal staff of 2 headed until recently by Postmaster Elbert Reinke. A lot of the mail is important messages to Santa Claus the man, laboriously handwritten missives with pleas for trains, trucks, dolls, buggies, and a baby brother or two.

Santa Claus the town, where the strains of "Frosty the Snowman" drift out across the sleeping fields, has gotten such letters almost from that holiday eve in 1852 when a town meeting was stalemated over a name for the three-year-old community, which then had a population of 30. Suddenly, it is said, waiting youngsters screamed "Santa Claus!" as he entered the church. And that became the town's name. Things were quiet then until 1929, when Ripley's "Believe It or Not" carried an item about the community. Apparently, many postal workers had the Ripley cartoon read to them because they started forwarding all the letters addressed to Santa Claus, North Pole, to Santa Claus, Indiana. It got so hectic here during the holidays that the annual Town Christmas Dinner was rescheduled to the first Tuesday in October, when there was more time for such things.

Just before World War II, Louis Koch, the father of nine little Santa letter writers in Evansville, Indiana, got the idea for a theme amusement park, even before Disneyland. Naturally, the park was named Santa Claus Land. It opened in 1946 and lost money for 10 years. Now, it is run by his son, William, who is also president of the town board and the recreational housing development.

The 40-acre park includes Santa's workshop, Mrs. Claus's kitchen, some trained animals, wax and circus exhibits, a host of rides, and ambitious expansion plans when Interstate 64 opens nearby. From Easter until Christmas each year, more than 300,000 patrons pay $2 to Frieda Foertsch at the gate. The busiest times are Sundays in August, and the slowest time is Christmas Eve. "We thought the gas situation would hurt our weekend business," said Mr. Koch, "but last Sunday we had more people than we did with the gas stations open."

Fortunately, no energy crisis could ever affect the park's star attraction, S. Claus, this community's own "Miracle on Route 162." No Santa's helper is he. Children in line rehearse their little lists as Santa Claus's Santa Claus sits in his chair with the tinkling bells on the back by the old desk overflowing with letters. Mr.

Claus's belly is round. His brows are bushy. His hands are chubby. Unconsciously, they grip his sides as he laughs deeply. And those tiny antique spectacles perch precariously on the end of his large nose. There is no air of department store, assembly-line chats that end with the flash of a camera. Instead, there is an unusual feeling that something special is happening.

"Well, hello, Jimmy, how are you this year?" asks Santa as a little boy stumbles up the steps.

The parents, who live many miles away and gave no one their son's name, exchange wondering glances. Jimmy is nonchalant with his pal.

"Hey," says Santa, "how's your truck doing?"

"O.K."

"Say, you didn't mean to get in that fight the other day, did you?"

"No, Santa, but he pushed me."

"I know," says the old man, pursing his lips, "I know. Now what are you wishing for this year?"

Later, another child is near tears. "Santa, you know the bike you brought last year?"

"The red one?" he replies. "Yes, I remember."

"Well, somebody stole it."

"I know," says Santa, "and his name is right up there in the Bad Boys' Book."

The child smiles, happy in the knowledge that justice will be done.

"Santa Claus should never ask anyone's name," says Santa Claus. "Santa Claus knows everybody's name. And if he forgets for a minute, well, he need only listen to the parents. They always say, 'Go on, Bobby, you're next.'" He explains his omniscience only by saying he uses a little imagination and observation. "Every boy has a truck," he says.

Mr. Yellig first realized he was Santa Claus in 1914 when, because his hometown was Santa Claus, his crewmates on the U.S.S. *New York* chose him as old Saint Nick at a Christmas party for neighborhood children at the Brooklyn Navy Yard. "I looked in those little children's eyes," says Santa, "and suddenly I knew." He has been Santa ever since, organizing the American Legion post here to help answer the flood of letters. Between Christmas and Easter, while the park is closed, Santa studies up on the latest toys. And he prepares his costume; the youngsters wear out the knees of four red-flannel pants every year.

"As soon as I put on my suit," Santa says, "I am Santa Claus and you better believe it." Visitors do believe. When he is wearing his Santa suit he doesn't answer to Jim. And even with no children present, it seems grossly inappropriate to call him anything but Santa.

"I love being Santa Claus," he says, "because when I'm Santa Claus, well, you know there's only one reason for Santa Claus to be—and that is to spread joy and happiness. That's my life." His biggest thrill is to watch the elderly who bring their grandchildren. "I believe there should never be any unhappy old people," says the 80-year-old man, "because, after all, their days are numbered. We have to take care of them." Santa has also noticed changes over the years in children's tastes. "Once they wanted marbles, tops, rolling hoops, and toy wash boards. Now they want talking dolls and scuba sets and airplanes that fly."

Still, there is one thing that never changes: the inevitability of Christmas Eve. "I go back," says Santa, "and take off these shiny boots and the red suit and I sit there. I just can't believe then that I can't come back the next day and be Santa Claus. It's about the saddest time of the year for me."

*The post office was doing away with postmarks. If people collect beer cans, I figured, then others collect postmarks. And they were plenty angry, too.*

# UNITED STATES POSTAL SERVICE OH 445

It used to be whenever anyone got a letter from this eastern Ohio city, all he had to do was look at the postmark next to the stamp on the front of the envelope and he would know immediately that the letter was from Youngstown. But soon, unless you are a zip-code zealot who has memorized the nation's entire list of numerical postal codes, you will have no idea of a letter's origin without reading on. For the United States Postal Service is in the process of eliminating, with the exception of a very few of the largest cities, virtually all town and city names from its postmarks. This, officials say, will help speed mail service.

It is a step that eventually will wipe from the letters of the land the old lyrical names of America, the artful names pioneers chose to describe their initial thoughts on their new homes. These names, however, will not die without a fight. From Tie Siding, Wyoming, to Fly Creek, New York, and Greasy Ridge, Ohio, the members of the Post Mark Collectors Club are becoming increasingly aroused. And matters may reach a climax at their upcoming annual convention in Findlay, Ohio. For more than 27 years, the members have collected millions of different postmarks, savoring the rich rural names in their albums and catalogs, and tenaciously trading duplicates with other collectors.

But now the postal service is installing automated sorting and canceling equipment around the country in Area Mail Processing Centers, or AMPCs as they are called. To justify their existence, however, these high-speed machines must have a large volume of mail to digest. The letters from several dozen smaller post offices, therefore, are now trucked unsorted and uncanceled to 357 widely scattered AMPCs. No one knows how many centers there will be eventually. The clacking machines have no way of knowing which little town produced which letter. So a growing volume of mail is now being postmarked: U.S. POSTAL SERVICE, with the date, state abbreviation, and first three digits of the area's zip code.

"This is an outrage," said Mrs. Erna Galske, a longtime collector who has filled her dining room in Elgin, Illinois, with postmarks that her husband calls "pure junk." "We sure don't like this number business one bit," Mrs. Galske continued. "I tell my friends if we live long enough we're not going to have any names. We're all going to be born with nothing but a number."

Some of the younger club members have adapted and now save the new numbered postmarks with the goal of possessing one of every zip code in the nation. Others hope the end of the postmark names will boost the value of their early collections in what is, admittedly, a somewhat limited market. No one knows yet exactly the effects of the postmark change on the postmark club's museum of 500,000 items displayed in an old school bus in Mrs. Bernice Mittower's backyard in Republic, Ohio. But Herbert H. Harrington will not quit. As the president of the 1000-member Post Mark Collectors Club, he is on the verge of writing several congressmen and throwing the entire weight of his club behind legislative steps to revive the old postal system. "These machines," he said, "are taking all the romance out of postmarks. They're ruining the poor man's hobby. It's getting so as you don't know where your mail is coming from. All the envelope has is a lot of cuckoo numbers on it."

Postal officials note that anyone can still get a named postmark if he asks the postmaster. Also, collectors may send themselves a letter via a particular post office. But this can become costly and time-consuming when, as in Mr. Harrington's case, you are talking about some 70,000 postmarks.

Generally, collectors, who call themselves commatelists for reasons none of them seem able to explain, mount their postmarks on three-by-five-inch cards. Some specialize in "topicals," that is, postmarks from towns with names that involve a theme—animals, flowers, occupations, or the weather. The latter might include Thunderbolt, Georgia, and Hurricane or Cyclone, West Virginia. Other collectors try for one postmark for each day of a particular year (holidays and Sundays are the hardest to get). Some raid the waste baskets of nearby businesses and the attics of friends in search of their treasure. Still others rely on trading (experienced collectors know they can mail exactly 25 postmarks for one first-class stamp). Mrs. Galske, for instance, has been trading with Ida Abbott of Tacoma, Washington, for 13 years, and someday they may even meet personally.

Usually members meet at the annual convention, which in previous years has been held in Newark, New Jersey; Sarnia, Ontario; Poultney, Vermont; and on Margie Pfund's farm in Columbiana, Ohio. Mr. Harrington, who lives near here in Warren, Ohio, has presided over recent meetings, which included a policy dispute that saw a dissident faction of postmark collectors secede from the club to form the American Postmark Society. But Mr. Harrington is tiring of the responsibilities of his office and plans to appoint a new president soon.

The 50-year-old Mr. Harrington is in a rather unusual position. For not only is his hobby being phased out by machinery, but his job is being phased out, too. He is a railroad-crossing guard. For eight hours every weekday Mr. Harrington stands guard in a tiny cement shanty here in downtown Youngstown. Whenever a train rumbles along the Erie Lackawanna tracks, Mr. Harrington steps to the middle of Hazel Street to stop the automobiles. "When I started in this business 22 years ago," Mr. Harrington said, "I was No. 160 in seniority. Now I am No. 3. . . . Of course, there's only 16 of us left in the area."

The job is not too taxing. So between the day's dozen trains, Mr. Harrington rests in his shanty, which is heated by a coal stove and lighted by electricity secretly tapped from a nearby illuminated billboard. Here, Mr. Harrington monitors the moods, schedules, and figures of regular pedestrians passing by at the same time every day. He has rigged a mirror so he can look out one window and see both ways down the tracks without having to turn his head.

He has also installed a tiny table, where he puts his briefcase, which serves as his desk. Then, in his frequent free moments, Mr. Harrington conducts the club's business, including writing for the monthly newsletter and accepting new members. (The club's address is P.O. Box 87, Warren, Ohio 44482. Dues are $4.) "If I didn't have something like this club to keep me busy," he said, "I'd probably go stark raving mad."

Sometimes Mr. Harrington leafs through his collection, scanning "the sharp names that never get fat," as Stephen Vincent Benet called American names in 1927. There are Lickskillet, Tennessee; Bug Tussel, Kentucky; Tight Wad, Missouri; Dog Bone, West Virginia; Shickshinny, Upper Black Eddy, and Fearnot, Pennsylvania; and Bowlegs, Oklahoma. Nearby in southeastern Ohio there are Rush Run, Businessburg, Whipple, Crooked Tree, Temperanceville, Rich Valley, Olivegreen, Moscow Mills, Coolville, Antiquity, Ruraldale, and Long Bottom, which is not to be confused with Round Bottom. There are Paradise and Hell, Michigan; Big Isaac, West Virginia; Cut and Shoot, Texas; Rough and Ready, and Gouge Eye, California; Gnawbone, Georgia; Accident, Maryland; and Rabbit Hash, Kentucky.

Postmark collectors, and perhaps other Peoples (Kentucky) Reading (Pennsylvania) this Odd (West Virginia) Little (Kentucky) Story (Wyoming), will miss these Nice (California), Rich (Mississippi) names. In addition, many of the collectors are shut-ins. And What Cheer (Iowa) and Good Times (South Carolina) they have are based on postmarks. So, Smartt (Tennessee) club members are United (Pennsylvania) in their Hope (New Jersey) for a Reform (Alabama), New Deal (Texas), or just a Normal (Illinois), Ordinary (Virginia) Miracle (Kentucky) against the Troublesome (Colorado), Nameless (North Dakota) postmark Rule (Texas).

The postal service says Okay (Oklahoma), but why stop Progress (Pennsylvania)? Pointblank (Texas), postmark collectors reply, Whynot (North Carolina)?

*What can I say about little-known people
like Dorsie W. Willis? You can't say
anything. You just tell their story.*

# MINNEAPOLIS, MINNESOTA

"Nowadays," said Dorsie W. Willis, "I just sit and eat and think." And what he thinks about most often is the night in 1906 when a gang on horseback rode through Brownsville, Texas, shooting at lighted windows and killing one man.

Mr. Willis remembers how the townspeople blamed the black soldiers at Fort Brown for the shooting, and how the furor reached Washington, and how President Theodore Roosevelt sent an investigator, and how without any trial the President ordered 167 black soldiers "discharged without honor" when they volunteered no information on the culprits.

Mr. Willis also remembers that on Sept. 28, 1972, Secretary of the Army Robert F. Froehlke called the incident a gross injustice and changed all the discharges to honorable. Mr. Froehlke simply wanted to right a wrong, an Army spokesman said. No official effort was made to find the soldiers, and it did not seem likely that any of them were still alive. But one still is.

He is Dorsie William Willis. Once he was a private in what was called D Company, First Battalion, 25th Infantry (Colored). Now he is 86 years old, arthritic, and resentful that an administrative order could have ruined much of his working life. After his dishonorable discharge, the best job that Mr. Willis ever had was as a porter and shoe shiner in the Northwestern Bank Building Barber Shop here.

For 59 years he opened the barbershop every morning, swept the hair off the floor, brushed lint off coats, rubbed dirt off shoes, and closed the shop at night. When he started in September, 1913, a shoeshine cost 10 cents plus tip. When he quit last September it cost 50 cents and maybe a tip. With income from that job and a little earned on the side, he supported his wife, reared his son, who is now 65, and at the age of 50 went $2,850 into debt to buy his own home.

247

"Some people feel the world owes them a living," Mr. Willis said as he sat in that same home on this city's southeast side. "I never thought that. And I never took a dime in welfare. I did figure the world owed me an opportunity to earn a living myself. But they took that away from me. That dishonorable discharge kept me from improving my station. Only God knows what it did to the others."

The Brownsville Raid was a 10-minute shooting spree by 16 to 20 men on the night of Aug. 23, 1906, in that dusty southern Texas border town. It began 24 hours after a white woman charged that a Negro had tried to rape her. After the shooting, one man was dead, another injured, and some Army cartridges were found in the street. Under Presidential orders, the War Department, assuming that the men from the all-black unit were guilty, took them to Oklahoma for questioning. When not one soldier admitted anything, they were all cashiered for their "conspiracy of silence."

"None of us said anything, 'cause we didn't have anything to say," said Mr. Willis. "It was a frame-up straight through. They checked our rifles, and they hadn't been fired. Those cartridges were empties we was sending back to the maker. And we was infantry. We never had any horses to ride." After a lengthy investigation, an author, John D. Weaver, concluded in *The Brownsville Raid: The Story of America's Black Dreyfus Affair* that some local vigilantes, angered by the black soldiers' presence, staged the shoot-out, and two people got in the way of the bullets.

Mr. Willis remembers his discharge paper well, although he said it was lost years ago. He squinted his eyes and recited, "Dorsie Willis is hereby discharged from the Army of the United States without honor and forever debarred from enlisting in the Army or Navy of the United States or holding any civilian employment under the Government." A check of Mr. Willis's yellowing military folder in the National Archives in Washington showed his memory to be sharp.

It also showed a 1972 amendment by the Department of the Army changing the discharge to honorable and noting, "No back pay, allowances, benefits or privileges shall occur by reason of the issuance of this order to any heirs or descendants." But, apparently because all involved were believed dead, there was no mention of what benefits were due those still living. So Mr. Willis's status is confused.

In an effort to clear that up and to help the descendants of the 167 soldiers, Representative Augustus F. Hawkins, Democrat of California, has said that he planned to introduce legislation soon to make available such benefits as payments to widows and medical care at veterans hospitals and perhaps to award some monetary compensation to survivors and heirs. "The entire case is a real disgrace," Mr. Hawkins said. "The Army must have felt there was some wrong committed when it amended the discharges. But to do so without considering the human tragedies and factors is cold-blooded. The Army owes these men something. Ironically, they were the ones who guarded Teddy Roosevelt's flank at San Juan Hill."

Mr. Willis is somewhat baffled, and apparently he is not alone. A Veterans Administration spokesman asserted that Mr. Willis lived in Saint Louis. Mr. Willis said that someone called from Washington recently to say that he was eligible now for veterans-hospital treatment, which might have saved him many insurance payments and recent hospital bills. When he called the local veterans hospital, however, he was told that he might still not be eligible.

He said someone telephoned from Washington last fall and said his honorable discharge papers were in the mail. No papers have arrived. But a spokesman explained the Army will help Mr. Willis prove he is the Dorsie Willis who served at Brownsville, a necessary step before an honorable discharge certificate is issued.

Meanwhile, finances are a bit tight for Mr. Willis and his wife. They have stopped exchanging Christmas presents with relatives. And soon it will be time for another $31 worth of medicine for Mr. Willis's arthritis, which keeps him indoors close to his big leather chair and the worn wooden cane that members of his Zion Baptist Church gave him. Mrs. Olive Willis earns $3.79 an hour boxing hamburgers for a restaurant chain. Then there's Mr. Willis's $180 social security check. "We get by barely," Mrs. Willis said. Mr. Willis's eyesight and hearing are deteriorating, and he moves very slowly. To protect their tiny home at 3724 Minnehaha Avenue, he bought Subrina, an energetic, menacing Doberman pinscher.

Long ago, Mr. Willis, who completed sixth grade in an Oklahoma Territory schoolhouse, considered many jobs other than shining shoes. But, he said, no one would post an insurance bond for him, he feared what would happen if employers discovered his discharge, and employment at the post office, popular work for many blacks here, was barred by his discharge. Meanwhile, Mr. Willis said he heard long ago that some of the other 166 men had changed their names to start new lives while some had fallen into crime or their children had gone to work to help family finances.

He was so happy and surprised last September when he read about the exoneration that he bought a dozen newspapers to mail to relatives. Since then, however, his enthusiasm has waned. "It seems," he said as he slowly filled his worn pipe, "that I ain't got nothing left but time."

*It wasn't the most pleasant assignment
I've ever had. How do you talk about death
with the friends and parents of the dead?*

# BEALLSVILLE, OHIO

The wind whips through the wires up on Cemetery Hill here these days, rustling the long, dried grasses and banging the rope on the new metal flagpole. At the foot of the pole down next to the soil in the lee of the wind is a plain plaque. It says: "In Honor Of Those Who Served Our Country. 'He causeth wars to cease.' Psalms 46:9."

"It's a darn shame it couldn't have ended a few years sooner," said Joe Decker, "at least for us here."

He was referring to the war in Vietnam and to this sleepy town which is home to 452 persons. For its population, Beallsville (pronounced Bellsville) was hit perhaps as hard as a town could be hit. It lost seven of its sons to the Vietnam war. In New York State the same proportion of war deaths would be about 278,000, or nearly 70 times the state's toll of 3,985. Today, the townspeople—the coal miners, aluminum workers, and farmers—talked about the war and the cease-fire. They said they would believe it when they saw it.

"The cease-fire is wonderful," said Mrs. Nelda Gramlich, "but I wonder if it was all worth it." Beallsville has had questions about the war before. In 1969, shocked by its casualty rate, the town asked the Department of Defense not to send any more of its young men to Vietnam. The request was denied. Like many residents along Beallsville's three curbless streets here in the Allegheny foothills, 100 miles southwest of Pittsburgh, Mrs. Gramlich was not too keen to talk about the war.

"We've lost more over there than we'll ever get back," said Sonny Lawrence, who works at the gas station, "but it seems like people are trying to forget about the war before it's even over." Last night, for instance, when the President went on television to

251

announce a cease-fire, many townspeople were up at the high-school basketball game watching the Beallsville Blue Devils lose to Bishop Donohue. Today, only one person mentioned the cease-fire as he picked up his mail from Harry Decker, the postmaster. And this morning when Henry A. Kissinger went on television to explain the peace accord, Mayor Olis Thornberry was too busy to listen as he installed a new washing machine over at Sam Britton's house.

It was, as old-timers here would say, a "peaceable day." Along the ridges and down in the hollows that George Washington surveyed 230 years ago the schoolchildren stood by the road, their lunch pails clutched firmly in the early morning darkness, as they awaited their school bus. Soon the sun was melting some of the inch-deep snow on the ground and shining weakly on the hand-lettered signs—"Fresh Eggs 4 Sale"—that stand by dozens of local driveways. Riley's Sunoco station, which has a "radar oven" to heat sandwiches, again sold several dozen cheeseburgers and "torpedoes" to students who opted against their school's luncheon menu. Barbecued potato chips were also a big item.

Out at the Earl Pittman house it was not so gay. For Jack Pittman, their 20-year-old son, died of a shrapnel wound in the head suffered in Vietnam in 1966. He was the first of Beallsville's boys to die there. Six more were to follow and another died at an air base in the United States. "I guess," said Mrs. Maegene Pittman, his mother, "when you lose all you've got, all you got to live for, you become a little bitter."

One day seven years ago the Pittmans got a telegram that their son was wounded but not seriously. For seven days they heard nothing more. When Mrs. Pittman called Washington to inquire about her son, a man said, "This happens every day."

"Not to me," she replied.

Then an Army sergeant arrived to say that their son had died in a California hospital. He is buried with most of the other dead from Beallsville up in the cemetery overlooking the high school and the football field where Jack once played. His picture in his football uniform, along with his basketball trophies and varsity letters, stands in a new trophy case in the Pittman living room. Mr. Pittman recently sold his peach and apple orchard. "Why not?" Mrs. Pittman asked. "We have no boy to leave it to."

Three years after young Pittman's death an enemy sniper shot and killed Beallsville's Robert Lucas, a medical corpsman, as he tended a wounded Marine. That incident, in March 1968, was the last straw for this town. Raymond Starkey, Monroe County Treasurer, and Keith Harper, the town undertaker, asked the Department of Defense to keep any more Beallsville boys from serving in Vietnam. The request was turned down, which prompted more bitterness about a military draft system that then exempted college students, which Beallsville's young men could not afford to be. A total of 35 local men were drafted in the war's later years.

So the town passed around a weathered baseball hat and collected $1,080 for the flagpole and plaque. But even then, townspeople were careful to point out that it was not so much opposition to the war that aroused them. It was the feeling that their little town with no traffic light had done its part and that those controlling United States participation in the war were not doing theirs. "As big as the United States is," Mrs. Pittman said, "we just got sucked in and in and in. I think we could have gotten a treaty sooner if we just put our foot down. They tied our boys' hands over there."

Mayor Thornberry feels the same way. "We should have had that heavy bombing a long time ago," he said. "Then we'd have gotten a treaty sooner. I think now maybe we'll have some peace for a while. We're getting out with some honor and Mr. Nixon is doing his part." His wife, Madeline, had some doubts, however. "You can't trust North Vietnam," she said, "even when they're signing a treaty. I'm afraid they may have other ideas on their mind. It all just seems too good to be true. And I'm a-wondering why."

There were others with suspicions. "I want to know why we couldn't have had the same settlement years ago," said Ed Witzberger, "and why does it take three days to stop fighting? How'd you feel if your boy got hurt or killed between now and then?" "It's a war for nothing but weapons experimenting," added Fred Riley. "You watch, the Communists are going to control that place within five years." An older woman who asked that her name be withheld said, "I'm not going to get excited till they quit fighting. I welcome peace, but you can't trust politicians any more."

"I'm like a lot of people here," said Postmaster Decker. "I don't think that war should even have been." "Me, too," said Charles McDougall, a construction worker who was picking up his mail. "It wasn't worth it. We could have had a cease-fire a long time ago. Now you watch, son, in a year's time they'll be back fighting again somewhere else. I just don't know why."

*Would you travel half a day to buy*
*some stamps? Well, I did.*


# NAZARETH, MICHIGAN

The cost of mailing one single letter increased by 25 percent yesterday to 10 cents, an increase that will cost Americans an extra $2 billion a year. There was a good deal of grumbling about that at many of the nation's 31,000 post offices. But no one swore at the postmaster here. It could have been because the postmaster is the friendliest person in town. It could have been because the postmaster is almost 60 years old. Or it could have been because the postmaster is a nun.

Sister Marciana Hennig is one of the country's very few sisters of the church who is also postmaster of the town, in this case a tidy hamlet nestled by the northeast corner of Kalamazoo. Here since 1889 the Sisters of Saint Joseph (Roman Catholic) have taught the young and tended the old. Here since 1899 they have run the neighborhood's full-service post office in the convent's basement. And here since 1970 Sister Marciana has presided over the postal facility in the truest Ingrid Bergman cinematic style.

She sells stamps and envelopes with subtle skill, the envy of any used-car salesman. She monitors the comings and goings in her basement bureau with sharp eyes, the envy of any hawk. And single-handedly she took on—and whipped—the government's bureaucracy with a zeal that puts Ralph Nader to shame. "This is a fun job," she says, twisting the key chain on the rope belt of her full flowing habit. "I like it."

And apparently the community's postal patrons—the nuns, convent employees, area residents, and Nazareth College students—like her, too. "It may be hard to imagine a pleasant postal worker," said Jim Willette as he bought a roll of the new 10-cent stamps, "but Sister Marciana makes it fun to come here. She knows everybody's name and she's always got something nice to say."

"Good morning, Mrs. Filiputti," says the 59-year-old Sister Marciana. "Did that package get to your folks all right? I see there's a strike in Italy now and I was afraid it got tied up." Sister Gregory arrived to mail some letters but was 20 cents short. "Bring it down later," said the energetic postmaster, who sends Christmas cards to each postal patron.

The post office, where letters were routinely hand-canceled as late as 1967, is decorated somewhat differently than most. Over the writing table hangs a mobile of four little bees. Over the counter hang wind chimes, not far from the vase of vines and the poinsettia plant. Missing, however, is the usual grim array of wanted posters. "I've got some prettier things to hang up," says Sister Marciana, who keeps the posters neatly filed away in a notebook where she can look up fugitives' names identical to customers'. Then she teases the patron about the activities of his alleged relative.

The sister has also hand-lettered a poster announcing the 75th anniversary of the post office, an event celebrated on special envelopes on sale for three cents each. And she posted two signs over separate mail slots. They give patrons their choice of cancellation marks—one from Nazareth, Michigan 49074, or one from the U.S. Postal Service 49074. Sister Marciana is something of a Nazareth chauvinist who has made it most clear to customers which postmark they should use to carry the community's name across the land. As a result, nine out of ten letters fall into the Nazareth slot. And those that don't somehow find their way into that box anyway.

It was similar strong feelings that prompted The Great Confrontation almost three years ago. Sister Marciana, a Michigan native who joined the order in 1929, was told that her post office might soon become a mere branch of the Kalamazoo post office. It is doubtful postal officials knew exactly what they were getting into, but the sister, like many residents of small towns, has long regarded a post office as an important focus of civic pride, a recognition of the community's identity by distant authorities and the world in general.

So the sister studied legal argument forms, financial records, and post office history. She gathered quarterly financial statements for the last decade, showing Nazareth's efficient operation. "I was really getting hot," recalls the sister, whose strongest chastisement is "Oh, you sinner you." The thrust of her argument was that merging Nazareth's post office with Kalamazoo's would reduce the postal services available to the 1000 or so area residents. And a reduction in service, Sister Marciana reminded her postal superiors, was something which they recently had said was out of the question anywhere.

Then one day a pair of postal inspectors visited Nazareth to make a report. First, the sister suggested, how about a tour of the order's facilities? The unsuspecting inspectors were in a hurry but found it hard to say no to a nun. Sister Marciana's tour route just happened to take the visitors into the Red Parlor, a somber room used for the wakes of deceased sisters. There, before the startled inspectors, were the remains of Sister Celestine Connors, resting peacefully in a coffin before her final mass and burial in the Gate of Heaven Cemetery out back. "She was our second postmaster," Sister Marciana told the men, "and I'm the fourth. I do hope I'm not the last."

Officially, it is unclear exactly what part the experience played in the men's report. But Sister Marciana had a new confidence. And soon afterward, on the Feast of Saint Anne, July 26, 1972, word came that Nazareth would keep its independent post office. That day Father John Selner offered a special prayer of thanksgiving at mass.

Every day now at 8 A.M. sharp Sister Marciana opens the post office with the retractable key chain that snaps back to her rope belt, and she sorts the eight bags of mail that Bert Roeloff has delivered. If anyone in town subscribes to *Playboy*, it doesn't come through the sister's post office. Instead, *Reader's Digest* is the most popular publication. On the counter there's a small dish of candy for customers' children. For their entertainment there's a battery-powered stuffed dog that jumps backward with joy when a child walks in. And in her drawer Sister Marciana stashes special stamps for collectors, including one youngster named Randy. Every Thursday he brings in a few more coins toward the cost of four $1 Eugene O'Neill commemoratives. So far, Sister Marciana has $2.04 in a tattered envelope.

But the sister, who gives her entire $13,000 salary to the order, can be firm, too. She once posted a sign: "No Mail Leaves Here Without a Zip Code." Just about everyone now includes those postal numbers. In addition, President Nixon, Michigan's senators, oil company executives, and the county road commissioner had best be warned. For Sister Marciana is increasingly concerned that Nazareth no longer appears on Michigan state maps. "I'm getting hot about that," she says.

*As a child I read about ole Jim Bridger.*
*Then one winter's eve I wondered if anyone*
*still did trap for furs. The answer was "Yup."*


# ASKOV, MINNESOTA

Terry Wolfe and Vern Ward had a few free hours the other day. So they drove to this little crossroads community 125 miles north of Minneapolis and set out into the woods, struggling several miles on snowshoes into a frozen swamp. When they got back to their homes in the city after dark, they were cold and tired, but they were happy. They had enjoyed the wilderness immensely and they had collected a frozen rabbit, and to them it all made for a beautiful day. For Mr. Wolfe and Mr. Ward are fur trappers, a rural profession that is all but forgotten in an age dominated by urbanization. Nonetheless, it is a profession that has left an indelible mark on America and still claims about 2 million part-time practitioners.

Depending on your viewpoint, they are lean, rugged, and self-reliant individuals, wise in nature's ways, or they are cruel, stubborn killers who, during these winter months, snare unsuspecting animals in steel traps and sell their skins so city folk can dress fashionably. "We despise any kind of trapping," said Mrs. Alice Herrington, president of Friends of Animals.

But fur trappers are as much a part of the American tradition and lore as the Pilgrims. Indeed, it was at Plymouth Rock that this nation's original white settlers loaded their first export cargo—furs. From then on the adventurous, greedy, and often short-lived trappers were the shock troops of advancing American civilization. As Meriwether Lewis and William Clark clawed their way upriver to explore the virgin western wilderness one day in 1804, they passed a band of trappers drifting back downriver to sell their catch. In their rootless and ruthless wanderings westward, hundreds of mountain men like Jim Bridger, Jedediah Smith, and Kit Carson gave the English language (and a later President) such colorful expressions as "Bring the coonskin home on the wall." The trappers followed

the beaver tracks and the settlers followed their moccasin tracks. The trappers' shoddy but well-located supply forts became the settlers' rest areas—and many of today's cities. Their once-crude paths are now interstate highways.

It was, in fact, an interstate highway that led Mr. Wolfe and Mr. Ward to this wild area of Piñe County where bobcat, coyote, and fox still roam. Like most of today's trappers, both men have trapped since childhood. They take great satisfaction in reading animal signs, intentions, and habits—natural challenges lacking in their daily work in the city. The 55-year-old Mr. Ward is a self-employed house painter; Mr. Wolfe, 25, who has a college degree in wildlife management, helps the state's Department of Natural Resources acquire new lands. "Trapping," observed Gerald A. Walkup, president of the National Trappers Association, "is a hobby, a sport, a recreation, and a supplemental income. And it's a challenge to outwit the animal."

Like many in this northern country, where weather dictates life-styles, Mr. Wolfe seizes the slightest excuse to get outdoors—on snowshoes, snowmobile, or foot. His vacations are scheduled during the hunting or trapping season. Overtime is taken not in money but in equivalent time off on weekdays so the traplines can be checked regularly. And, as it happens, Mr. Wolfe's first child is due in June, when trapping is poor. In November and December both men trap full-time daily from dawn until darkness. Last fall, in three weeks of trapping fox, mink, muskrat, and raccoon, Mr.

Wolfe grossed $750, or two and a half times his state salary for that period. The animals are skinned at home. The remains become garbage. The furs, which Mr. Wolfe stores in his pantry in Saint Paul, are sold to traveling buyers and go to New York City or abroad.

Trapping was slow one day recently as Mr. Wolfe and Mr. Ward, who share the driving, gas expenses, and profits, awakened at 6 A.M. at their city homes. "Actually," said Mr. Wolfe, "trapping is just an excuse to get outside. It's so peaceful up here. I'd go buggy in the city all winter."

Four days before, each man had set about 20 traps on state land. They were after foxes, bobcats, or coyotes, which are unprotected by established trapping seasons. During other seasons they set around 200 traps many miles apart. The temperature had risen to zero that day as the two men shuffled their snowshoes over the three-foot snow among the bare trees. The silence was intense. "Hey, Vern," Mr. Wolfe called as he spotted some tracks, "that fox is back, but he's afraid to cross the trail." Later, in hopes of snaring the animal on his next round of the woods, the men carefully set a seven-inch trap nearby, wrapping it in a cellophane bag to prevent it from freezing open, then adding a thin covering of sifted snow.

The other traps were set by stumps or logs with pungent dead fish or animal remnants nearby as bait. Of 40 traps checked that day only one yielded anything—a snowshoe rabbit that had wandered to its doom, struggling before dying and freezing solid. Mr. Wolfe took it home to eat. At other times, however, the animal is still alive when the trappers come by. A few days later the two men dispatched a trapped fox with a knockout blow to the head and a stomp on the chest. To shoot the animal would have marred its pelt with bullet holes.

Each year almost 9 million fur-bearing animals are trapped in the United States, according to the Federal Division of Wildlife Services. About 190,000 are foxes, 48,000 coyotes, 13,000 bobcats, and 5.2 million muskrats. Last year Mr. Wolfe caught 100 foxes, 12 raccoons, 10 wild mink, 60 muskrats, 7 badgers, and 25 skunks. Depending on the condition of the market and the pelts, Mr. Wolfe might get as much as $20 for a fox. A bobcat might bring $15 from a fur buyer and $40 from a taxidermist. The beaver skins may bring $8 to $20.

Last year Mr. Wolfe grossed $1,500 trapping. But he spent more than $300 on gas and another $350 on special lures and traps (20 percent of his traps are stolen annually). "It may seem like a lot of earnings for a hobby," Mr. Wolfe said, "but when you figure out how many hours I spend just looking for good sites, digging the car out, and tending empty traps, it doesn't pay so well. You have to love it, that's all."

*The call came from my New York desk at noon. "We know who the New Orleans sniper was," they said. "He's from Emporia, Kansas." Minutes later I was airport bound.*

# EMPORIA, KANSAS

The 1967 edition of *The Re-Echo*, the student yearbook of Emporia Senior High School, was just about the most prized piece of property in town today. Copies of the book were passed from student to student, teacher to teacher, and parent to parent. And each shook his head as he thumbed through the shiny pages. They all stopped at page 36. It bore senior portraits of Stephen Floyd, Larry Fields, Margaret Flynn, and Joyce Goodell. And there at the top of the page, looking out at the world as jovial as ever, was a photo of Mark Essex.

No one could believe that that fellow who was always smiling, who was so respectful, and who never got into any major trouble here had died violently. No one could believe that the little guy who had had difficulty carrying a saxophone in the school band had been identified by the New Orleans police as the sniper who carried a .44 caliber Magnum deer rifle to the roof of the Downtown Howard Johnson's Motor Lodge and picked off six persons as if they were rabbits in a field out by the turnpike here. But he was.

And today his friends, teachers, and neighbors tried to understand why. It was most difficult because urban unrest, racial disorder, and killing are topics totally foreign to Middle Western towns such as Emporia, which has a population of 23,327, only 569 of them blacks. Seemingly more relevant was the winter weather, which came two months early in November and coated most streets here with several inches of slick ice. These included Cottonwood Street, where at No. 902 Mr. and Mrs. Mark H. Essex, their two daughters, and two surviving sons gathered to mourn.

No. 902 is a simple, single-story white frame house where giant icicles hang from the gutter, where a large dog sleeps on the porch, and where a neighbor politely answers the door to say the Essexes are not receiving company. A family respected for their hard work, the Essexes learned yesterday of their 23-year-old son's death from the local police. Mr. Essex was at work as a foreman at the Fanestil Meat Packing Co. His wife, Nellie, was counseling preschoolers at a Head Start center.

"It is difficult for me to believe that this baby-faced kid with that good family background could conjure up all this killing," said Robert Lodle, a high-school guidance counselor who was acting principal in 1967. "He was never any problem here." Upstairs at the school in Room 301, the biology room where an impressionable Essex distastefully dissected frogs a few years ago, his teacher, Frank Nelson, remembered him as someone "who didn't make an A and didn't make a D. He was average. Some of these faces that go through here you figure will wind up dead in some alley," Mr. Nelson continued, "but I figured Jimmy would probably start college, then fade, but get a job and go back to night school to finish up."

Mr. Nelson was right in part. Mark Essex, who was known as Jimmy, did start college several times. He variously attended Labette Community Junior College, Kansas State College in Pittsburg, and Kansas State Teachers College here. He withdrew in the fall of 1968.

A few months later the changes began. On Jan. 13, 1969, Jimmy, once a Cub Scout, enlisted in the Navy, as many boys here do. He trained in San Diego and began work nearby as an apprentice dental technician. According to local police records, however, he was reported absent without leave in 1970. And then on Feb. 10, 1971, halfway through his four-year enlistment, he received a general discharge "for character and behavior disorders." He returned to this east Kansas town an embittered man. His friends noticed. Renee Green, a high-school classmate, said he was not jovial any more. "At parties he'd always sit in the corner," she said.

"He was a changed boy," recalled the family pastor, Reverend William A. Chambers. When Mr. Chambers met Jimmy on Sylvan Street one day, he asked him why he hadn't been in church recently. Jimmy shocked the pastor by bluntly saying he did not believe in Christianity any more because "it is a white man's religion." "He wouldn't talk openly with me like before," Mr. Chambers said.

Mrs. Essex said a series of incidents in the Navy influenced her son. She said these included white guards stopping her son more often than they did whites; white policemen, presumably in San Diego, frisking her son more often than whites; and complaints by white sailors about soul music being played too loud in her son's barracks. "You know," she said, "you just keep on putting a little snow up on top of snow and pretty soon it's going to break. Jimmy wanted to be a man."

Then, last April 11, Jimmy Essex specially ordered the high-powered rifle and ammunition at Emporia's Montgomery Ward store. Later, he visited Louisiana, where he stayed. Christmas Day he called his mother to say he had "found himself." A week later, the New Orleans police say, his rifle was used to kill a police cadet.

Last Sunday Jimmy Essex climbed to the top of the Downtown Howard Johnson's Motor Lodge and opened fire. At almost that precise moment, Mrs. Essex rose here and asked the congregation of Saint James Baptist Church to pray for her son who "doesn't want to go along with the Lord and the church."

*I'd seen life on an ore boat. Now how about the guys who slice open the ice?*

# ABOARD THE ICEBREAKER MACKINAW

For Charles Faircloth, a father of three boys who lives in Cheboygan, Michigan, it all began as another typical workday. He ate breakfast and left home in time for work at 8 A.M. But then the weather turned colder. And Micheline Faircloth, along with the wives of dozens of other Cheboygan men, began to suspect that her family would not be together for dinner that night. And perhaps for some time to come. She was right.

By 2 o'clock that afternoon, with the family car still locked on the dock, Commander Faircloth and 128 other men were many miles from Cheboygan. They form the crew of the Coast Guard icebreaker U.S.S. *Mackinaw*. When everyone else in the Middle West retreats from the bitter cold to the warmth of family living rooms, the men of the *Mackinaw* and a dozen other Coast Guard vessels go out to work.

Their job—slicing open a path through the treacherous ice on the Great Lakes—has been in increasing demand in recent years as the efficiency-minded steel companies send their lumbering, thin-skinned iron-ore boats to the northern mineral ranges far into the winter months. They used to lie idle in southern lake ports while awaiting the spring thaw. But no more. As a result, the life of an icebreaker crew in these waters is a little-known one. Sometimes they cruise silently by within 200 yards of unsuspecting families at their dinner tables.

Aboard this powerful, gleaming-white 290-foot ship, life is insulated. For all the crew knows of winter life ashore, they might as well be in mid-Pacific. At times some crewmen are even unaware of their own ship's destination. The ship itself is a self-contained community. She can carry fuel and supplies for several months' cruising. She has her own band; her own social life, cliques, and traditions; her own movies; and sometimes her own floating flu

epidemic. Yet the ship is rarely more than a few dozen miles from shore.

At times "the other world"—life ashore—is presented only by a disembodied voice on the radio: "Coast Guard Cutter *Mackinaw*, this is Soo Control. Over."

"Roger, Soo Control. This is the *Mackinaw*. Over."

"Yeah, good day, captain. It's getting colder up here and we've got some ships due down tomorrow. I think maybe you ought to head up right away. Over."

"Ah, Roger on that, Soo Control. We'll be under way shortly."

Similar messages went out to the *Southwind*, the *Arundel*, the *Sundew*, the *Naugatuck*, and other ships that soon were casting off frozen mooring lines and steaming for Sault Sainte Marie, Michigan. At the Soo, winter had already closed three of four locks that carry the giant ore boats down the 22 feet from Lake Superior to the Saint Marys River on a tricky 45-mile voyage to the Straits of Mackinac, then on to the steel mills of Ohio, Illinois, and Pennsylvania. Soon the ore boats tie up until spring. But ferries and tankers will still need help. Then, in the summer, there is much training to do.

At 11 P.M. the day she left Cheboygan, the *Mackinaw* tied up at Soo Control, a tiny Coast Guard base just below the locks. There, Captain John H. Bruce, the *Mackinaw's* 51-year-old skipper, learned that United States Steel's new *Roger Blough*, a mammoth metal box 858 feet long and 105 feet wide, was due at the locks with 34,750 tons of iron-ore pellets bound for Conneaut, Ohio.

The *Blough*, he decided, would need help above the locks in ice-clogged Whitefish Bay. The *Arundel*, a Coast Guard tug with a reinforced hull, sailed. The *Blough* would also need help in the river. The *Mackinaw* prepared.

The crew of the *Mac* rose at 6 A.M., donning long underwear and Arctic parkas. "This is going to be a cold one," remarked John Higgins, a 17-year-old seaman from Brooklyn.

8 A.M.—The *Mackinaw* backs into the harbor, her stern crunching open the new ice that flashed across the water last night.

8:10 A.M.—The sun rises over Sugar Island. Temperature: 2 degrees above zero. Wind: 16 miles an hour. Wind-chill factor: 33 degrees below zero.

8:25 A.M.—The *Cason J. Callaway*, an upbound ore boat, reports tough ice down river. The *Blough* is delayed; lock gates are jammed with ice. *Mackinaw* idles in mid-river.

9:53 A.M.—The *Blough* heaves into view, three miles astern of the *Mackinaw*. Even at that distance, she appears to fill the river. "Hello, Neil," Captain Bruce radios to Captain Neil Rolfson, the *Blough's* skipper. "Can we help you with the ice?"

"Yes," replies Captain Rolfson, "take it all with you."

9:58 A.M.—The *Blough* moves into a narrow passage. The ice, with no place to go, grips the hull. The *Blough* slows. "If she has trouble there," Captain Bruce says, "this will be a long day." The *Mackinaw* leads, reopening "the track," the path of broken ice that refroze overnight. Her heavy, much-scraped bow slams into the ice cakes. They explode in a white spray. Below decks, crewmen must yell over the thunder as ice chunks hit the hull, then bump and scrape along the side.

11:18 A.M.—Decrease speed to watch the *Blough* make first turn. No problem.

12:35 P.M.—Here comes Winter Point, always difficult. This time is no exception. The *Mackinaw* takes the turn wide, aiming

to slice off some of the three-foot-thick ice to give the *Blough* more turning room. The icebreaker shudders, her 10,000-horse-power diesel engines pushing hard. Outside, the ice moans audibly. Then a crash. A jagged crack sprints across the snow-covered ice like frigid lightning. Under the ship's pressure, sheets of ice, some 20 feet across, tilt majestically on their side, then smack down or slide slowly under the pale green water, only to bob up astern like surfacing whales.

12:44 P.M.—"*Mackinaw*, this is the *Blough*. We're in trouble." The ship, almost one-sixth of a mile long, cannot make the turn. The more maneuverable *Arundel* cuts a half circle around the *Blough* to relieve the pressure. "A couple more bow whacks, then I'll give her the gun," Captain Rolfson radios.

1 P.M.—The *Blough* is freed.

3:05 P.M.—The *Mackinaw* comes about just above Detour Village. "It looks good from here on, Neil," says Captain Bruce.

"OK, John," Captain Rolfson radios in reply. "Many thanks. See you next trip."

4 P.M.—Upbound, the *Mackinaw* meets the downbound ore boat *Leon Fraser*. "Hey, that's a swell track you made," says Dave Parsons, the skipper.

"Yeah, thanks, Dave." Captain Bruce radios. Like old friends, both wave as the ships pass in the dusk about 100 yards apart. They have never met in person.

4:30 P.M.—On deck, Seaman Higgins mumbles under his parka. "It never got this cold in Flatbush."

5:36 P.M.—Sunset. In the crew's quarters, Bob Sova, 22, of Ogdensburg, New York, sleeps soundly. Bob Lafean, 18, writes to his fiancée. Dennis Bosio, 25, grouses. "I had my choice between the Army in Vietnam, running to Canada, or the Coast Guard," he says. "I chose the draft dodgers' yacht club."

6:45 P.M.—The *Mackinaw* eases to her mooring by Soo Control. New ice, caught between the dock and the ship, shatters like window panes.

6:55 P.M.—Engines all stop. "Well," says Captain Bruce, who is still standing after 12 hours on his feet, "only four more months and we'll be through with the ice."

*I never saw Bronko Nagurski play football.*
*But I had my hand and my arm and my*
*shoulder shaken by him once.*

# INTERNATIONAL FALLS, MINNESOTA

The hands are the same large, meaty paws that totally envelop a visitor's handshake firmly. The arms are muscular logs heading up to shoulders that virtually fill the doorway and a neck that measures more than 19 inches around. The hair, way up there 6 feet 2 inches off the ground, is thinner. The weight has crept up to 265, or 30 over his playing trim. That sly smile may bring a few more wrinkles these days and arthritic knees and ankles have curbed his walks in the woods. But he's still none other than "The Bronk," that legendary Paul Bunyan whose fabled football feats of the 1930s and '40s still draw a half-dozen letters a day from youngsters and adults.

Bronko Nagurski, at the age of 63, is long since retired from football and professional wrestling. And he says he doesn't even remember his rushing total (4013 yards in nine seasons). But his name recalls the epics of his strength and skill, of how his bulky shoulders left countless tacklers bruised in his wake, or of how he'd carry three or four tacklers into the end zone. Opponents plotted many means to halt him, but Steve Owen of the Giants had the only sure way: "Shoot him before he leaves the clubhouse."

Now with his six children and four grandchildren scattered about this state, the charter football Hall of Fame member enjoys a peaceful retirement in his beloved North Country, where spring is still several hundred miles south. The former Chicago Bear great, who last played in 1943, lives with his wife, Eileen, who works for the county welfare department, on the shores of Rainy Lake on the Canadian border. Nagurski, who likes to work with his hands, has twice remodeled their handsome three-bedroom home.

His days are low-pressured now, filled with reading magazines about the outdoors, answering mail, cooking, fishing in one of his boats for walleyes, gardening, and watching television (his favorite show, "All in the Family"). He also likes to watch hockey, a game his four sons played. But baseball, he says, "is too slow and dull." Of course, he watches football games. "If they're playing interesting ball," he says, "I follow them. If they're playing stupid ball, who wants to watch?"

He sees many changes in the game that never brought him more than $5,000 a year. "I sometimes think there's less enjoyment in the game now," he muses. "The quarterback always handles the ball. The games all seem so much alike. Only the faces and numbers change. And, of course, the platoons. We had 18 men on a team and you played 60 minutes, sometimes twice a week." Those were pre-pension-plan days, too, when the star who personified the big and vicious Bears, the Monsters of the Midway, made no personal fortune from his sports career. Nagurski doesn't seem bitter, though. "We used to say Coach [George] Hallas tossed nickels around like they were manhole covers," he recalls.

Nagurski wrestled professionally until 1960. "I'd be the good guy or the bad guy, whichever I thought would bring in the most people," he says. Then he ran a gas station here until 1970. Now he rises about 6 A.M. to listen to the news, later heading to town on errands and for the mail. Most of it comes from adoring youngsters eager for an autograph, and Bronko answers every one of those. At home after a light lunch he reads, prepares the family dinner (often stews or short ribs), and awaits warmer weather. "Actually," he says, "we don't have any summer up here. We just have a season in the middle of the year when sledding is poor."

In the fall there is always hunting, although Bronko stays pretty close to camp, where he does the cooking while his sons (including Bronko, Jr., who played tackle eight seasons for the Hamilton, Ontario, Tiger Cats) and their children wander in the woods. "These old knees and ankles aren't much good on uneven ground," he says. But he does get invited for at least a dozen appearances a year at banquets, at grand openings, and on television. On one recent sports show, the panel guessed his identity immediately as soon as they heard the mystery guest was the only player to be All-America at two positions (tackle and fullback at Minnesota).

Nagurski recalls his greatest thrill was returning for a season after six years' retirement to lead the Bears to a 41–21 championship victory over Washington in 1943. "But," he adds, quietly, "I don't reminisce much any more. That's all behind me now."

*After the turkey races, I wasn't surprised*
*by Ely, Minnesota. Not surprised.*
*Just frozen stiff.*

# ELY, MINNESOTA

"Hike!" the driver yelled, and 14 growing dogs burst off the starting line in the fourth annual All-American Championship Sled Dog Races. Their breath made steamy little clouds in the frigid air as the dog teams raced the clock, lunging across 16.5 miles of brushlands, forests, and frozen lakes. Much of the trail was lined with thousands of cheering, chattering, parka-clad Arctic aficionados in the latest of this North Country's cherished celebrations of winter.

The races are an eagerly anticipated three-day series of multimile jaunts by 100 "mushers" ages 9 to 73—participants in an expensive, rapidly growing hobby whose feverish followers have seen the value of a quality husky or malamute racing dog climb in recent years from $100 to $3,000 in some cases. Part of the high price is due to the increasing number of Americans buying sled dogs. But racers here said that a prime reason was that Alaskan natives, who for centuries have bred the animals for work and their own survival, have now switched their interests to faster snowmobiles and are no longer breeding the dogs.

More important locally, the races represent an attempt by a financially struggling summer-resort community to take advantage of the nation's growing amount of leisure time and broaden its economic base into a four-season resort town, a transition eagerly sought by dozens of Middle Western communities. Economics, however, was just about the last thing on the minds of Ely residents and visitors this weekend. Much more urgent were the sled-dog buttons, sled-dog patches, pancake breakfasts, sled-dog programs, dances, parties, sled-dog beauty queens, and, oh yes, the sled-dog races.

From Friday afternoon until today's awards ceremony, teams of from 3 to 14 dogs leaped from the starting chute next to the

abandoned iron-ore mine and charged out across the snow toward Canada in quest of $5,300 in prizes. Such competition has developed its own rules, etiquette, fashions, language, and rigorous regimen as it spread from Alaska's native villages into the 19-state northern snow belt.

Basically, the races consist of four classes—novice (a team of 3 dogs over 2.5 miles), C class (3 to 5 dogs over 5 miles), B class (5 to 7 dogs over 10 miles), and A class (an unlimited number of dogs over 16.5 miles). The 30-pound sleds are made of lightweight wood with Teflon runners. The surprisingly small, but taut dogs weigh no more than 65 pounds.

The driver, or musher, stands on the rear runners, muttering affectionate orders to his attentive team, much like radio's old Sergeant Preston of the Yukon. Sometimes the driver may run or push with one foot to help the animals. The dogs, which sometimes collapse when working in temperatures as warm as 32 degrees, live in their own compartments on specially modified camper trucks that often have the racing team name emblazoned on the side. Sometimes dog-food concerns sponsor teams.

Along with snowmobiling, which true mushers disdain, sled-dog

racing is the outdoor activity adopted by residents of this area, where winter is a way of life rather than just a season. There are two seasons here—winter and a slightly warmer time occasionally called summer. The latter occurs between May and September, when temperatures on a torrid day might shoot up around 75 degrees or so. The residents almost revel in the climatological hardships they face. Tim White, a 24-year-old musher who uses his dog team to ferry state employees to remote lakes, recalls with great amusement the time last winter when his hands froze so quickly on his sled that he did not feel the cold and had to pry his fingers open with his teeth.

At race time the temperature had climbed all the way to zero, a veritable heat wave for this town of 4848, which seems much more than 700 miles north of Chicago. Last year the dogs ran in minus 52-degree weather, described here as "chilly."

Around the starting line, tension was mounting as a team prepared to take off. "Thirty seconds," the announcer said.

The dogs were barking and moaning and straining in their harnesses, eager for the race they knew was near. "Fifteen seconds."

A half-dozen handlers helped to hold the sled steady. "Ten seconds."

The driver adjusted his gloves and grabbed the handle for dear life. The crowd grew silent.

"Five     seconds . . . four . . . three . . . two . . . one . . . zero."

"Hike! On boy!" And the sled whizzed across the snow at almost 20 miles an hour. Every three minutes another team left. An hour later the first team and driver returned, each panting, each with ice on his face. The best total time in two tries wins.

"It's incredible," said Mr. White, the fifth-place finisher in B class, "to see how much a dog will put out on faith. They don't know if they won, just if you're happy." "You win races today by having the least trouble—lame dogs, fights, and spills," said Dick Moulton, a 56-year-old musher from Center Harbor, New Hampshire, who drove dogs to the South Pole with Admiral Byrd. "To me," added Mr. Moulton, who has won the class A races two years in a row, "there's nothing like training a team to run well. That's the romance."

"The dogs become like your children," said Jean Bryar, who is also from New Hampshire and one of the top women mushers, "only you have a few more. You get to know each of your 60-odd dogs not only by sight but by their bark." Mrs. Bryar talks to them during a race, watching for the slack harness that means a dog is loafing and then saying its name firmly. "Now, Sparrow." Then its ears perk up and the dog is striving once more.

Merv Hilpipre, a Cedar Falls, Iowa, musher who came here three weeks ago to begin final training, and his son, Craig, 13, who also races, rarely talk to their dogs in a race. "Then when we do talk, they pay attention," Mr. Hilpipre said.

Suddenly, he was interrupted by a sad-faced fellow driver. "I'm terribly sorry to hear about Tom," he said.

"Yes," said Mr. Hilpipre, "it was quite a blow." Tom, it turns out, was Mr. Hilpipre's lead dog who died in a recent fight with some canine followers.

"You can't scare a dog into running," said Dr. Roland Lombard, 62, a veterinarian from Wayland, Massachusetts, who finished second in the A class. "They run because they want to, because you've built that in them," he said. Dr. Lombard, who will not

return home until April after a series of races between here and Alaska, spends countless hours and dollars on his "addiction" with little hope of breaking even financially. "But," he says, "I wait for that perfect day when the weather is just right, the snow is fast, the dogs are running in unison, and you move through the woods effortlessly with only the rhythmic panting and jangling of harnesses to hear."

It will be a sound heard more often in these rugged woods, splotched with hundreds of lakes, where you can walk 150 miles and see no other human. That is, if it is up to Ely (which, according to civic literature, is named for Samuel Ely, a Michigan miner who never came here). "When you get 10,000 people in a wilderness outpost like this," said Mayor J. P. Grahek, "it's bound to have a beneficial impact. We don't want to make this a Disneyland. But we want a viable year-round economy."

Already Ely's 20 bars report that race night is busier than New Year's Eve, and the canoe outfitters who closed during previous winters are now open and selling cross-country skiing equipment. It isn't too surprising, then, that exactly 14 days from the end of this year's races Ely's Official Sled Dog Committee will hold its first meeting to plan next year's races.

*"You remember your article about*
*Dorsie?" the old lady asked on the phone.*
*"Well, it sure 'nuff worked."*

# MINNEAPOLIS, MINNESOTA

Dorsie W. Willis was honorably discharged from the United States Army today, 66 years after he was dishonorably discharged from the same Army. In an emotional ceremony in his church on his birthday, the 87-year-old Mr. Willis finally won a seemingly endless fight to clear his name.

In 1906 President Theodore Roosevelt discharged without honor —and without a trial—Mr. Willis and 166 other black soldiers from what was then called D Company, First Battalion, 25th Infantry (Colored). They had failed to volunteer information about a 10-minute shooting spree in Brownsville, Texas. Later evidence indicated that the black soldiers had no information to volunteer about the shooting, which killed one man and became known as "The Brownsville Raid."

Despite Mr. Willis's petitions, phone calls, letters, and wasted hours, the official record of the case was not corrected until last fall. By then, however, all but one of the men had died without ever having been relieved of the burden that a dishonorable discharge inflicts.

But today Mr. Willis, who shined shoes in a barbershop here for 59 years, leaned on a worn wooden cane in front of his congregation at Zion Baptist Church and heard an Army general apologize to him. Mr. Willis, whose declining health usually confines him to his giant leather easy chair at home, stood by his wife, Olive, and his son, Reginald.

"I stand here today," said Major General DeWitt Smith, Jr., "before the friends of Dorsie Willis to make absolutely and officially clear what has been true and clear in the minds of those who have known Mr. Willis. That is, that he rendered honest, faithful, and entirely honorable service to his country while in the uniform of the United States Army."

General Smith continued, "We are trying to substitute justice for injustice, to make amends, to say how much we of this generation—white men as well as black—regret the errors and injustices of an earlier generation. Mr. Willis, you honor us by the quality of the life you have led, by your outstanding citizenship, and by the faithful service you rendered the United States Army."

Then Mr. Willis looked out at the congregation, a beaming smile covering his face. They gave him a standing ovation. The choir sang "The Battle Hymn of the Republic." And grown men wept. Mr. Willis could not speak to the audience. He just could not stop smiling.

But later he said, "It was a tough fight. I'm happy. But I feel so weak." It had been a tiring time for Mr. Willis, who has arthritis, deteriorating eyesight, and poor hearing. He learned only Wednesday that the Army was sending General Smith and Lieutenant Colonel William Baker from the Pentagon to deliver his honorable discharge certificate (backdated to Nov. 25, 1906), a new United States flag, and copies of his amended service record to send to relatives.

Then on Friday, Mr. Willis came down with the flu. And yesterday morning, when the full impact of today's ceremony had dawned on him, Mrs. Willis found her husband in bed sobbing uncontrollably. "I just felt like I had to cry, that's all," he said. Unknown to Mr. Willis, however, his 77-year-old sister, Julia, died in California at about that time. Friends were keeping that news from him until after today's happy celebrations.

"I think I'll just keep that flag to put on my coffin," Mr. Willis said tonight at a party in his home at 3724 Minnehaha Avenue. He bought the house 37 years ago with the tips he earned at the Northwestern Bank Building Barber Shop.

Mrs. Willis, who packages hamburgers for a restaurant chain, rose early this morning to prepare the party food. There were roast beef and sweet potatoes and beans and spinach, and after church this afternoon Mrs. Willis raced home to fry up some chicken. "I want this to be a happy time," she said.

. Things have been happier for the Willises since last fall when Secretary of the Army Robert F. Froehlke called the mass punishment of the soldiers in the Brownsville case "a gross injustice." He ordered their discharges changed to honorable. The men were all presumed dead. And the matter seemed closed until a newspaper article called attention to Mr. Willis and his financial plight. Readers, including a class at New York City's High School of Music and Art, promptly sent him several hundred dollars to help buy medicine. A few days after the report appeared, the Army sent a three-man team, including Colonel Baker, to verify Mr. Willis's identity.

Now that the Army has admitted its mistake, Mr. Willis feels that he is entitled to some compensation, perhaps $1,000 for every year that his dishonorable discharge kept him from work in the post office or from getting an insurance bond for a new job or perhaps from following an Army career with its pension possibilities.

Such a sum does not seem likely, unless special legislation is passed in Congress. But Colonel Baker will meet tomorrow with Veterans Administration officials here to assure Mr. Willis's eligibility for hospitalization benefits.

And, Army officials noted, Mr. Willis is now eligible for burial in a national cemetery. But because of his age, health, and previously dishonorable discharge, Mr. Willis had already bought his own plot at a cost of several hundred dollars.

*Everybody knows what a farmer does in
the summer. But what about those
winter days when the fields are sleeping?*


# FESSENDEN, NORTH DAKOTA

"This time of year," Norman Rudel said slowly, "these short winter days sure can seem mighty long." Mr. Rudel is a farmer, one of 9.4 million farm residents across the country now passing through the slowest, least productive, yet in a way the most important, time of year. In these windblown parts, the weather dictates the entire rhythm of life. And in winter here the weather dictates minimal outdoor work.

It is a time of little physical labor but intense planning, careful calculations, and crossed fingers. It is a time when the fields are dead and frozen, but when family and civic activities, freed from the summer burdens of demanding farm work, can blossom and flourish indoors. And it is a time of year that has recently changed drastically as farming became less a way of life to follow and more a sizable business to run.

A farmer's winter life is a little-known one beyond the boundaries of the Rural Free Delivery mail zones that still dot the Middle West. Yet it is during the thoughtful winter months that crucial family decisions are made: when and how much of what to plant where for what projected income.

At present, for instance, the 44-year-old Mr. Rudel (rhymes with doodle) spends much of each day in his tiny basement office poring over aerial photographs of his 1435 acres. Comparing the photos with records for previous years, he can tell how "tired" each field is, what crop should best grow where, and what types and quantities of fertilizer he will need.

He must be careful also to maintain the four-year crop cycle for each field—wheat, wheat, barley, fallow—which allows the land to rebuild moisture and natural nutrients. Fallow fields, however, must not be too large, for that would give the prairie winds too much opportunity to bite off vital topsoil. And he must weigh the demand and price for his crops and what he thinks these might be in August.

Last year on his 1344 tillable acres Mr. Rudel planted 260 acres of hard, red spring wheat, which makes bread flour; 260 acres of durum, which makes macaroni; and 334 acres of barley, which goes into beer. The remaining 490 acres he simply plowed a half-dozen times to keep the weeds down. To avoid an oversupply of wheat, which would undercut the price, the federal government paid him $35.72 for each vacant acre designated for wheat.

But this year President Nixon said the demand for wheat was strong, so such "set aside" payments and other government subsidies would not be offered. As a result, Mr. Rudel must decide how to reapportion his land among the various crops. Tentatively, he has decided to leave 344 acres fallow, plant 375 acres in durum, 375 in wheat, and only 250 in barley, because the bushel price for barley is only about half the price of wheat. Mr. Rudel also must manage 70,000 bushels of grain, some of it harvested five years ago, that are stored in his 10 silos. So he listens to the noon grain-market report from Minneapolis. Should he sell some grain at today's price? Wait until tomorrow? Or borrow on it from the government, hoping that the price will go higher in months to come?

"It gets more complicated every year," Mr. Rudel said while he was punching figures into an adding machine and shuffling papers into a filing cabinet. In fact, according to Mr. Rudel, his farm is a $42,000-a-year business, which is considerably greater than some of the businesses that line the main street of this town (pronounced Fezenden) of 815 people seven miles west of his farm. Mr. Rudel had the figures at hand because a farmer's income taxes are due March 1, when the federal government knows farmers have more time for such work.

But winter is not all work. For one thing, Mr. Rudel does not get up until 7:30 A.M., two hours later than his summer schedule. At 8:30 sharp Leonard Martin wheels a school bus down the family's two-mile-long dirt driveway to pick up Mr. Rudel's two school-age daughters, Carol, 15, and Rene, 13. After a morning of office work, there is a light lunch, a far cry from the huge summer lunches that must last the family and Wesley Sanderson, the hired hand, until 11 P.M., when they return from the fields. After lunch Mr. Rudel often stretches out on his davenport to relax, which upsets the routine of his wife, Norma. "Who can get up for housework," she said, "when you see your husband snoozing over in the corner?"

However, about three times in a normal winter a blizzard blasts by. Schools, which build four "storm days" into their annual schedule, close, and farm families huddle together at home, perhaps to play Monopoly, bake cookies, have wrestling or tickling matches, or paint or clean a room together. It is a happy time fondly remembered for years. Storms blow so fiercely in this land of the "sideways snow" that family members leave the house only in pairs and follow a taut rope to the barn they cannot see for the snow.

But soon the afternoons will be filled with preparing and treating this year's seeds. By April 1 it will be warm enough to work outdoors on Mr. Rudel's $50,000 worth of machinery. Mid-April means plowing time. May to June is planting time. Then there is spraying to be done against weeds. In July there is the county fair and a long weekend of camping in Minnesota. Before leaving for the holiday last year it took the Rudels some time to find the keys to lock their house. They never do any other time.

In August the six-week harvest begins, first barley and then wheat. Afterward, the fields are cleared of "new" rocks, fertilized, and cultivated to a precise depth to reduce winter wind erosion, a step that saved Mr. Rudel much soil this winter because there has been little snow to protect the ground.

By November 1 those 100-degree summer days are only a memory. Ahead lie those beautiful, star-filled but minus 40-degree nights. "I never look forward to winter too much," Mr. Rudel said.

But winter does have some social life. There is regular dining out with friends, choir practice, the Fessenden Oriole basketball games where Carol Rudel is a cheerleader, and an occasional Kiwanis fund-raising play. This year in rehearsals for *Room No. 13,* Mr. Rudel exasperated the director, Lloyd Hehr, because he often forgot his lines. "Wait just a minute. It'll come to me," Mr. Rudel would say.

Two nights a week Mrs. Rudel, a registered nurse, works at a nearby hospital. On other evenings friends drop by to chat, or they might visit a cafe in town, where all social activities are drowned out by the first tractor chug of spring. "When the good weather comes," one local bartender said, "it's so dead around here that we go out on the sidewalk and watch for a car to pass."

By 10 o'clock on winter nights the Rudel family is back at home, preparing for bed. "We usually watch Johnny Carson on TV," Mrs. Rudel said, "until he puts us to sleep."

Every two years the family breaks up the long winter with a two-week vacation to see a new part of the country. This year it was Washington State. "After each trip," Mrs. Rudel says, "we ask each other, 'Would you swap lives with them?' And always we answer, 'No.'"

*The countryside is dotted with thousands of weathered old windmills, sitting in the field or by the house like some retired spirit helplessly watching the seasons pass by. I was curious why they were unemployed.*

# PUMPVILLE, TEXAS

The windmill, that tall, graceful lady whose spinning blades harnessed the prairie wind and gave rural America its vital water for generations, is falling victim to rot, rust, and electrification.

By the thousands, the proud mills once marched across the land, their endless revolutions fascinating many a youth while pumping life-giving water from the earth's depths to millions of isolated farm families and livestock. A windmill's existence was reason enough to found a city or build miles of railroad tracks, while disputes over control of a mill sparked many a frontier fight.

Windmills have been long gone from the Middle West. But they have clung stubbornly to their role in the West and Southwest, where their ability to draw up water from beyond man's reach made human settlement possible in arid areas. Now, one by one, ranchers and farmers from this dusty Texas rail siding near Mexico to the distant Canadian border are disconnecting their windmills from the pipes and installing more efficient electric or gas-powered pumps. The old mills are then either torn down or left to idle and decay.

"Let's face it," said an official of one of the nation's two remaining windmill manufacturers, "windmills are a disappearing market."

Here in Pumpville, an arid array of five buildings on a dirt road hard by the Southern Pacific tracks, the windmill is gone—along with the last of the thirsty steam engines that trekked their way from well to well across the sandy wastes of west Texas. Only the windmill's tower remains. Like many mills across this region, it stands out starkly against the seemingly limitless sky that covers this land.

284

Down the road a piece and back in the hills Jack Skiles has disconnected his giant windmill, which was built sometime between 1880 and 1920. He has installed, instead, a 2.5-horsepower electric motor. It pumps water from a 400-foot well for his sheep and horses. That costs $8 a month. Automatically, every 150 minutes, the electric motor turns itself on. It runs for 15 minutes. The weather does not affect it. Towering 50 feet overhead, the windmill sits idly, its tail locked to the side to keep the wheel turned from the wind. The weathered wooden blades, much like those in discarded window blinds, vibrate in the brisk east wind. The only sound is a soft-tired creaking, like that of an old sailing ship at anchor, as the mill turns slightly, stops, then turns back, as it has for years. "Shutting her down was a pragmatic decision," said Mr. Skiles.

Generally, a windmill can pump 3 to 5 gallons of water a minute on a windy day. An electric pump spews out 20 to 30 gallons every 60 seconds, rain or shine, calm or storm.

Nowadays, since electricity is arriving on more remote ranches, some windmills are relegated to supporting television antennas. Antique dealers, sentimental for old windmills, or alert to a good investment, also buy some discarded mills.

"There is a certain nostalgia about windmills," said one manufacturer. "They were the first sign of civilization a settler saw on the horizon as he worked his way west. Windmills are majestic—standing up there, churning away by themselves. And there's no cheaper power than the wind."

Mr. Skiles's father, 74-year-old Guy Skiles, built and fixed windmills in this area for more than 50 years. He even built one that pumps spring water over 200 yards to water his lawn and fill his swimming pool.

"There's something fascinating about a windmill," he said, "like watching a fire." But he added, "Sometimes it's hard to get romantic about them when you're up there on the platform in the wind and ice."

He used to erect an entire windmill in three or four days, sometimes spending hours gouging foundation holes in solid rock with a crowbar. "We used to build them in the vegas [small valleys]," he said, "so we wouldn't have to drill so deep. Then we put them up on the hills to catch the wind better and the water could run downhill to the stock. But the old ladies are dying off," he continued. "Used to be a windmill cost $400. Now it's over $1,000. They last 40 years or more, you know. The electric pumps only last 5 years if you're lucky. But they only cost a few hundred. Still, I'd rather have me a windmill."

Apparently he is not alone. The two windmill makers left—the Heller-Aller Company in Napoleon, Ohio, and Dempster Industries, Inc., in Beatrice, Nebraska—report a growing number of inquiries from Easterners, many of whom have no intention of using the windmills to pump water.

Charles Buehrer, the Ohio concern's general manager who recently stumped the panel of "What's My Line?" said, "Windmills have a connection with the past, with your youth. So when a lot of Easterners buy a country place, they say, 'I'm going to have a windmill to sit there and watch.'"

Robert Murray, Dempster's sales administrator, says he, too, gets many inquiries from Easterners, many of whom want to fill a pond by a pollution-free power source. "A lot of people are on this ecology kick," he said, "and they think about buying one, too, until they find out the price." Dempster's most popular mill is 33 feet tall with an 8-foot diameter. It goes for $839 plus shipping and installation. Electric pumps cost $150 to $350, plus $100 in accessories.

Though domestic demand for windmills has dropped considerably, both companies said that their exports of windmills were growing, especially to Africa and South America. One former American windmill manufacturer even moved to Venezuela to be closer to the market. Even so, each company makes only 700 to 800 windmills a year, a sharp decline from the days when Dempster made annual model changes like automobiles and turned out 3500 windmills a year. As a result, Dempster now makes windmills only two months each year, and the time may come when a decision on whether to continue will be necessary. "We're not killing the windmill," Mr. Murray said. "It's just dying." Like Heller-Aller, Dempster has diversified its production lines and now turns out a variety of electric pumps and allied items.

But perhaps the windmill's demise proves in a way that there are no endings, only beginnings. Some years ago another windmill manufacturer found its orders dwindling, despite a very popular free premium offered to the children of every farmer who ordered a mill. Approaching financial disorder, the company realized where its future lay. It abandoned the production of windmills and began marketing the premium full time. The premium was the Daisy air rifle.

*If this is Thief River Falls, Minnesota,*
*then it must be winter.*

# THIEF RIVER FALLS, MINNESOTA

An eerie humming sound, much like the buzzing of bees in their hives, fills the crisp air around Thief River Falls these nights. Unusual lights, resembling frigid fireflies, dance across the flat fields, which carry the smooth, meandering tracks of some monster dragging its weight through the deepening snow. Then, suddenly, several strange creatures streak by, plummet down a slope, scoot out on the frozen river, and disappear in the darkness at 60 miles an hour, their red tails glowing softly. What were they? They were the Sno-Drifters, the masked men of Thief River Falls astride their snowmobiles, wending their way to the woods for a sub-zero winter wiener roast.

Here in what you might call the capital of United States snowmobiling—it boasts this country's No. 1 manufacturer—the noisy, 30-horsepower machine has clearly revolutionized winter life and created its own special culture complete with costumes, regulations, and rites. Snowmobiling is a burgeoning national phenomenon that in recent years has seen some 2 million Americans in the 19-state northern snow belt take to it for both recreational and utilitarian purposes.

The snowmobile's new popularity has brought with it a number of problems, though. There are thoughtless and careless riders, some of them now deceased; at least 20 died in Minnesota this season. And there is the peculiar noise, similar to an outboard motor's, but which, in a pristine wilderness, sounds much louder. Such characteristics have prompted a growing number of states and towns to set curfews, mark out prohibited areas, and establish a number of other rules to curb the sound and the as yet undetermined environmental impact of the sometimes smoky machines.

Except for closing downtown to snowmobiles, Thief River Falls, however, doesn't go in much for snowmobile rules. It is too thank-

ful for the economic prosperity the machine has brought—indeed, the town's first "boom" in 76 years—and for the relief it provides from the boredom of long, silent winters. Thief River Falls—once said to have been the headquarters of marauding Indians (the thieves) who lived on the river (the river) near the rapids (the falls)—had a sawmill once, but it closed. Farming and rural business have not been too good either. As a consequence, the young people had been leaving this compact collection of single-family homes on the eastern edge of the prairies and heading for Minneapolis and Saint Paul, 300 miles to the southeast. In 1960 the population was 7151 and aging.

Then came Arctic Enterprises, now the nation's largest producer of the snowmobile, which is a winter tractor first built more than 30 years ago. And life here will never be the same. The company has grown in about seven years from 3 local employees to 2300 with an annual business of $120 million. In 1966 Arctic sold 1100 snowmobiles; in 1972 it built 112,000. And what was thought by some to be worthless stock that early employees got in place of pay now trades for around $30 a share after splitting several times.

The town's population is now over 10,000, the young people are returning, and the three local banks advertise savings accounts instead of loans. The snowmobile boom has also meant more housing, sewage, and schoolchildren, which mean higher taxes. Arnie Johnson paid $132 a year in property taxes on his $12,000 home in 1955; now he pays $565. But he is not complaining; he sells snowmobiles.

Old-timers no longer recognize every passerby, who all seem in more of a rush. The boom has also brought more stores, other industries, regular air service, more traffic, full motels, a year-round resort season, better business for local gas stations, and a better selection of liquor on local shelves. And with more new babies, plus more old folks and more snowmobile injuries (they average three a week now, up from one), Northwestern Hospital erected new additions recently and Norman Peterson, the administrator, finds it easier to attract qualified personnel.

Practically every yard here contains a snowmobile, often three, lovingly parked and waiting for that delicious moment of freedom when the owner yanks the starter rope, clambers aboard, and steers out across the frozen fields for nowhere in particular. Of course, if you aren't dressed properly, the wind-chill factor at 30 miles an

hour equals 70 degrees below zero. One recent snowmobiler froze
an eyeball into uselessness. Or if you are careless for a second, the
machine could rip your kneecap off against a tree or, as is more
frequently the case, splinter your leg against an auto bumper. Two
snowmobilers had their heads severed by barbed-wire fences while
their machines continued on riderless.

Nonetheless, the other night Stan Gibson, a real-estate agent,
pocketed his $12 snowmobile registration, threw on his special
snowmobiling suit—boots, helmet, goggles, gloves, and mask—and
jumped on one of his five $1,200 Arctic Cats for a short spin. Three
hours and 50 miles later he returned, saying: "I just couldn't stop.
The snow and wind and the moon. Once I just sat in the middle of
nowhere. It was beautiful." Mr. Gibson also organized the recent
wienie roast by the Sno-Drifters, the snowmobiling club whose
more than 100 members give safety lessons to young enthusiasts. It
was 15 below at 7:30 that night. But, said Dick Sculthorp, "We
only cancel when it gets cold."

The members rode upriver, then cut across the sleeping fields,
which Mr. Gibson had checked for hidden obstacles that afternoon. From a distance their bobbing headlights resembled a religious procession. Thirty minutes later they roared into the Gibson

farmyard to down a few drinks and roast hot dogs by a roaring bonfire that cooked one side while the other froze.

Other riders pull sleds loaded with steaks and tents for weekend outings. Some go barhopping on their snow machines, drawing one playing card at each stop, ending at the fifth with a poker hand. A few chase wildlife until the animal collapses from exhaustion and freezes to death or dies under a snowmobile's churning tread. This is now illegal, however. "Like any new sport, there are bound to be excesses," said the town's mayor, a 77-year-old retired dentist, A. E. Jacobson. "But like everything else young, it matures."

And so the snowmobile has come to be as much a part of life in Thief River Falls as television or the telephone or the automobile; it, too, is a piece of technology whose principal impact is probably not material. But what it means to the people here may not be easy to grasp by city people who yearn for the quiet beauty and repose of a country winter. Norman Peterson, the hospital administrator, put it succinctly: "Winter here is no longer something to endure sitting indoors drinking beer, watching television, or playing pinochle. The snowmobile has freed us from captivity, from being spectators. Now, winter here is a time of action and fun. And you can't find anyone at home on a Sunday afternoon."

*"I can't believe it's finally gonna happen,"*
*said the same old lady on the phone.*

# MINNEAPOLIS, MINNESOTA

Dorsie W. Willis, an 87-year-old retired shoeshine man who was dishonorably discharged from the United States Army by President Theodore Roosevelt, received a tax-free government check today for $25,000—as an official penance. Mr. Willis was one of 167 Negro soldiers dishonorably discharged without a trial in 1906 for what Washington officials assumed to be their part in a 10-minute Texas shooting spree that left one man dead and came to be known as the Brownsville Raid. Later research exonerated the men of B, C, and D Companies, First Battalion, 25th Infantry (Colored), as the unit was called. But it wasn't until recently after years of fruitless appeals and petitions that Mr. Willis, now the sole survivor of the dishonored men, got his honorable discharge papers.

The long legal struggle came to an end today as a spirited Mr. Willis, his eyesight, hearing, and lungs failing, donned his best blue suit, leaned on his shiny "Sunday cane," and came downtown to receive the check from an Army general about half his age. At a special luncheon in the Marquette Inn, 19 friends, relatives, and Army men paid tribute to Mr. Willis, who suffers from arthritis and emphysema. It was the first meal the Army had bought Mr. Willis since Nov. 25, 1906, when he was discharged.

"I prefer buying my own lunch," said Mr. Willis, who was one of 10 children and never finished grade school in Oklahoma. "I can look the world in the face," he added, "and say, 'Oh, man, everything that I got, I got myself.'"

Mr. Willis rose early on this special day. "I had to," he said, "just to get to the bathroom before all the womenfolk."

Alfred Allen, his brother-in-law, had shoveled the snowy sidewalk at Mr. Willis's tidy little home at 3724 Minnehaha Avenue. Then at 11:30 A.M. Lieutenant Colonel William Baker arrived to escort Mr. Willis and his second wife, Olive, downtown.

After a meal of veal cordon bleu, peas, potatoes, salad, and chocolate sundaes, John Cornelius, a longtime family friend, spoke. Mr. Cornelius, whose shoes Mr. Willis shined for many of the 59 years he worked at the Northwestern Bank Building Barber Shop, recalled how every six months Mr. Willis quietly handed him a paper bag full of quarters to help support one youth in the Minneapolis Boys Clubs. "The money totaled $50 a year," said Mr. Cornelius, "and the way I figure it, that's 200 shoeshines every 12 months." So he gave Mr. Willis the clubs' Man and Boy Award, a gold statuette.

"It's wonderful," said Mr. Willis, "it's wonderful. It's wonderful." He began to cry. But he was not alone.

"Mr. Willis," said Major General DeWitt Smith, Jr., "we are honored by the quality of life which you have led over these long years." The general recalled the 166 other dishonorably discharged men. "They asked no favors because they were Negroes," he said, "but only justice because they were men. Our debt is really unpayable." Then he handed Mr. Willis United States Treasury Check No. 82680 for $25,000, or 10 times the most annual income that Mr. Willis ever made sweeping up hair and shining shoes. The check was recently authorized by Congress, which also granted $10,000 each to the five known living and unremarried widows of other Brownsville dischargees. Mr. Willis will use the money to add a downstairs bathroom to his house because he has trouble climbing stairs. He is also pestering his doctor, Donald Brown, Jr., for permission to fly to Los Angeles for a vacation with relatives.

Mr. Willis thanked everyone and with a shaking hand endorsed the check for deposit in a savings account, where it began earning $4-a-day interest. And Sergeant James Wittman whispered in Private Willis's ear, "It's a pleasure to serve with you, sir."

General Smith proposed a toast. Raising his glass of wine, he said, "To a distinguished human being, Dorsie W. Willis." The guest of honor sipped his Coca-Cola. The Reverend Curtis Herron offered the benediction. "O Lord," he said, "we seek your continued blessings. And we pray that when evening shadows lengthen and Brother Willis goes down to the River Jordan you shall meet him there and take him into your everlasting arms."

"Phewee," said Mr. Willis. "Phewee."

*I've heard of looking for trouble. But*
*this is ridiculous. And it tasted funny.*

# SWEETWATER, TEXAS

Glenn Wortham, a 35-year-old food-store operator, didn't have much to do here last weekend. So he went out back and played with some rattlesnakes. Diamondback rattlesnakes. The five-foot-long kind. The ones with the fangs that drip deadly yellow venom.

Now, this might seem like a somewhat offbeat pastime for the father of four children. But it isn't. Not in Sweetwater, Texas, near the end of winter. For this is the time of the Sweetwater Rattlesnake Roundup, those fun-filled three days when men and women travel hundreds of miles to poke around on ledges and caves littered with sheep dung, listening for that familiar, chilling rattling sound that indicates a deadly reptile is nearby—and annoyed.

For Sweetwater, a town of 12,000 not far from Stink Creek and Big Spring, the rattlesnake roundup is a combination picnic, carnival, coin-and-gun show, fund-raising circus, celebration of spring, and vigilante party that helps rid this rangeland area of West Texas of some pesky critters that outnumber humans. But whether weekend festivities like these deal with snakes or buzzards or plowing or mules or snow, they are repeated thousands of times in America each year in honor of a local agriculture or industry or hobby or wildlife.

"It's a good way to have a good time," said Lydia Palacios, the high-school freshman who was sponsored by the Union 76 Truck Stop and is now Miss Snake Charmer 1974. Like some visitors here, though, the 14-year-old Miss Palacios is not particularly charmed by the rattlesnakes, which are hauled by the boxload to the Nolan County Coliseum for display. Still, the boxing and hauling are all part of the fun—except, of course, for the snakes. Their heads are removed by machete.

In these windblown parts of Texas, 240 miles west of Dallas, rattlers are as common as raccoons elsewhere. And a couple of times each month each snake paralyzes a rodent by pumping venom through a hollow set of foldaway fangs and then unhinges its jaws to swallow the victim whole. Too often, however, those same fangs sink into the snout of a valuable—but overly curious— lamb, goat, calf, or sheep dog. And to ranchers, the resulting carcass is less tragic than costly.

Some humans, too, including Mr. Wortham, have felt that sudden sickening sting like a cigarette burn. Very slowly, the poison spreads and starts the snake's digestion inside the victim. If not treated by the snakebite kit that everyone here carries as routinely as a New Yorker carries subway tokens, the venom can kill a human, especially a youngster.

So it is with a certain sense of purpose, as well as enjoyment, that each year before the sleepy reptiles become too alert, hunters pull on their double-thick boots, grasp their metal snake hooks, sign up for special insurance, and trek out to distant dens that some- times yield more than 100 snakes.

"Watch your hand there," said Mr. Wortham, who has nine fingers left. "You just never know where you're gonna find these dudes." Minutes later, he spotted one. There in the cliff crevice at the end of his flashlight beam was a rattler. "All right," said Jim Hixon, the other guide, "let's gas him." A long copper tube was run into the crevice behind the snake and gas vapors pumped out. Theoretically, the snake or snakes would seek fresh air and crawl toward captivity, and an alert hunter would be watching the correct hole. The day's first snake didn't know the theory, however.

Soon, Mr. Wortham spotted a diamond-shaped design in an- other hole. More gas. It moved.

"He's comin' out your way," shouted one man.

"I see him," said Mr. Wortham. The rattling grew louder. "That's it. Keep a-comin'. A little more. Gotcha!" And the pincers at the end of a three-foot pole clamped down on the 40-inch snake's middle. Then, swiftly into the wooden box that muffles the rattling beneath a locking lid.

Another snake was spotted in the canyon, but it wriggled back down a dark rock ledge. More gas. "I wonder if maybe he's fixing to come out the bottom," said Mr. Wortham. He was. The rattling sound started again. The men crouched under the overhanging cliff. "He's pretty angry," someone said. Then a flat head peeked around a corner and flashed a forked tongue. Mr. Wortham missed with the pincers, and the reptile sped off through the reddish dirt. But the chase was on. "He's a big one. Back, everyone, back. Easy now. Gotcha!" Apparently, the pincers were warm because the rattler struck at the metal and broke a fang. Within minutes, though, a spare set would fall into place.

"There's another one here!" said Mr. Hixon, "and another one!" They, too, were caught, making it four for the morning—part of the 6000 for the rattlesnake roundup, which the Holiday Inn marquee has billed as the world's largest. "Snakewise, this is not the best year, though," explained Mr. Wortham.

The hunters earn 35 cents a pound from the Jaycees, which sponsors the roundup. At the Coliseum the snakes are weighed and placed in securely walled enclosures where they pile up in corners by the dozen as spectators, who pay $1, peer over at the mass of moving reptiles. Bill Ransberger and other handlers step among the snakes, explaining how the reptiles move at night and how the king snake and roadrunner are the rattler's natural enemies. Many snakes strike at the handlers' boots as they talk. Mr. Ransberger then milks the snakes' venom by pressing their mouths against the rim of a glass. The crowd mumbles at the sight of the yellow liquid dripping down the side.

Most snakes then meet Don Stanley, the executioner. While the snake is skinned for the crowd, Mr. Stanley carefully nudges the head toward a distant corner. Even though severed, the head can still strike and kill for a while. The heads go to biology laboratories, and the venom is used to make antivenom serum. The skin is sold to spectators or wallet and belt companies, and some live rattlers are bought by snake farms. The meat is sold raw for $2.50 per pound or deep-fried by Corkey Frazier in buttermilk batter and cracker meal for 50 cents a slice. (It tastes like slightly fishy chicken.) All proceeds finance Jaycee civic projects.

There have been some complaints about rattlesnake hunts from persons who don't live near the snakes. Mr. Hixon, however, says Sweetwater's snakes are handled as little as possible, are sold only to reputable dealers, and are not burned alive, as some are elsewhere. Besides, the females, the ones with the shaplier rattle, have 10 to 20 babies a year. So the roundup's annual catch seems as steady as the reptile's population.

Or as steady as a human's curiosity about rattlesnake roundups. "Well," said Nancy Hutchins of Arlington, Texas, as she carefully backed away from the rattling snake pit, "it's something a little unusual to do on a weekend."

*For this story, I talked with everyone in town.*

## T U W E E P ,   A R I Z O N A

Everyone in Tuweep owns an airplane. Everyone in Tuweep gets drinking water from the rain. Everyone in Tuweep is 62 years old. Everyone in Tuweep is John H. Riffey. Few individuals can say they are the entire population of any town. Even fewer can say they are the entire population of a town that for 19 years has been misplaced on just about every map that includes northwest Arizona. That in itself would be enough to set Mr. Riffey apart from most Americans. But in addition, for more than 30 years now Mr. Riffey has worked here full-time as a park ranger—the most isolated in the nation.

For more than 30 years he has lived in this valley in the morning shadow of a nameless mountain where he cares for the wildlife, fights range fires, tends 40 miles of fence, rescues lost travelers, and helps the range grasses reclaim these colorful wild lands from the brush and tumbleweed. Like a number of little-known Americans scattered about the country, Mr. Riffey has had a distinct impact on his locality. And like many of those little-known Americans, he'd just as soon stay little-known.

It is always difficult, and at this his most isolated time of year it is generally impossible, to find out about Ranger John Riffey. His sole contact with the world is an 8 A.M. daily radio transmission to Grand Canyon National Park headquarters, a transmission he sometimes skips if he feels like it. In Tuweep, a corrupted version of Toroweap that some nameless postal bureaucrat mistakenly attached to the post office here decades ago, there is no mail service from either Saint George, Utah, or Fredonia, Arizona, from December until April. Between April and December there is weekly mail delivery—sometimes.

And visitors to Tuweep these days are by and large infrequent, if only because the shortest branch of John Riffey's driveway is 57.1 miles of dust, snow, and sloppy mud past 16 gates, a few hundred nonchalant cattle, and countless hills and over 6 suspiciously ancient wooden bridges spanning dried riverbeds. Two Mile Creek, the neighborhood's only flowing waterway the other day, has no bridge and must be forded by vehicle with a zeal that borders on insanity. The road ends at an unguarded, 3,000-foot sheer drop into the northern end of the Grand Canyon, where the green Colorado River still gnaws its way through rock layer after rock layer.

But not far from the cliff, a handmade stone house stands in front of a handmade stone root cellar near a handmade catchment basin that traps the year's rainfall for John Riffey's sink and toilet. The yard—if that is the word for it in this awesome area where the nearest human lives several mountains away—is dotted with rusty red rocks, a goldfish pond with a heater to ward off ice, a half-dozen homemade animal and bird feeders, some breakfast garbage left out for anyone or thing that wants it, and a small dirt excavation that a coyote dug the other night for some unknown reason.

"Living here," says John Riffey, who volunteered for the job, "is like alcoholism. You get addicted. And I'm too busy to be lonesome." Mr. Riffey, a former agriculture instructor who is something of a legend to the area's younger rangers, presides over the 200,000 acres of the Grand Canyon National Monument, an area, not a thing, that includes part of the Grand Canyon National Park and equals in size the entire mass of New York City. For these duties Mr. Riffey, perhaps the ultimate do-it-yourselfer, is charged $30 a month rent for his home. He receives $16,000 in salary, much of which is invested since his only sizable expense is the frozen meat and vegetables he buys every few months.

He lives here alone, except for a couple months each year when his wife, Marybeth, a biology professor at Western Washington State College, comes to visit and catalog the valley's plants. Some friends do fly by for a chat. There is an occasional cowboy. And tourists now and then try to drive in. However, since few know the mud freezes at night here, they try by day and end up being pulled from the mire by Mr. Riffey's bulldozer, spending a few nights on his living-room couch, and eating his delicious flapjacks before dawn. Many of the rescued become close friends by Tuweep standards and annually send Mr. Riffey Christmas cards or presents, which he generally receives by Easter. Last year, however, Mr. Riffey saw no one from January to April, which was okay with him. "I like people fine," he says, "but I don't seem to miss them."

Ever since a younger John Riffey went rabbit hunting, though, and learned he could not kill, Mr. Riffey has seemed to have a special understanding with wildlife. Although a scorpion or tarantula sometimes wanders in, the bobcats and mountain lions keep their distance. Numerous bands of birds visit his juniper-shaded yard daily. Porcupines chew up his wooden ax handles for the salt from his sweat, and pack rats hide his shiny tools. When he needs them, Mr. Riffey hunts the tools down, but carefully returns them to the pack rats later so they won't hide them somewhere else.

Occasionally an eagle drops in, the one Mr. Riffey once helped over an injury. And Robert, an abandoned baby rock squirrel "no bigger than a minute" when Mr. Riffey first fed him with an eye-dropper, has moved into the garage permanently. When Mr. Riffey calls, Robert comes, sits up, and eats. "Robert is so dumb," says Mr. Riffey, "he thinks he's a people."

Perhaps Mr. Riffey's closest friend here is Pogo, a weathered Piper Super Cub that he keeps in a shelter marked "Tuweep International Airport." While the Los Angeles-bound jets flash by high overhead, Pogo and John fly low over the range together searching for stranded people, injured animals, or fire. Often they fly down the grassy valley toward some rocks that suddenly open beneath the speeding plane to reveal a seldom-seen Grand Canyon. "People can't change the canyon up here," he says. "It's too far away and too big."

"I leave here no oftener than I have to for supplies," adds the ranger, who favors frayed flannel shirts and can't remember watching television. "I get too far out of this valley and I get claustrophobia. Oh, there's a lot I haven't seen. But there's a lot I'll never see. So I'm not going to fret about it." He's also not fretting about his town being dislocated every year by the nation's map makers. The error apparently stems from the movement over the years of Tuweep's post office, an informal facility that shifted from the old Kent place to the Cunningham house to Mattie Kent's spread before closing in 1955. It is Mattie Kent's abandoned shack that is marked as Tuweep now and not Mr. Riffey's tidy little bungalow 10 miles to the south.

Mr. Riffey is often busy this time of year removing snow from his driveway. "Usually," he says, "I only have to plow the first 25 miles." But nightfall comes suddenly in this valley. The bright blue sky turns paler. A piece of cloud turns pink over the western mountain. A shadow races across the grasses. Then, like a lid slamming shut, darkness falls. The air turns cold. And soon thousands of bright stars burn overhead. By then, however, Mr. Riffey has checked his diesel generator, closed the shed, and started dinner. Afterward, he does his job's necessary "blessed paperwork," lights a fire, and reads a book on philosophy or Chinese archeology until 11.

Then, every morning at 5:30 Mountain Standard Time, when the rush hour is at its peak in far-off New York City, Mr. Riffey awakens without an alarm. At 8, after breakfast, he checks in with the world by radio. At 8:30 the quails arrive for their breakfast. By 9 the coyotes are down by the waterhole. And at 10:30 the shadow races across the nine-mile-wide valley again and the sun suddenly pops up over the eastern mountain. "I keep thinking I see something new every day that I'm alive," says Ranger Riffey. "But maybe I just have a poor memory."